"In *Race in Psychoanalysis: Aboriginal Populations in the Mind*, Celia Brickman illuminates the manner in which our colonialist and enslaving past continues to reverberate within the construction of psychoanalytic theory and practice. Taking a thoughtful and detailed tour through the history of Freud's relationship with the sociopolitical forces within Europe during his time, Brickman chronicles the various iterations of the use of the darkened masses as timeless and primitive. Illuminating the way race and racialized object relations permeate our canonical texts, her perspective is a wonderful new resource to locate pathways to a multicultural, racial, and ethnically diverse discourse within theory construction and training in psychoanalysis. 'The pitfalls and paradoxes concerning race that are embedded within the field' become points of access for those perceived as other, not-white, and different from whiteness to become psychoanalysts. Brickman points to the lived psychodynamics of racialization as the way to further Freud's wish that his project be for the people."

—**Annie Lee Jones, Ph.D.**,
clinical psychologist/psychoanalyst,
member of *Black Psychoanalysts Speak*

D0218171

Race in Psychoanalysis

Race in Psychoanalysis analyzes the often-unrecognized racial assumptions in psychoanalysis by examining how the colonialist discourse of late nineteenth-century anthropology made its way into Freud's foundational texts, where it has remained and continues to exert a hidden influence. Recent racial violence, particularly in the US, has made many realize that academic and professional disciplines, as well as social and political institutions, need to be re-examined for the racial biases they may contain. Psychoanalysis is no exception.

When Freud applied his insights to the history of the psyche and of civilization, he made liberal use of the anthropology of his time, which was steeped in colonial, racist thought. Although it has often been assumed that this usage was confined to his non-clinical works, this book argues that through the pivotal concept of "primitivity," it fed back into his theories of the psyche and of clinical technique as well.

Celia Brickman examines how the discourse concerning the presumed primitivity of colonized and enslaved peoples contributed to psychoanalytic understandings of self and raced other. She shows how psychoanalytic constructions of race and gender are related, and how Freud's attitudes toward primitivity were related to the anti-Semitism of his time. All of this is demonstrated to be part of the modernist aim of psychoanalysis, which seeks to create a modern subjectivity through a renegotiation of the past. Finally, the book shows how all of this can affect both clinician and patient within the contemporary clinical encounter.

Race in Psychoanalysis is a pivotal work of significance for scholars, practitioners and students of psychoanalysis, psychologists, clinical social workers and other clinicians whose work is informed by psychoanalytic insights, as well as those engaged in critical race and postcolonial studies.

Celia Brickman, Ph.D., is scholar-in-residence at the Center for Religion and Psychotherapy of Chicago, where she practices psychotherapy and previously was the Director of Education and a faculty member. She received her Ph.D. from the University of Chicago, has been a visiting lecturer at the Chicago Institute of Social Work and a senior fellow at the University of Chicago's Divinity School, and has given talks throughout the United States. In addition to this book, the first edition of which was nominated for a Gradiva Award, she is the author of several articles and book chapters on psychoanalysis, race and religion.

RELATIONAL PERSPECTIVES BOOK SERIES
LEWIS ARON & ADRIENNE HARRIS
Series Co-Editors

STEVEN KUCHUCK & EYAL ROZMARIN
Associate Editors

The Relational Perspectives Book Series (RPBS) publishes books that grow out of or contribute to the relational tradition in contemporary psychoanalysis. The term *relational psychoanalysis* was first used by Greenberg and Mitchell[1] to bridge the traditions of interpersonal relations, as developed within interpersonal psychoanalysis and object relations, as developed within contemporary British theory. But, under the seminal work of the late Stephen A. Mitchell, the term *relational psychoanalysis* grew and began to accrue to itself many other influences and developments. Various tributaries—interpersonal psychoanalysis, object relations theory, self psychology, empirical infancy research, and elements of contemporary Freudian and Kleinian thought—flow into this tradition, which understands relational configurations between self and others, both real and fantasied, as the primary subject of psychoanalytic investigation.

We refer to the relational tradition, rather than to a relational school, to highlight that we are identifying a trend, a tendency within contemporary psychoanalysis, not a more formally organized or coherent school or system of beliefs. Our use of the term *relational* signifies a dimension of theory and practice that has become salient across the wide spectrum of contemporary psychoanalysis. Now under the editorial supervision of Lewis Aron and Adrienne Harris, with the assistance of Associate Editors Steven Kuchuck and Eyal Rozmarin, the Relational Perspectives Book Series originated in 1990 under the editorial eye of the late Stephen A. Mitchell. Mitchell was the most prolific and influential of the originators of the relational tradition. Committed to dialogue among psychoanalysts, he abhorred the authoritarianism that dictated adherence to a rigid set of beliefs or technical restrictions. He championed open discussion, comparative and integrative approaches, and promoted new voices across the generations.

Included in the Relational Perspectives Book Series are authors and works that come from within the relational tradition, extend and develop that tradition, as well as works that critique relational approaches or compare and contrast it with alternative points of view. The series includes our most distinguished senior psychoanalysts, along with younger contributors who bring fresh vision. A full list of titles in this series is available at https://www.routledge.com/series/LEARPBS.

---

1   Greenberg, J. & Mitchell, S. (1983). *Object relations in psychoanalytic theory.* Cambridge, MA: Harvard University Press.

Race in Psychoanalysis

Aboriginal Populations in the Mind

Celia Brickman

Routledge
Taylor & Francis Group

LONDON AND NEW YORK

First published 2018
by Routledge
2 Park Square, Milton Park, Abingdon, Oxon OX14 4RN

and by Routledge
711 Third Avenue, New York, NY 10017

Routledge is an imprint of the Taylor & Francis Group, an informa business

First published as *Aboriginal Populations in the Mind: Race and Primitivity in Psychoanalysis* by Columbia University Press, New York, 2003.

British Library Cataloguing in Publication Data
A catalogue record for this book is available from the British Library

Library of Congress Cataloging in Publication Data
Names: Brickman, Celia, author.
Title: Race in psychoanalysis : aboriginal populations in the mind / Celia Brickman.
Other titles: Aboriginal populations in the mind
Description: Abingdon, Oxon ; New York, NY : Routledge is an imprint of the
    Taylor & Francis Group, an Informa Business, [2018] |
Series: Relational perspectives book series ; 98 | This book is revised edition of a
    book with a new title previously published with Columbia University Press
    called Aboriginal Populations in the Mind : Race and Primitivity in
    Psychoanalysis, NY, 2003. | Includes bibliographical references and index.
Identifiers: LCCN 2017030960 (print) | LCCN 2017036530 (ebook) |
    ISBN 9781138749382 (hbk : alk. paper) | ISBN 9781138749399
    (pbk : alk. paper) | ISBN 9781351718523 (ebk) | ISBN 9781315180168
    (Master) | ISBN 9781351718523 (Web PDF) | ISBN 9781351718516 (ePub) |
    ISBN 9781351718509 (Mobipocket/Kindle)
Subjects: LCSH: Psychoanalysis. | Freud, Sigmund, 1856-1939. | Psychoanalysis and
    racism. | Psychoanalysis and colonialism. | Psychoanalysis and anthropology. |
    Primitivity (Psychoanalysis)
Classification: LCC BF173 .B79 2018 (print) | LCC BF173 (ebook) |
    DDC 150.19/5—dc23
LC record available at https://lccn.loc.gov/2017030960

ISBN: 978-1-138-74938-2 (hbk)
ISBN: 978-1-138-74939-9 (pbk)
ISBN: 978-1-315-18016-8 (ebk)

Typeset in Times New Roman
by Swales & Willis Ltd, Exeter, Devon, UK

The content of the Ucs. may be compared with an aboriginal population in the mind.

Freud, "The Unconscious" (1915)

Contents

Foreword

Celia Brickman's masterpiece, *Race in Psychoanalysis: Aboriginal Populations in the Mind*,[1] is one of only a handful of books that I would describe as having profoundly changed the way I think about Freud and the development of psychoanalysis. Much of my own attempt to revision psychoanalysis, as described in my co-authored work with Karen Starr, *A Psychotherapy for the People* (Aron & Starr, 2013), was the result of years of thinking about Brickman's arguments in the wider context of the New Freud Studies along with changes in contemporary psychoanalytic theory and practice. Brickman's book will remain a classic and generations of analysts will need to study it to understand and reconceptualize the most fundamental assumptions and tenets of psychoanalysis, and it is for this reason that I encouraged a new edition within the Relational Perspectives Book Series of Routledge.

The key that Brickman uses to unlock many of the mysteries and quagmires of psychoanalysis is the concept of "primitivity" and its post-colonial critique. In a variety of forms and terms, the archaic, pre-Oedipal, feminine, early, regressed, unformulated—"the primitive"—is ubiquitous in psychoanalytic literature. Developmental lines, regression, and progress are all ideas that are intrinsic to the theory and continue to play an essential role in clinical theory and practice. Brickman, however, demonstrates that the ubiquitous psychoanalytic concept of "primitivity," as an early stage of psychological development, has inevitable and troubling anthropological connotations. The anthropology of Freud's day had inescapable racial implications, and until now these have not been identified in Freudian theory, nor have their ethnic and racial associations been identified in the clinical situation.

Other important works have stimulated the contemporary historical recontextualization of Freud's contributions. Among those that have been most central to my own work is Sander Gilman's (1993) *Freud, Race and Gender* which presented Freudian thought as arising in the context of Viennese antisemitism in which the feminization of male Jews was a prejudicial stereotype. Central to Gilman's thesis is the notion of Jews as primitive, but it was not until Brickman systematically articulated the place of "primitivity" at the core of psychoanalysis that I could grasp the overall significance of this new understanding and its relationship to race, gender, and ultimately to health, illness, growth, maturity, and therefore to the overall psychoanalytic value system. *A Psychotherapy for the People* is in large measure an attempt to examine numerous polarities that structure psychoanalytic theory and practice, all of which line up with the fundamental dichotomy of civilized/primitive, health/illness, adult/child, rational/irrational, male/female, white/black, gentile/Jew, psychoanalysis/ psychotherapy—among numerous other polarities that require careful deconstruction.

Brickman, it should be emphasized, is not accusing Freud or psychoanalysts of being racists. Hers is not a variety of Freud bashing. She appreciates that Freud's intention was to universalize primitivity as an aspect of the unconscious that exists in all humanity. But in its very attempt to be universal, psychoanalysis inadvertently overlooked the impact of ethnicity and culture in its theory and clinical practice, and thus inadvertently perpetuated racist assumptions and racial prejudice.

There has never been a one-to-one relationship between psychoanalysis and any specific political philosophy. Psychoanalytic ideas have historically been used by those on the political left, middle, and right wings. Psychoanalytic ideas have been used to rationalize communist and Nazi policies as well as democratic and anti-democratic ideologies. Despite the left-leaning politics of most contemporary American psychoanalysts that makes many of us take for granted that psychoanalysis is a liberal, if not radical, orientation, we know that historically psychoanalysis can have both normative-conservative as well as socially critical implications (Herzog, 2017).

Consider how the notion of "primitivity" has played a role in such political positioning. Following World War II, Ernest Jones, then president of the International Psychoanalytical Association, used all his power and prestige to urge psychoanalysts to refrain from taking political positions or from commenting on political matters. He called for a purely intrapsychic focus for psychoanalysis, avoiding any discussion of the social, political, or any extra-psychic factors. His rhetoric is most relevant here, calling on psychoanalysis to attend exclusively to "the primitive forces of the mind" and to eschew any interest in sociological factors that were construed as superficial and non-psychoanalytic (quoted in Herzog, 2017, p. 3). Hence, it was specifically "the primitive" that was defined as the object of psychoanalytic study and investigation. In this one move, "the primitive" not only became the object—the Other—of psychoanalysis, but this positioning also served to rationalize and justify the psychoanalytic avoidance of the socio-political, and especially of the study of race and culture—the very analysis that would ultimately come to challenge and complicate the notion of "the primitive."

At the New York University Postdoctoral Program in Psychotherapy & Psychoanalysis, of which I have been director since 1998, we have established a Committee on Ethnicity, Race, Culture, Class, and Language (CERCCL). We provide several scholarships to promote diversity by supporting students from underrepresented populations within the psychoanalytic profession, as well as assisting those who serve diverse populations. While psychoanalysis has opened up, first to non-medical doctors, then to women, and then to gay, lesbian, and queer analysts, we have not yet been successful with other forms of diversity. Unfortunately, our well-intentioned efforts to recruit a diverse group of students and faculty have so far yielded only minimal results. While there are many factors that need to be considered in understanding why psychoanalysis has remained so homogeneous, we must carefully and systematically examine and change any racist and misogynistic assumptions that remain deeply embedded in the theory, as only such an intellectual project will allow the psychoanalytic community to become a welcoming home for a more diverse group of contributors.

A young African-American graduate student asks why she should consider investing time and money pursuing postdoctoral analytic education when there is little likelihood she can conduct four or five times a week individual treatment within her own community. An enthusiastic young Latino psychologist who practices in a community health center asks what benefit there would be in his coming for psychoanalytic training when he is determined to reach out to larger numbers of people than he could possibly reach with a psychoanalytic approach. These psychologists might even think of themselves as "psychodynamically oriented," but would not necessarily want to invest time and money in learning to do psychoanalysis proper. Yet although most psychoanalysts today have little opportunity to practice formal psychoanalysis, they understand that psychoanalysis, defined broadly, can make a significant contribution to psychotherapy and to community mental health.

These non-white, potential analytic candidates are exactly the students we want to attract to our program; but they sense some exclusionary, elitist, classist, and racist sensibilities within psychoanalytic institutions. If we fail to make the necessary changes so as to attract these students and future contributors, then we cannot possibly thrive, nor do we deserve to do so. But to do that, we psychoanalysts must start to reflect the broader population. Certainly, there are practical considerations of time, finances, and social class that affect our attracting such students to our programs, but some of what keeps them from joining us is our embeddedness in colonial assumptions. It seems to me that if Kurt Lewin was right, that there is nothing so practical as a good theory, then to effect the practical changes that are required we must begin with a detailed, systematic, and comprehensive deconstruction of racist, misogynistic, classist assumptions in psychoanalytic theory and how these have become embedded in our institutions. We have all internalized colonialism as a way of being in the world (Maldonado-Torres, 2007, as summarized by Esprey, 2017), and there is no transcending race as we internalize both sides of the relationship, the colonizer and the colonized, the oppressor and the oppressed (Suchet, 2007). Studying and teaching Brickman's *Race in Psychoanalysis* may be our best way to initiate the critical engagement with the legacy of racism in our theory that is essential to the continuity and growth of psychoanalysis.

Lewis Aron, Ph.D., Director,
New York University Postdoctoral Program
in Psychotherapy & Psychoanalysis

Note

1 Originally published as *Aboriginal Populations in the Mind: Race and Primitivity in Psychoanalysis* (New York: Columbia University Press, 2003).

Preface to the new edition

Psychoanalysis has not commonly been understood to be implicated in questions of racial bias, just as, until a generation ago, it had not been associated with any bias concerning gender and sexuality. On the contrary, Freud's vision of psychoanalysis as a universal theory of the psyche has, with a few exceptions, been accepted at face value for most of its existence. But towards the end of the twentieth century and by the beginning of the twenty-first, this veneer of universality has begun to be called into question.

In the last few decades, there has been an increase in the number of non-white psychoanalysts and psychoanalytic candidates who, attracted by a discipline holding the promise of a liberating understanding of self and other, have encountered racist elements within the theory and practice of psychoanalysis itself. Similar to the way women who entered psychoanalytic training in the final decades of the twentieth century went on to challenge outdated psychoanalytic theories about women, investigating new conceptions of gender, sexuality and the formation of subjectivity, here too we have begun to see the emergence of discussions of the difficulties and possibilities posed by the conjunction of the lived problems of race and the theory and practice of psychoanalysis.

This book aspires to further these discussions by investigating outdated psychoanalytic assumptions about race from a postcolonial perspective. It aims to reveal the colonialist theoretical network that underlies and engenders racist elements within psychoanalysis; to locate the origins and trace the ramifications of this network throughout the foundational texts of Freud; and to analyze the implications for our contemporary understanding and practice of psychoanalysis. It is a revised edition of my 2003 book,

Aboriginal Populations in the Mind: Race and Primitivity in Psychoanalysis
(Columbia University Press), offered anew as a resource for psychoanalysts
and students of psychoanalysis, white and non-white, academically as well
as clinically oriented, to assist in coming to grips with the pitfalls and paradoxes concerning race that are embedded within this field.

One of the predicaments in recent attempts to come to terms with the
topic of race in psychoanalysis has been the tendency to focus on raced
difference and racism as they are found within the individual mind and
within the interpersonal dynamics of the psychoanalytic relationship. Of
course, psychoanalysis, like psychology, is the study of the psyche, and
the psyche has for much of western history been conceived of as a characteristic internal to the individual subject. This fits only too comfortably
with the (white) American predilection to think of racism as a personal
outlook that an individual either does or does not have, or that does or
does not occur within a particular setting or relationship. The results,
therefore, are psychoanalytic essays which, though often very subtle and
penetrating, are limited to discussions of the ways in which issues of race
and racism are negotiated within the psychoanalytic relationship.

This is a very necessary and important task, but it does not fully
address the issue that racism is not, fundamentally, solely a characteristic
of the individual subject and his or her associated interpersonal interactions, even though quite obviously, individuals can and do espouse and
act upon racist views which dovetail with their particular psychological
dispositions; and individuals can and do both repress and express these
views in a variety of ways. But by discussing race and racism in terms of
individual and interacting psyches, these accounts help obscure the wider
political and structural dimensions of racism. Although some recent psychoanalytic authors have begun to recognize the thoroughly social and
political nature of individual subjects and interpersonal interactions,[1]
they have largely not yet taken into account the role of racism within the
theoretical structure of psychoanalysis itself.

Racism is a foundational sociopolitical and epistemic division of human
beings into the fully human and the not-quite human, with reference to differences in skin color and ethnicity. A key moment in the inauguration of
this type of categorization was the emergence of the modern idea of Man,
more or less concurrent with the aftermath of Columbus' encounter with
the Americas. The modern conception of Man and the modern western
capitalist economy on which it depended were developed together with,

and as a result of, expropriation and slavery in Europe's exploited colonies and their plantations.[2] This political-social-epistemic categorization of different types of people into the fully human, entitled to rights, land and liberty; and the not-so-human, lacking entitlement not only to the above-mentioned desirables but to life itself, has continued on in different shapes and forms to this day. It continues to influence our ways of conceptualizing relationships between different groups of human beings. Embodied in our institutions of governance, it is often referred to as institutional or structural or systemic racism.

In the last several years the systemic nature of racism in the United States has gained more mainstream acknowledgment due to the galvanizing and well-publicized works of such writers as Michelle Alexander and Ta-Nehisi Coates,[3] to the widely disseminated cell-phone videos of unprovoked police violence against unarmed African Americans and to extensive public protests against this violence. All of this has caused some segments of white America to begin to recognize what black America has been aware of all along: the systemic nature of the racism that shapes our governance, law enforcement, work and educational opportunities, and the geography of our living arrangements.

Among the institutions that help perpetuate and normalize the division of humans into the entitled and those vulnerable to degradation, we must also count our disciplines of knowledge. They too are "institutions" that create, embody and mold our ways of understanding ourselves, others and the world around us. Psychoanalysis is one such discipline of knowledge, as are the social sciences, the humanities and the professions. In several of these fields, scholars have begun the work of teasing out the racist elements in their intellectual traditions, in spite of the often canonic status of these traditions. For example, in his book *The Racial Contract*, philosopher Charles W. Mills systematically unveils the centrality of racial bias in the classics of western philosophy, demonstrating the racism propounded in the writings of (among others) Immanuel Kant, "in complete opposition to the image of his work that has come down to us and is standardly taught in introductory ethics courses."[4] Psychoanalysis is one of the great cultural projects of western modernity, and it too harbors a racial bias that seems to contradict its distinguished image. More than other academic disciplines, psychoanalysis, like all forms of psychology and psychotherapy, is susceptible to playing a pivotal role in the transmission of racism because of its ability to represent social and cultural conventions as norms of mental health. While psychoanalysis was created to challenge these norms rather than perpetuate them, it nonetheless lends its considerable cultural authority both within and outside of the consulting room to a range of differing interpretations, many of which remain unaware of their troubling racial assumptions.

Freud's work entered the world as a radical subversion of the conventional wisdom concerning not only sexuality and the unconscious, but also of Victorian notions of the mental abyss thought to separate so-called "primitive peoples" from modern Europeans. Instead of an abyss separating Europeans from their cultural others, Freud saw the "primitive unconscious" as the inheritance of all of humankind. In describing a universal psyche common to all, Freud saw Otherness as a quality *within* all humans, rather than a barrier between different groups of humans. Nevertheless, at the same time Freud's work can be seen to be pervaded by his often inadvertent racial, if not racist, assumptions.

In 1915, in his essay on "The Unconscious," Freud wrote that "The content of the Ucs. may be compared with an aboriginal population in the mind."[5] I chose this sentence as subtitle and epigraph because it neatly sums up the problematic this book addresses: the self or subject of psychoanalysis has been constructed, in part, via the use of now-outdated, raced representations of Europe's others. These representations are not restricted to Freud's more speculative works about civilization and the history of society; as with the essay in which this quotation is found, we find such representations throughout his works on the agencies and dynamics of the mind, where they continue to wield an often unsuspected influence.

In this reading of Freud's work, then, I lift out the threads of his assumptions about race and connect them to the hidden theoretical networks to which they belong. These assumptions may seem too literal or beside the point in view of the larger significance of Freud's work. Nonetheless, similar to many of his pronouncements on women, they are objectionable and unjust, and can be recognized as such without invalidating the continued relevance of the discipline he created. Let me be clear: Freud's ambitions were not racist. Indeed, he developed psychoanalysis as a universal theory of the mind in part as a riposte to the racist discourse of his day. Nonetheless, the susceptibility of psychoanalysis to a casual racism has been played out all too often in the analyses, training, supervision and professional lives of black analysts and trainees, as the recent movie *Black Psychoanalysts Speak* so eloquently attests.[6]

As I argue throughout, Freud worked within a conceptual network strongly influenced by the late nineteenth-century racist anthropology which had helped legitimate Europe's colonizing and slaving enterprises. This nineteenth-century anthropology contributed to the basis of Freud's works on culture and society, from where it made its way into his works on the agencies of the psyche and on clinical technique. But just as the recognition that the Enlightenment discourse of liberty took place in tandem with the practice of slavery in Europe's colonies does not diminish our ideals of liberty, this book is not meant to diminish our appreciation of the very real capabilities of psychoanalysis to illuminate both psychic and social ills. Indeed, it is the imposing significance of Freud's work that calls for this critique. Psychoanalysis will be better suited to our contemporary world once we reckon with, and begin to free it from, its colonial baggage.

Notes

1 Frantz Fanon was the pioneer in this respect, in his *Black Skin White Masks* (Paris: Editions de Seuil, 1952; New York: Grove Press, 1967), and Homi Bhabha's *The Location of Culture* (London; New York: Routledge, 1994) has also become centrally significant. See also Derek Hook, *A Critical Psychology of the Postcolonial: The Mind of Apartheid* (New York: Routledge, 2012); Kelly Oliver, *The Colonization of Psychic Space: A Psychoanalytic Social Theory of Oppression* (Minneapolis, MN: University of Minnesota Press, 2004); Phillis Isabella Sheppard, *Self, Culture and Others in Womanist Practical Theology* (New York: Palgrave Macmillan, 2011); Hortense J. Spillers, "'All the Things You Could Be By Now, If Sigmund Freud's Wife Was Your Mother': Psychoanalysis and Race," *Black, White, and in Color: Essays on American Literature and Culture* (Chicago, IL: University of Chicago Press, 2003), 376–427. See also the discussion of Ranjana Khanna, *Dark Continents: Psychoanalysis and Colonialism* (Durham, NC: Duke University Press, 2003, 2004) in note 10 of the Introduction, as a significant addition to these works.
2 For this periodization, see David Scott, "The Re-Enchantment of Humanism: An Interview with Sylvia Wynter," *Small Axe* 8 (September 2000): 119–207.
3 Michelle Alexander, *The New Jim Crow: Mass Incarceration in the Age of Colorblindness* (New York: The New Press, 2010); Ta-Nehisi Coates, *Between the World and Me* (New York: Spiegel and Grau, Random House, 2015).
4 Charles Mills, *The Racial Contract* (Ithaca, NY: Cornell University Press, 1997), 72.
5 Sigmund Freud, "The Unconscious," in *The Standard Edition of the Complete Psychological Works of Sigmund Freud* (London: Hogarth Press, 1914–16), 14: 195.
6 Basia Winograd, *Black Psychoanalysts Speak* (PEP Video Grants, 1:1, 2014).

Acknowledgments

Fourteen years have passed since this book was first published, and many of the people who helped shape my thinking about these issues and kept my spirits buoyed during the original writing have continued to sustain me with their wisdom and generosity as I have prepared this edition. Among them are Anne Blackburn, Susan Gooding, Elise LaRose, Maureen McLane, Linda Diamond and Mark Shapiro, Laura Slatkin, and Bruce Thomas. In addition, I must, very belatedly, thank Sara Bershtel and Laura Slatkin for their crucial role in getting the original edition of this book published in the first place. My thanks to my family for the pleasure they've given me over the years and for the newest little ones who now grace our lives.

I remain deeply appreciative of the scholarship of the many people cited in the footnotes whose work has made mine possible, in particular that of Jessica Benjamin and George W. Stocking Jr. Others have provided indispensable assistance along the way: Lynn M. El-Hoshy, former Senior Cataloging Policy Specialist at the Library of Congress, patiently instructed me on the intricacies of CIP data (the Library of Congress' cataloging record that selects the key words used in the search engines of libraries and bookstores for each book) and kindly established several new headings to accommodate the subject matter of this book; the Center for Religion and Psychotherapy of Chicago and its related Mason Fund provided funding at the early stages of this work; Jennifer Crewe, Associate Provost and Director of Columbia University Press, graciously smoothed the transition from one press to the other; Kate Hawes, Senior Publisher and Charles Bath, Editorial Assistant, both at Routledge (of Taylor & Francis), as well as Caroline Watson, Production Manager at Swales & Willis, have provided generous assistance in the preparation of the revised manuscript. Finally, I am indebted beyond measure to Lewis Aron, Director of the New York University Postdoctoral Program in Psychotherapy and Psychoanalysis, for his keen interest, appreciation, and ongoing support of this work, and for shepherding this edition into the Relational Perspectives Book Series at Routledge. Many thanks!

Introduction

What assumptions concerning race are embedded within psychoanalysis? What do we learn when we consider the origins of psychoanalysis from the postcolonial perspective of the cultural legacies of colonialism? These issues first began to press themselves on me as I pursued graduate studies in the humanities and the social sciences, at the same time as I was training to become a psychoanalytically oriented psychotherapist. Within these two different frameworks I repeatedly encountered markedly differing conceptions and evaluations of the category of "the primitive." In the academy I was confronted with the trenchant critiques of postcolonial theorists who considered the idea of the *primitive* to be a long-abandoned relic of anthropology's colonialist and racist ancestry, where its evocation of the presumed inferiority of non-white and non-western peoples had contributed to the legitimation of Europe's colonial and slaving enterprises around the globe. In my clinical training I was guided toward the care of psychological suffering within a framework that made liberal use of the term *primitivity* to describe the feelings and behaviors that characterized the painful situations in which our patients found themselves. In the clinic I was struck by the common and casual use of this term: "S/he's so *primitive*," I often heard; "that behavior is so *primitive*." Indeed, patients themselves sometimes took up the same language to complain about the intractable nature of their distressing feelings: "it's just so *primitive*."

An overview of recent psychoanalytic literature reveals that this usage is ubiquitous, and thus receives the full legitimating support a prestigious field can confer. At first, I accepted it at face value: after all, psychoanalytic theory tells us that our patterns of behavior and the roots of our pathologies lie in the earliest experiences of our lives, when our mental organization and abilities are at their most rudimentary. Why not call this level of organization *primitive*? Why not describe certain behaviors understood to be immature and childish as *primitive*? Surely the term *primitive* is commonly used in everyday life, not only within psychoanalytic theory, to convey the raw and the rudimentary, the undeveloped, the archaic.

But this psychoanalytic usage continued to bother me because it seemed remarkably indifferent to the postcolonial critique which I found so urgently persuasive. Just what did this clinical usage imply? Was *primitive* behavior meant to refer exclusively to characteristics of infants and to psychologically regressive episodes in adults, or did its psychoanalytic meaning also somehow apply to those who used to be—and apparently sometimes still are—referred to as "primitive peoples"? Why was psychopathology characterized as *primitive*, along with femininity and religious experience? If the psychoanalytic meaning of *primitivity* extended to so-called primitive peoples as well, as it often seemed, was contemporary clinical psychoanalysis proffering a covert social Darwinism in its developmental coding of behavior? In short, how could the clinical usage of the term *primitive* not be connected with the racist category which, for centuries, had classified the non-white, non-western world as eligible for colonization and domination by the west?

It finally dawned on me that what I was witnessing in these casual and not-so-casual remarks were unacknowledged traces of the racially inflected anthropological theory that had provided Freud with the foundational premises of his social thought. Freud read widely among the anthropological writings leading up to his day; understandably, it was on these writings that he based his knowledge of non-white and non-western peoples and of their presumed relation to a universal human prehistory and a universal evolutionary history. I became convinced that although the problem extended far beyond the use of a single term, the term *primitive* in psychoanalysis is as central to the problem of race as the term *feminine* has been to the problem of gender. I saw how frequent, subtle slippages between the two registers of the term *primitivity*, the anthropological and the psychological, contributed to the effortless way in which psychoanalytic interpretation could convey, and thereby unobtrusively help reinforce, racist stereotypes.

An example offered itself at a case conference I happened to attend one day, conducted by a group of white, psychoanalytically oriented psychotherapists. The patient under discussion was a young white man who had lost his mother at an early age and was now having difficulty deciding on his vocation. One way or another, he hoped eventually to go to Africa to do good works. His desire to go to Africa was immediately taken up by the clinicians at the conference: he wished to visit the dark continent! they exclaimed. What could this mean, except that he was now ready to explore the darker reaches of his own mind? What could this mean, except that he was now ready to explore the painful memories surrounding the loss of his mother, *primitive* memories buried so deeply in those darker reaches? He wanted to go to a developing country: clearly, he was signaling his interest in carrying forward his own arrested self-development. The remarks tumbled out in enthusiastic profusion.

No one for a moment questioned the implications of endorsing stereotypes of Africa as dark and developing and primitive, or the strategy by which these stereotypes could be used to represent the psychological situation of a young white American man. Indeed, raising such issues would have been perceived as an unwelcome disruption to the clinical work at hand. Yet there it was: the most intimate details of this white man's psychological development configured through the use of racialized stereotypes of Africa. We might well imagine what role such assumptions would play in clinical work with African-American and other overtly raced subjects.

Of course, one might protest that this vignette demonstrates nothing more than the taking up of culturally available stereotypes in a chain of interpretive associations, and that it is not psychoanalytic theory itself that has produced or even condones these associations. Indeed, it is quite unlikely that the many psychoanalytic practitioners and writers who might make use of such associations and in particular the term *primitivity* to account for a range of psychological phenomena would intentionally endorse the racist anthropological theories that gave this term and its network of meanings their currency. They would most probably disavow several of the texts in which Freud explicitly made such anthropological and evolutionary arguments. But it will be my claim in these pages that traces of these anthropological theories are to be found throughout Freud's work, giving rise to a covert racist subtext within the discourse of psychoanalysis.

This study asks the question: What attitudes toward its raced others does psychoanalysis harbor within its configurations of subjectivity? Rather than a psychoanalytic investigation of race or racism, this is an investigation of psychoanalysis from the perspective of the question of racial difference. It is concerned with the implications of the relationship of the foundational texts of psychoanalysis to the colonial construction of race as a system of unequal power and privilege indexed to skin color.[1] The beginnings of psychoanalysis coincided with the heyday of nineteenth-century European colonialism, and Freud borrowed liberally from the colonialist discourse of the anthropologists of his time. Although occasionally acknowledged as part of the "tarnished origins" of psychoanalysis,[2] this colonial influence has commonly been held to be peripheral and of little consequence to the main body and import of Freud's work. I intend to demonstrate, however, that its effects have been more pervasive than generally recognized, having permeated not only Freud's works on culture and society but his texts about the agencies of the mind and his therapeutic approach as well.

It is to a considerable degree through the figure of the primitive that a colonialist anthropological perspective was able to find a foothold in psychoanalysis. *Primitivity* is central to Freud's concerns: both its repudiation and its reclamation are at the heart of the psychoanalytic project. *Primitivity* in psychoanalysis is not simply a disinterested term signifying the earliest and often repressed stages of individual psychic development, as is often assumed. That the term *primitive* functioned for Freud both as a psychological category and an anthropological one points to its location at the intersection of numerous colonial signifiers that converged, at the turn of the last century, on the topic of race. For the nineteenth-century anthropology from which Freud borrowed, the *primitive* referred to the earliest and most rudimentary stages of a universally conceived human evolution. In this anthropological sense, it referred to "savages" who were considered, by virtue of their differences from European cultural norms and their darker skins, to be less evolutionarily advanced than their European cousins. But for Freud *primitivity* also referred to the earliest psychosexual stages of development of the white, European child. The overlap of these two meanings meant that the concept of *primitivity* would move throughout Freud's work with metonymic force, allowing for the possibility of a continuous slippage between psychological and anthropological registers. *Primitivity* is thus the key to the racial economy of psychoanalysis, the watchword of a psychologizing discourse behind which is concealed an ideology of race. For this reason, my investigation of issues of race in psychoanalysis will revolve around the ramifications of various conceptions of *primitivity*.

Freud's corpus radically subverted the imperialist arrogance of late-nineteenth-century European thought, ushering in a critique of western civilization and a profound skepticism concerning its "progress." Freud used the notion of *primitivity* to undermine the supreme self-confidence of modern European self-understanding, contending that what had been consigned as primitive actually lived on in the structures of contemporary European subjectivity and institutions. But although *primitivity* was the term through which Freud affirmed the universal commonality of the psyche, it was also the racially indexed term of derogation he used to discredit the pretensions of civilization.[3] This ambiguity of the term *primitivity*, embedded within Freud's critique of western civilization, meant that his critique covertly sustained, while overtly dismantling, the colonialist theses with which this term was linked. Hence the racially ambiguous nature of the emancipatory intent of Freud's project: his critique often retained the terms of the underlying assumptions it challenged.

Because *primitivity* signifies both an anthropological and a psychological meaning, it allows us to investigate how anthropological assumptions about racial difference found in Freud's cultural works were absorbed into his metapsychological formulations to become constitutive elements of his representations of the agencies of the mind. By the time it reached Freud, the concept of primitivity had accumulated a host of now-outmoded assumptions linking racial differences to degrees of sociocultural evolution and from there to the psychological development of the contemporary European subject. It was associated with a range of European policies that had coordinated the relationships between western and non-western peoples at least as far back as Columbus's arrival on the shores of the New World. Because so much in psychoanalysis came to be apprehended under the sign of the primitive, this concept not only leads us to the relationship between colonialist anthropological thought and Freud's model of the psyche, but also gives us access to connections between race and psychopathology, race and gender, race and temporality, and race and religion. These interrelations demonstrate the interwoven and reciprocal influences of the three main bodies of Freud's texts: his metapsychological texts, where he describes the agencies and dynamics of the psyche; his cultural texts, forays into the history and workings of the psyche, culture and society; and his texts focusing on the protocols of clinical work, as found in his *Papers on Technique*. Often enough, clinicians read primarily Freud's metapsychological and clinical texts, while students of the humanities read primarily his cultural texts: there is in general little communication between the two approaches. Clinicians often discount Freud's texts about culture and society as peripheral and speculative. They are his "scientific myths," his cultural daydreams, and therefore held to be unnecessary to the principal intent of his work. But it was Freud himself who taught us that the (day) dreams and (scientific) myths we may consider inconsequential are often the hidden but royal roads to the underlying significance of the matter at hand. Reading these three groups of writings with and through each other helps us see how assumptions about race written into Freud's seemingly peripheral works on culture and society have implications that resonate throughout his works on metapsychology and clinical technique.

In this book, then, I trace a covert racial subtext within psychoanalysis through an examination of the sociocultural, metapsychological and clinical dimensions of Freud's thought. Over fifty years ago Philip Rieff wrote that "the connection between psychoanalysis and Lamarckianism cannot be overemphasized,"[4] stressing Freud's wholehearted adoption of the theory of the inheritance of acquired characteristics that was a staple of nineteenth-century social evolutionary and anthropological thought. More recently Mary Ann Doane has written that "the force of the category of race in the constitution of Otherness within psychoanalysis should not be underestimated."[5] Taken together, these two remarks point to my contention that the hidden category of race is omnipresent in psychoanalysis within the Lamarckian (and Haeckelian) category of the primitive which it adopted and made its own.[6] The racial subtext in psychoanalysis arises not from any personal racist animus on Freud's part, but from the logical force and implications of the colonialist anthropological theories from which he drew. This network of meanings became part of the modernist temporal framework of psychoanalysis, which saw the modern present as overcoming, by coming to terms with, the primitive past.

This book might have been more modestly titled "Race in Freudian Psychoanalysis" since it focuses predominantly on Freud's texts. However, I purposely chose the broader title to indicate that, rather than a work of purely historical interest, my intent was to write, in Foucault's phrase, a "history of the present": By focusing on Freud's texts as the common foundation of all the various schools of psychoanalysis that have developed over the past century, I hope to elucidate what I see as a contemporary predicament within the larger family of psychoanalytic schools by tracing its hitherto unexamined roots.

There are, of course, many schools of interpretation within psychoanalysis itself, some of which are in acute opposition to others. They can, perhaps, be loosely encompassed within two broadly drawn tendencies, both deeply woven into its very fabric. The first emphasizes our essential incompleteness and disorientation, the disturbing existence of the alien within what is closest to home, and suggests that elements of our being are in fundamental conflict with one another. The second emphasizes our desire for coherence and for the containment, if not the resolution, of anxiety and conflict; it suggests that the elements of our being are functional parts of a larger whole and that what is disturbing is contingent rather than elemental. For some, narrative coherence redeems us from the inner chaos we suffer; for others, as Adam Phillips suggests, it is the very "making coherent of a life—the forcing of a pattern—that people often suffer from."[7] These two trends are represented by two phrases found in close proximity in *The Ego and the Id*, where Freud wrote both that the ego was "a poor creature owing service to three masters and consequently menaced by three dangers" and that "psychoanalysis is an instrument to enable the ego to achieve a progressive conquest of the id."[8] Freud's evolutionary pronouncements on race and primitivity find their most congenial—although not exclusive—home in those aspects of his works which lend themselves to the second, more positivistic view of the psyche, where the ego or self is the paramount agency of the mind whose structuration and stability is the telos of psychological development. But of course Freud's work both includes and exceeds this positivistic dimension: as a multivocal text with numerous and differing possibilities and problems, it can be read equally for its intentions to normalize as well as to disturb.

Psychoanalysis remains invaluable for its exploration of the constitution of subjectivities and for an approach to psychic suffering that privileges the roles of inner desire, fantasy, anxiety and conflict. It has generated the indispensable insight that our behaviors and symptoms speak to us, giving testimony to hidden layers of meaning which, when articulated, can lead both to a deeper self-understanding and to an increased capacity to participate more fully in the world around us. Although this book is devoted to the racial subtext embedded in psychoanalysis which I believe we have an obligation to confront and come to terms with, this subtext by no means exhausts all of what psychoanalysis has to offer. Susceptible to multiple readings that can support a range of political perspectives, psychoanalysis contains the resources to illuminate as well as to reproduce dilemmas of racial difference. As a critical discourse it is eminently suited to analyze racist and colonialist discourse, as has been shown in the works of Frantz Fanon, Homi Bhabha and an ever-growing number of others.

But despite its ability to furnish the tools for such emancipatory interventions, psychoanalysis retains its own ideological blind spots. As with questions of gender, Freud's outdated assumptions concerning race and primitivity are likely to be reproduced whenever his theories (or those of his descendants) are used, until and unless these assumptions have been explicitly examined and challenged. My aim is to confront the assumptions concerning race within psychoanalysis in the service of a reading that is responsive to the racial dilemmas of our time. This examination is not meant to indict Freud or psychoanalysis as purveyors of racism. Rather, I am claiming that the concept of primitivity and its associated network of meanings in psychoanalysis are part of a broader colonialist discourse and constitute a problem that requires our critical attention. By considering its ramifications throughout Freud's work, together with the history that is its semantic freight, my hope is that we can begin to reckon with the fact that this concept, and the network of meanings to which it is ineluctably connected, "demands," as Hortense Spillers has written of the problematic of race itself, "an endless response."[9]

This project lies at the intersection of a number of different bodies of literature that engage psychoanalysis from different disciplinary perspectives. There is the long anthropological tradition of the application and critique of psychoanalysis in relation to non-western cultures; there are those who have sought to expose the role and outdated nature of nineteenth-century evolutionary thought in Freud's work. There are some who, in addressing the relationship of psychoanalysis to religion, have been obliged to contend in various ways with the "primitivity" of religion. Still others have written about Freud's racial—Jewish—identity and its impact on his creation of psychoanalysis, some of whom have pointed to the relationship between anti-Semitism and colonialism. Practicing psychoanalysts, too, have recently begun to grapple with ways of dealing with questions of ethnocentricity and racism in western clinical practice. And cultural critics have begun to examine more closely the interwoven assumptions about gender, sexuality and race that have been part of the psychoanalytic enterprise. Thus far, however, little systematic attention has been paid to the colonial and racist ancestry of the anthropological thought which Freud made use of, and its relationship to the historicizing framework of psychoanalysis that seeks to create a modern subjectivity through a renegotiation of the past.[10]

The conversation between psychoanalysis and those viewed as its racial or cultural others has, historically, been largely the province of anthropologists who understandably have had no particular concern with the implications of their arguments for what we might call the indigenous practice of psychoanalysis: the practice of psychoanalysis in the western cultures from which it emerged and in which it has developed. A conversation within this anthropological/psychoanalytic tradition would begin with the anthropologist Bronislaw Malinowski, who, in his *Sex and Repression in Savage Society* (1927), vigorously challenged the universality of the oedipus complex, contending that family complexes were not universal but instead varied with social structure. This conversation would proceed to Ernest Jones's condemnation of Malinowski's critique the following year, and would continue down the years through the ensuing anthropological endorsements, modifications and criticisms of psychoanalysis until reaching the contemporary literature of psychoanalytic anthropology.[11] Whether psychoanalysis is found, in these anthropologically oriented discussions, to be a suitable critical or therapeutic practice for cultures other than the west has not been understood to have any bearing on its domestic practice and utility. After all, the focus of these anthropological discussions has been on cultures far away (for instance, the Trobriand islanders, the highlanders of Papua New Guinea, various peoples of South Asia, the Kagwahiv of Brazil). But as has become increasingly clear and as postcolonial and critical race theorists have been pointing out for some time now, "cultures far away" have all along been implicated in "our" everyday, contemporary lives, through the legacies of slavery, colonialism, immigration and now globalization. How the western self's raced/cultural Other is imagined is at the very heart of how that self or subject is represented. Given the invidious racial situation of his own day, Freud attempted to transcend the racial taxonomies of his time by creating a model of the psyche as held in common by all humans. But his universalist solution shared with the project of modernity, of which it was a part, the problems of deep-seated connections to racism, colonization and slavery. As anthropologists John and Jean Comaroff have written, "The colony was not a mere extension of the modern world. It was part of what made that world modern in the first place."[12] Colonization and slavery created the economies that made the modern world possible, as has been argued by C.L.R. James, W.E.B. Du Bois, Eric Williams, Frantz Fanon, David Brion Davis and others. Since Freud's psychoanalysis was one of the discourses that helped shape the culture of western modernity, it is of key significance that we examine the contribution of the colony and the plantation—and of the presumed "primitivity" of the peoples who lived there—to psychoanalytic understandings of self and raced other.

The debate between psychoanalytic and anthropological perspectives on those other to the west began with Malinowski's challenge to the universality of the oedipus complex; but before Malinowski was challenging Freud, Freud himself was reading earlier anthropologists such as E.B. Tylor and Sir James Frazer, whose evolutionary notions of "primitive culture" represented the culmination of centuries of European thought concerning non-European others. Thus, rather than beginning with Malinowski and the history of the disputes between psychoanalytic and anthropological disciplines, I devote the first chapter to a genealogy of the figure of the primitive in western thought, tracing the contexts in which Europe's raced others came to be understood as representatives of the European past and came to furnish the basis for theories of "the primitive mind." These theories eventually fed into the colonial and evolutionary anthropology of the latter half of the nineteenth century which provided Freud with the foundations of his social thought. The perplexity with which my contentions were often met when I first started out on this project ("What's wrong with the idea of the primitive?") and the continued justifications for the persistence of the psychoanalytic use of this concept ("It's a scientific term") have convinced me that this intellectual history and its sociopolitical contexts provide a crucial background for a fuller understanding of the hidden complexities of Freud's theories of primitivity.

Chapter 2 begins by discussing some of the specific writers, forerunners of today's anthropologists, on whom Freud relied, particularly in his writing of *Totem and Taboo* and other works on culture and society. Through his adoption of these writers' Lamarckianism and recapitulationism, Freud mapped their racially coded scale of cultural evolution onto his model of contemporary psychological development, correlating psychological with anthropological primitivity. The chapter argues that *Totem and Taboo*, by virtue of its function as the "origin myth" of psychoanalysis, provides the paradigmatic reference point for Freud's descriptions of the origins of the agencies of the psyche. This, in turn, gives us the background for a demonstration of the pervasiveness of the continued entanglement within psychoanalysis of anthropological and psychological meanings of primitivity. The chapter goes on to examine regression as the mechanism in psychoanalysis that forged the link between its raced others and psychopathology.

Chapter 3 examines *Group Psychology and the Analysis of the Ego*, the sequel, in a sense, to *Totem and Taboo*, where Freud, in the guise of an analysis of the psychodynamics of groups, presented his theory of the emergence of modern subjectivity from "primitive" groups and, in so doing, sketched out his implicit psychology of primitivity. This implicit psychology of primitivity is characterized as an emotional enthrallment with authority, an enthrallment cast by Freud at some moments as the racial characteristic of "primitive peoples" and, at others, as politically produced by relationships of domination and submission. The chapter then explores the relationship within psychoanalysis between race and gender by comparing Freud's psychologies of primitivity and femininity: it is the repudiation of these related positions on which the normative subjectivity of psychoanalysis is seen to rest. The representation of both primitivity and femininity as repudiated positions is traced to the premise of separation as the psychic operation necessary to the constitution of subjectivity, and the chapter ends by examining this premise and proposing an alternative to it.

Chapter 4 contextualizes Freud's discourse of primitivity in two ways: by placing it within the larger historicizing framework of psychoanalysis, and by relating it to the social and cultural situation in which Freud lived and wrote. The first part of the chapter places psychoanalysis under the postcolonial critique of the historicizing or "temporalizing" tendencies of anthropology that have consigned non-western cultures and non-white peoples to the past of the modern west. This leads to the topic of religion in which, for Freud, was crystallized the authority of the past from which psychoanalysis was to release us. The discussion reveals the political dimension of Freud's critique of religion as the ideology of primitivity and demonstrates the racialized framework in which this critique was inscribed. An investigation of secondary works on psychoanalysis and religion examines how well their authors respond both to Freud's criticisms concerning religion and to postcolonial criticisms concerning the temporal mapping of cultural differences. The chapter concludes by placing Freud's work in the context of his position as a Jew in fin-de-siècle Vienna, where he repudiated the racist Aryan and anti-Semitic discourse of his day as part of a religious past that was to be superseded by a contemporary, universal scientific culture—all the while retaining his Jewish identity.

The way psychoanalysis is understood to figure subjectivity and raced difference has, of course, a profound effect on its therapeutics. Authors who have addressed the question of race and psychoanalysis from a textual perspective have not evinced much interest in the clinical scene, whereas those whose primary interest in psychoanalysis is in its clinical application have not paid much attention to the historical contexts of the theoretical constructs that inform that scene. Chapter 5 examines the clinical psychoanalytic situation, drawing connections between Freud's *Papers on Technique* and texts analyzed in earlier chapters, to demonstrate how the colonial perspective written into psychoanalytic theory through its anthropological foundations became part of the blueprint for the clinical relationship. Freud's fluctuating perspectives on the therapeutic use of suggestion and influence, along with his conceptualizations of regression and resistance, are examined for their contribution to disturbing resonances that can be seen between the psychoanalytic encounter and the relationship of colonizer to colonized.

Finally, the Epilogue reflects on some of the epistemological changes within current trends of psychoanalysis that open up possibilities of disengagement from its colonial legacy.

Freud read widely among the colonialist anthropological works of his day; through his incorporation of these works into his own, their theories became staples of psychoanalytic thought. Contemporary anthropologists, together with postcolonial and critical race theorists, have subjected these ideas, as they have appeared in anthropological works as well as in western political, philosophical and legal thought, to considerable critical scrutiny. This study seeks to extend such scrutiny to the career of these ideas in the foundational works of psychoanalysis.

Notes

1 Although there is no doubt as to the reality of racism, "race" itself, as biologists and anthropologists have been telling us for some time, is not a scientifically meaningful category: the number of genetic differences between groups commonly understood to be racially different is smaller than that found between members of a single group considered racially homogenous. See Luigi Luca Cavalli-Sforza, *Genes, Peoples, and Languages*, trans. Mark Seielstad (New York: North Point Press/Farrar, Straus and Giroux, 2000), esp. chapter 2,

"Genes and History," 3–32, for a geneticist's explanation of the pointlessness of attempts at racial classification. Race is politically, socially and culturally ascribed rather than found in our genes. Nevertheless, the categorization of human beings in terms of visible differences understood as racial is ubiquitous and lines up not only with cultural differences, but with the entitlement of some and the oppression of others, and with the inequitable distribution of wealth and resources within and among the nations of the world.

2 Christopher Lane, "The Psychoanalysis of Race: An Introduction," in Christopher Lane, ed., *The Psychoanalysis of Race* (New York: Columbia University Press, 1998), 1–37, quote at 13.

3 cf. Ashis Nandy, "The Savage Freud: The First Non-Western Psychoanalyst and the Politics of Secret Selves in Colonial India" in *The Savage Freud and Other Essays on Possible and Retrievable Selves* (Princeton, NJ: Princeton University Press, 1995), 81–144, esp. 81–2.

4 Philip Rieff, *Freud: The Mind of the Moralist* (Garden City, NY: Anchor Books, 1961 [1959]), 219.

5 Mary Ann Doane, *Femmes Fatales: Feminism, Film Theory, Psychoanalysis* (New York: Routledge, 1991), 211.

6 While Lamarck remains well known for his theory of the inheritability of acquired characteristics, Ernst Haeckel was responsible for the recapitulation hypothesis, also known as the biogenetic theory, according to which "ontogeny recapitulates phylogeny"; that is, the developmental beginnings of the individual subject recapitulate the evolutionary beginnings of the human race. Freud made ample use of both these theories. See Chapters 1 and 2 of this volume.

7 Adam Phillips, *Terrors and Experts* (Cambridge, MA: Harvard University Press, 1995), 71.

8 Sigmund Freud, *The Ego and the Id*, in *The Standard Edition of the Complete Psychological Works of Sigmund Freud* (London: Hogarth Press, 1953–74) (hereafter referred to as *SE*), 19:56.

9 Hortense J. Spillers, "'All the Things You Could Be By Now, If Sigmund Freud's Wife Was Your Mother:' Psychoanalysis and Race," *Black, White, and in Color: Essays on American Literature and Culture* (Chicago, IL: University of Chicago Press, 2003), 378.

10 An important exception is Ranjana Khanna, whose *Dark Continents: Psychoanalysis and Colonialism* (Durham, NC: Duke University Press, 2003, 2004) begins with the premise of psychoanalysis as a colonialist discipline. She too excavates some of the colonialist anthropology (and archeology) from which Freud fashioned his theories, and maps Freud's conceptions of the psyche onto theorizations of modern western nationalism. She then follows the role played by psychoanalysis, in conjunction with other theories, in the work of a range of post–WWII anti-colonial writers, and, through a complex discussion of colonial melancholy, points toward a psychoanalytically inflected postcolonial, transnational, feminist ethics.

11 Bronislaw Malinowski, *Sex and Repression in Savage Society* (Chicago, IL: University of Chicago Press, 1985 [1927]); Ernest Jones, "Review of *Sex and Repression in Savage Society*, by Bronislaw Malinowski," *International Journal of Psycho-Analysis* 9 (1928): 365–9. For a collection of essays that gives an overview of recent trends in psychoanalytic anthropology, see *Cultural Imagination and Individual Creativity: New Directions in Psychoanalytic Anthropology, The Psychoanalytic Review* (special issue) 84, no. 2 (April 1997).
12 John and Jean Comaroff, *Ethnography and the Historical Imagination* (Boulder, CO: Westview, 1992), 293.

Chapter 1

The figure of the primitive
A brief genealogy

The use of the idea of *primitivity* in psychoanalysis is so ubiquitous and taken for granted that it is difficult to recognize its function as the key to the code of racial difference embedded in psychoanalytic theory. This chapter will examine this term to demonstrate how its psychoanalytic usage conceals within it an anthropological and racial meaning by tracing the colonialist contexts in which it had developed by the time it reached Freud.

In spite of the apparent straightforwardness of its meaning, the psychoanalytic term *primitive* is overdetermined, drawing on two differing but overlapping genealogies. On the one hand, the term has a neutral, impartial meaning when used scientifically, in mathematics or in logic, or when applied to geological or anatomical structures. The definitions offered in the massive entry in the *Oxford English Dictionary* under the heading *primitive* all circle around the interrelated ideas of *first*, *early*, *original* and *simple*. These definitions are both temporal and structural. As a temporal designation, the word *primitive* points to the idea of the first or earliest time(s): of the earth, of humankind, of anatomical development. As a structural designation, it denotes the idea of simplest forms: of crystals, of mathematical figures, of logical propositions, from which other, more complex ones derive. These two meanings—priority in time and simplicity in structure—combine in the idea that the structurally simple is prior in time to the structurally complex; the complex derives over time from the simple.

Psychoanalysis, which often regards itself as a science and a member of the medical arts, assumes that it derives its usage of this term from the scientific lexicon and wields it with the associated assumption of scientific neutrality. Its use of *primitive* leans on definitions of originary stages of organic and inorganic structures that progress from the simple to the more complex. Primitive levels of the psyche are understood to be its earliest levels, without the complexity and capacity for differentiated response that come with development. Designating the behavior or experience of an adult as *primitive* casts it as an undeveloped remnant of the rudimentary stages of psychic life, on the analogy of primitive crystalline substances that have not yet been elaborated into complex structures, or of primitive geological formations that date back to the earliest eras of the earth's existence. As Freud wrote in *The Interpretation of Dreams*, "What is older in time is more primitive in form."[1]

On the other hand, the term *primitive* is also suspended in a web of social and cultural meanings that have played a prominent role in the discourse of European colonialism. The term *primitive* in psychoanalysis draws on these meanings as well, ascribing the simplest stages of psychological functioning not only to earliest infancy but also to so-called primitive peoples (Freud will call them *die Primitiven, die Naturvölker, die wilden Völker*). Applied to peoples rather than to geological formations or logical propositions, the evaluative dimension of the word becomes evident, as can be further seen from its associations with the terms *barbarian* and *savage*, all three of which have been used to designate the inferiority of those seen as outside the western human community. From this perspective, the word *primitive* is not a neutral and innocent scientific designation but, together with its opposite, *civilized*, it embodies the history of Euro-American civilization's evaluation of the unequal relationship between itself and its cultural others. Together, these three terms—*primitive, savage* and *barbarian*—have served to articulate these often racialized relationships. These terms, along with their religious counterparts—*heathen, infidel* and *pagan*—have been pivotal organizing figures in the multiple European frames of reference for representing those peoples conceived of as outside and other to the white European Christian community.

From the great European Age of Discovery (and before), European explorers, travelers, colonizers and missionaries journeyed to non-European lands, where they encountered places unlike any they had known and peoples radically different from themselves. The travel documents they produced contributed to the growing store of Europe's knowledge about its cultural others. From Columbus on, these early journeys of "discovery" and trade were animated by what Stephen Greenblatt has called "a particularly intense dream of possession";[2] and the swift colonization, expropriation, enslavement and decimation that followed hard upon these initial encounters became the material context in which such travel documents were produced. European thinkers, challenged to understand themselves now in relation to peoples wholly or largely unknown to them prior to the fifteenth century, turned to these documents to create universal theories of human origins, history and development; their theories in turn became sites of new and powerful figurations of the European self in relation to its cultural others. Conceived in the exuberance of Enlightenment social thought, these theories were recycled back through colonial administrations where they were used as the basis of colonial policies around the world.

Freud's use of the idea of primitivity, which correlated the infantile stages of the development of the contemporary European psyche with early stages in the psychological evolution of humanity, made use of this legacy of European theorizing about so-called primitive peoples, drawing on its culmination in the anthropology and social evolutionism of the late nineteenth century. Whereas later chapters will attend to the ways Freud enlisted the category of primitivity and its associated ideas in his development of psychoanalysis, and will investigate the resulting assumptions concerning racial/cultural difference embedded in the foundational texts of psychoanalysis, this chapter asks: What were the circumstances in which the meanings of the European figure of the primitive were elaborated? What roles did this figure play in the discursive schemata that governed the European relationship with its cultural others? What were the layers of meaning sedimented in "the primitive" and its related terms by the time Freud was to borrow them from his reading of the leading anthropologists of his day? Although the answers to these questions are to be found in the colonizing and enslaving relationships Europe held with non-European populations around the world, it was often the native American Indian who was taken by European social theorists as the quintessential emblem of the very first, primitive stage of human development.[3] Therefore this chapter begins by focusing largely on the history and resulting representations of primitivity that emerged out of the European encounters with the Americas.

Frameworks of encounter

Two sets of interlocking terms—*primitive, savage, barbarian*, together with *heathen, pagan, infidel*—appeared in the popular, literary, religious and legal frameworks with which Europeans represented lands and peoples they encountered from the fifteenth century on, and became critical elements of the discursive framework that would shape the modern colonial enterprise. Each term in the first set—*primitive, savage* and *barbarian*—focused on a somewhat different standard by which to measure cultural otherness. The term *savage* placed its subject within nature as opposed to culture. Deriving from the Latin *silva*, meaning forest, *savage* designated animals and people outside the boundaries of human settlement and domestication. Living in the wild, outside the bonds of communication and the responsibilities of human society, such animals or people were deemed ferocious, cruel and violent.

Rather than in the wild, the word *barbarian* placed its subject outside the particular political arrangements of European society. The early Greeks, from whose language this word derives, were proud of their form of governance in which the resolution of conflict took place through the exercise of speech and reason in public assembly. They looked down on those who did not manage their affairs in this way, and thus barbarians—from the Greek *barbaros*—"babbled": they did not share the political *language* through which membership in human society was understood to be constituted. Because of this the barbarian was considered an inferior being, not quite fully human, "rude, uncivilized, wild, savage and barbarous." In medieval Europe, the term *barbarous* meant both non-Christian as well as savage; and from the early seventeenth century, the inferiority of the barbarian was seen to rest not simply on the lack of (European) language but, more precisely, on the lack of alphabetic literacy.[4]

The term *primitive*, anchored in the meaning of temporal or structural beginnings, placed its subject at the historical origins of the evolution of humanity. Close to—or even part of—nature, untrammeled by the burdens of society and history, the primitive was idealized as the embodiment of an undeveloped, innocent and uncorrupted nature, still living in a terrestrial paradise before the fall. However, the absence of civilization could also mean that the primitive engaged in cannibalism and other forms of brutality. Primitive peoples were those who had existed at the threshold of the transition from animal to human, and the term became prominent in accounts that arranged cultures within a hierarchical developmental scheme, from most primitive to most advanced or developed. As evolutionary schemata emerged to range the peoples of the world in relation to one another, so-called savages and barbarians were placed at the earliest, hence primitive, rungs of the scale, with the result that by the nineteenth century each of these three terms—*barbarian, savage, primitive*—tended to merge and to function as somewhat interchangeable designations. Within each term the meanings of the other two were encoded, all three defined by their inferiority and opposition to that all-embracing term representing the self-congratulatory measure of western humanity: *civilization*. Thus in the idea of the *primitive* as it concerned humans, meanings pertaining to historical origins and structural simplicity joined with notions of a simultaneous idealization and disdain for the alien, the suggestion of innocence, wildness and violence; and a lack of development of language and reason. What was primitive was first, original and simple, and therefore so-called primitive peoples were seen as prior to and outside the realm of an enculturated humanity, the site of a noble innocence now lost, or of an ignoble, frightening and threatening inhumanity.

Similarly, *heathen, pagan* and *infidel* made up a triad of religious terms by which the Christian church characterized those outside its community. This community could be described broadly as including the three Abrahamic traditions of Judaism, Christianity and Islam, or it could be restricted to the Christian community alone. These three terms, like the first three, were each encoded within the other as they inscribed cultural otherness on a religious map. *Heathen*, derived from Germanic languages, referred to "dweller[s] on the heath" and was "applied to persons or races whose religion is neither Christian, Jewish or Mohammedan."[5] *Infidel*, Latin for "unfaithful," designated those who lacked faith in the "true religion," as Christianity fashioned itself; it was most commonly used to describe Saracens, as Muslims were known in the Middle Ages, but was also used to denote Jews, pagans and heathens. *Pagan*, from the Latin *paganus* for "rustic" or "villager," referred to non-Christians, "indicating," as the *Oxford English Dictionary* tells us, "the fact that the ancient idolatry lingered on in the rural villages and hamlets after Christianity had been generally accepted in the towns and cities of the Roman Empire."[6] A pagan was a heathen and an infidel, sometimes considered outside the Abrahamic traditions, sometimes considered outside the Christian tradition alone.

The first European understandings of newly encountered cohabitants of the earth made use of these terms and contributed to their development. When Columbus set sail for the Indies and found himself instead in the New World, already in place were two distinct frameworks for comprehending outsiders. The first was a medieval literary and popular discourse about outsiders as barbarians, wild men and noble savages, while the second was a religious-legal discourse, consolidated during the Crusades, concerning the treatment of infidels and the lawful right of Christians to the confiscation of uninhabited and non-Christian lands. The first, literary and popular discourse was composed of medieval European conceptions of non-European peoples which had been shaped by tales brought back by travelers in exotic lands together with religious notions of otherness. These conceptions coalesced in the figure of the Wild Man, which drew upon European traditions that saw the cultural other as outside the human community and outside the political or religious laws through which a person's full humanity could unfold. They also drew upon medieval notions, circulated in tales of foreign lands such as *Mandeville's Travels*, of such fantastic beings as trumpet-blowing apes, anthropophagi and blue people with square heads. The Wild Man took part of his persona from the barbarian who could not speak, part from ideas of savagery associated with wildness and part from the heathen outside the religious community.[7]

In addition, biblical thought taught that to be wild was to have been cast out from God's presence: Adam and Eve had been expelled from the garden, cursed to live in the wilderness. This in turn was allied with notions of blackness and bondage through the story of Ham, son of Noah. Because of the assumed etymological connection of the name Ham with words for both "dark" and "hot," by the Middle Ages Ham's descendants were believed to have been banished to Africa, thereby becoming dark-skinned. The figure of the Wild Man combined these notions with the Greek understanding of the *barbaros*: outside both religious and political constraints, the dark, Wild Man of medieval lore could give full range to his passions, for which he was both feared and envied. The resulting image of the Wild Man was a demonic, hairy being who lived in the forest, often black in color and likely to be a cannibal. Lacking the power of speech and any knowledge of God, he was without any mental capacity; he (and sometimes she) lived a life of unbridled lust and aggression in the wilderness, uncontained and unconstrained by community.[8]

Toward the end of the Middle Ages there developed a counterpart to the Wild Man as hostile opponent of the values of social and religious community: the savage as emblematic of a natural freedom of which civilization stood in the way. This figure, which hearkened back to Greek and Roman classical traditions, was to embark on its own career as the Noble

Savage who embodied the natural goodness of the uncivilized. The idea of the Noble Savage had, since the time of the Greeks, expressed a tendency within western thought to rue the burden of civilization and to dream of a simpler life.[9] By the time of the Renaissance, ancient Greek traditions of the Golden Age—a lost paradise of simplicity and happiness—had emerged to combine with medieval visions of the "Land of the Blest" and an Earthly Paradise to create the myth of a land "of peace and plenty hidden afar in the western seas,"[10] where the Noble Savage lived in innocence and peacefulness, without want, conflict, property or laws.

Representing the idealization rather than the demonization of the state of nature, the Noble Savage's wildness was seen to be a blessing, not a curse; he lived *in* the Garden of Eden, not yet having been cast out of it. The state of nature was the seat of the virtuous life rather than exclusion from it, and his natural abode made of the savage not a ferocious person but a virtuous one. The Noble Savage was praised and envied for living without the technological encumbrances of society, without agriculture or private property or government. He was seen as generous and hospitable and, depending on the proclivities of the writer, as either chaste or promiscuous in his sexual conduct. His lack of true religion made him not a fearful heathen but one whose equanimity was to be admired (and then brought within the orbit of Christianity). Philosophers such as Montaigne and Rousseau borrowed from the accounts of early voyagers to the Americas, accounts that perpetuated as well as added to these ancient figures of thought, to launch critiques of their own culture. The natural virtue, selflessness and gentleness of the Noble Savage was meant to put the civilized world to shame, whether as an emblem of rational common sense in the eighteenth century or as the object of romantic reverence in the nineteenth.[11] The contrasting images of the Wild Man and the Noble Savage, together with the varying purposes and experiences of those Europeans who would encounter and write about the natives of the Americas, contributed to a contradictory discourse which represented non-Europeans as both idealized and depraved, fulfilled in their simplicity yet lacking in their humanity.

When Columbus encountered the Amerindians on Caribbean soil, he believed he had arrived at, or very close to, the terrestrial paradise, and in his letters proclaiming his "discovery," he invoked the representation of the primitive as uncorrupted nature. "They are a people guileless and unwarlike," he wrote. "They are a loving people, without covetousness and fit for anything . . . and their speech is the sweetest and gentlest in the world, and always with a smile."[12] Further accounts of the generosity, hospitality and liberty of the inhabitants of the New World added to the repertoire of virtues of the Noble Savage. Explorers from Columbus to Jacques Cartier spoke of the warm welcome they received from savages "who as freely and familiarly came to our boats without any fear, as if we had ever been brought up together."[13] Common among the qualities described in early accounts of these peoples was their lack of "mine and thine," i.e. their holding of property in common; and the "independence and liberty of which they appear extremely jealous."[14]

But Columbus came armed as well with a second, legal discourse based on precepts of religious law, which stated that uninhabited land was available for possession by the first Christian European to set foot on it. He brought with him royal documents from the Spanish crown that authorized him to "*ganar, descubrir, regir* (acquire, discover, govern)" in order to "*comprar, trocar, hallar, haver* (buy, barter, locate, possess)."[15] Columbus's first acts were to take possession of and rename the land he had just "discovered." Stephen Greenblatt has written at length about this tragicomic ritual of possession, which required the juridical erasure of the existence of the inhabitants whom Columbus had just met to construe the land as uninhabited, and a feigned ignorance of their inability to understand Spanish to justify his statement, required by the legal ritual itself, that his claim to possession "was not contradicted" by them.[16]

By the time Columbus wrote the letters that made his discoveries widely known throughout Europe, the economic and legal imperatives of his mission had become framed in an explicitly religious language whose purported goal was to redeem the natives. As the legal historian Robert Williams has meticulously documented, this religious language had been shaped by a church militant, which, by the fifteenth century, had established the interpenetration of its military and religious prerogatives.[17] The struggle between Christians and Muslims waged in the Iberian Peninsula over centuries had just culminated in the Christian *Reconquista* of Granada, and the edict compelling the expulsion of the Jews from Spain had just come into force when Columbus set sail. Over the preceding centuries the church had issued a succession of papal bulls (edicts) concerning the Crusades in the Middle East, the creation of orders such as the Knights Templar and the forcible Christianization of pagans in Slavic countries and Lithuania.

According to medieval church doctrine the pope, as God's vicar on earth, had been charged by Christ with the spiritual care of all peoples, including those outside the community of Christian belief. This meant that it was the responsibility of the pope—and, through him, his princes—to convert barbarian, infidel peoples to Christianity. Should they resist, it was his further responsibility to dispossess them of their *dominium*, their lands and autonomy. This papal position was "readily incorporated . . . into [the] Discovery-era colonizing ventures and legal discourse" of the Spanish crown, which had been invested by the bull of donation of 1493 with the necessary apostolic powers and responsibilities. Through the legal structures that were the legacy of the Crusades, the necessity of converting such peoples to Christianity would provide the mandate for the conquest of their lands and the appropriation of their wealth and labor.[18]

These, then, were the popular, literary, religious and legal themes which influenced the first Europeans encounters with the inhabitants of the Americas. The explorers who wrote the very first accounts of these newly "discovered" peoples to reach European readers did not, of course, speak the languages of the people they were describing. Not knowing the languages, faced with incommensurate worlds of cultural practice and self-understanding, and motivated by powerful acquisitive energies, they represented indigenous peoples in terms of their lack of similarity to Christian Europeans. Columbus's first descriptions of the people he met seemed to indicate that what he could not recognize, they did not have: no clothes, no religion, no reason, no laws or private property, and even no language. Their lands were characterized as belonging to no one: *terra nullius*, nobody's land. What was unintelligible simply seemed not to exist, and thus these peoples were seen as deficient and inferior compared to European standards. The shock of intercultural contact—the exhilaration of encounter and the terror of difference—would be tamed and the impulse for acquisition fed, by assimilating this "lack" to familiar categories of inferior otherness: savage and barbarian, wild and noble, heathen and infidel, all of which would later converge in the figure of the primitive, laying the basis for theories that would be constructed to locate these peoples in relation to their European discoverers.[19]

The American native was seen both as lacking the attributes of the European and as embodying the attributes of the idealized exotic other. Both characterizations functioned to further whichever colonial policy was to be promulgated at the moment and to explain the availability of native peoples for European exploitation as due to their very natures. In Europe, the idea of the Noble Savage may have functioned as a living critique of the burden of civilization; but when peoples were so described by explorers and settlers in the New World, it was often to indicate the gentleness and ease with which it was hoped they would become subservient to that same civilization by taking up the twin yokes of Christianity and slavery. When trade and settlement were to be encouraged, the indigenous peoples were seen as friendly, peaceful, dignified and hospitable, since "it was only a friendly Indian who could be a trading Indian."[20] But when they were to be enslaved and land was to be wrested from them for European settlement, Amerindians previously seen as gentle and loving would suddenly appear to be brute beasts who were idle, godless and cannibalistic. Resistance to or retaliation against expropriation and enslavement was interpreted as a hostility that was in the very nature of the native. Noble or wild, the "normative divergence" of these indigenous peoples from Europeans was assigned an inferior status that would later be inscribed in theories elaborated to further inform colonial policy.[21]

Thus when Columbus encountered the peoples of the Caribbean and described them as "open-hearted and liberal," "guileless and unwarlike" and "fit for anything," he conjured up the image of the Noble Savage at the same time as he indicated the presence of conditions that would legally justify placing them under the tutelage of the Spanish crown, a tutelage that would dispossess them of their freedom and land and coerce their labor. Within three years of discovering this "sweetest and gentlest" of peoples, Columbus had instituted a policy of forced labor for gold mining and a feudal tribute system, and was exporting slaves from the Caribbean to Spain. Queen Isabella put an end to the outright enslavement of these people whom she considered her subjects, but the *encomienda* system of forced labor that Columbus had instituted endured.[22]

In 1513 the convergence of religious and military prerogatives inherited from the Crusades was inscribed in the Spanish document known as the *Requerimiento*, which was to be read aloud by conquistadores to any Amerindians they might encounter (but which seems to have been recited as often as not to empty fields and forests). This document announced—in Spanish—to the unsuspecting natives the requirement that they be subjected to Christianity and Spanish rule or else

[we] shall take you and your wives and your children and shall make slaves of them, and as such shall sell and dispose of them as their highnesses may command; and we shall take away your goods and shall do to you all the harm and damage that we can, as to vassals who do not obey and refuse to receive their lord and resist and contradict him.[23]

The Amerindians' salvation was to entail their colonialization and indentured labor; their refusal to be saved would entail their enslavement and death. Sixty years after Columbus first set foot on the territories of the New World, the Dominican friar Bartolomé de las Casas estimated that fifteen million Amerindians had perished.[24]

This rapacity and "genocidal fury"[25] was documented by Las Casas who, having himself served as an *encomendero* in what is now Cuba, underwent a change of heart that led him to become a chief advocate for the rights of the indigenous peoples of the New World. Las Casas's descriptions of Spanish brutality in his *Devastation of the Indies* make for harrowing reading: millions upon millions tortured and exterminated; innumerable people dismembered and cut "to pieces as if . . . sheep in the slaughter house" or hung on gallows and burned alive by fires set at their feet; infants taken "from their mothers' breasts [and pitched] headfirst against the crags"; attack dogs set upon people to "tear [them] to pieces." Although the Spaniards feared the purported cannibalism of the Amerindians, Las Casas reports that it was the Spanish themselves who "killed, cooked, and [ate]" children, and hung corpses of Indians in butcher shops where they were sold.[26] As Tzvetan Todorov remarks, "without [the] essential premise [of the Indians as inferior beings], the destruction could not have taken place."[27]

Amerindians perished in great numbers due to the violence inflicted upon them by the Spanish and as a result of European diseases to which they were unaccustomed. On the recommendation of Las Casas, distressed by the decimation of the native Americans, the Spanish government began to send Africans to the New World to take their places as enslaved laborers. To images of the "normative divergence" of the native Americans were henceforth added those of the Africans who were imported to the New World to labor in the plantations that would make commodities such as sugar, coffee, coca and cotton commonly available throughout Europe. The development of the Atlantic slave trade together with European interactions with the dark-skinned peoples of such lands as Australia and Tasmania provided further ample context for the development and deployment of European notions of savagery and primitivity.

Slavery in one form or another had existed in European lands since the time of the Roman Empire. Although by the fifteenth century Europeans were disinclined to enslave other European Christians, they had no such reservations when it came to the enslavement of infidels who, it was believed, could in this way be brought to the true faith. Even before Columbus embarked on the initial journey that would bring him to the shores of the Americas, Europe was engaged in the beginnings of the Atlantic slave trade: Portugal had begun trading slaves from the sub-Sahara in the mid-fifteenth century. From as early as 1502, and over the next three hundred years, more than fifteen million Africans endured the horrors of the Middle Passage to be sold as American slaves. C.L.R. James's descriptions of the Atlantic slave trade rival Las Casas's descriptions of the treatment of Indios in their sheer depth of depravity.[28] The sale of slaving licenses, in addition to the plundered wealth of the New World, provided important income for the Spanish crown. European development of the New World depended on this imported slave labor, and revenues from investments in the slave trade contributed to the financing of the infrastructure of the developing industrial economy in Europe. In these ways and others, the Atlantic slave trade made a crucial contribution to the development of burgeoning American and European capitalist economies.[29]

Africans had been known to Europeans before their first encounters with the peoples of the New World, not only through the European slave trade but also through the six centuries of struggle between Christians and Muslims on the Iberian Peninsula culminating in the *Reconquista* in 1492, during which both sides had enslaved their enemies. That the Islamic Moors were darker than the Iberians who enslaved them, and that they themselves had African slaves in their armies, fostered the Iberian association between infidels, slavery and dark skin. This association gave new life to the myth of Ham, which, through the above-mentioned assumption of an etymological connection of the name Ham with words for both "dark" and "hot," was understood to suggest that that Africans had been biblically fated to be enslaved: Ham had come upon his father Noah's nakedness, and therefore Noah had cursed his descendants—believed by medieval Europeans to have been banished to Africa and become dark-skinned—to become the "slave[s] of slaves."[30]

Whereas the Amerindians of the Caribbean could be seen as "a very handsome people" and as having a certain "aristocratic bearing, restraint and modesty,"[31] the peoples of Africa were considered by Europeans to be ugly and disfigured; they were often likened to beasts.[32] Thomas Jefferson, in his *Notes on the State of Virginia*, contended that while the native American could "astonish you with strokes of the most sublime oratory," he had seen no evidence of such ability in black slaves. Indians were capable of strong "reason and sentiment," while he judged the reasoning capacity of blacks to be "much inferior" to that of whites.[33] Blackness had long been associated in European languages with darkness, dirt and the stain of sin, and color came to be the unifying sign under which all the elements of African difference were subsumed: Africa was called the Dark Continent as early as the mid-sixteenth century. The fateful conjunction of the first European encounter with both African and ape in the sixteenth century set in place an almost unshakable conviction in the similarity, if not the identity, of the two in the European mind.[34] This conviction, bolstered by the occasional "report" of the sexual compatibility of Africans and orangutans, gave rise to the notion of the animal-like and excessively libidinous nature of Africans at the same time as it reinforced the sense of the propriety of slavery: Africans were animal "slave apes," and God had given (European) man dominion over the animals.[35]

All these deep-rooted assumptions caused it to seem "obvious and natural"[36] that Africans and other black-skinned peoples were bestial, sinful and deserving of enslavement. Savagery was associated with slavery as though to suggest that the institution of slavery was not a historically imposed condition but had arisen out of the dark and savage nature of Africa itself.[37] By "nature" a slave, the status of the African brought to the Americas was that of chattel property, as later codified in the US Dred Scott ruling of 1857. Whereas the Amerindian living in a state of nature was seen as emblematic of a wildness to be conquered, the African's relationship to nature was that of the beast to be enslaved, whose labor was necessary for the development of (another) civilization. Even Las Casas, so ardent a champion of the rights of indigenous Americans, suggested that the Spanish replace Amerindian slaves in the New World with African ones.

The curse on the son of Ham has been called the central justification for racial slavery."[38] Christian theologians from Augustine to Aquinas had argued that slavery was a divinely ordained punishment for sin.[39] Africans were believed to be so deeply mired in the darkness and sin of their continent of origin that slavery was deemed by many Europeans to improve their condition. Slavery was considered to better both Amerindians and Africans by civilizing and/or Christianizing them. Medieval Christianity found no moral difficulty in supporting slavery: the Iberian clergy in the New World possessed thousands of slaves.[40]

Las Casas's damning denunciation of the treatment of the Amerindians at the hands of the Spanish, quickly translated and circulated throughout Europe, stirred up indignation and controversy. Treatises were written and councils were convened by the Spanish crown where respected theologians were called on to justify Spain's activities in the New World. They debated who and what the Amerindians were understood to be to determine appropriate imperial policy toward them, and thus began some of the first forays into systematic theorizing about them and about what relationship they bore to Europeans.

Theologians framed their arguments in both religious and philosophical— Christian and Aristotelian—terms. According to each of these frameworks, the infidel and barbarian nature of the Amerindians meant that they lacked qualities essential for their own best development and governance, which the Spanish should therefore provide for them.[41] In the first of these councils held in Burgos in 1504, the policy of enslaving the Amerindians was justified by the view that their freedom was a form of idleness and a lack of Christianity. Forced labor, it was argued, would give the Amerindians the communication with Christians by which they could best learn Christian virtue. As the Spanish crown had decreed,

> Because of the excessive liberty the Indians have been permitted, they flee from Christians and do not work. Therefore they are to be compelled to work, so that the kingdom and the Spaniards may be enriched, and the Indians Christianized.[42]

Other arguments appealed to Aristotle's theory of natural slavery. The natural slave, according to Aristotle, was a person ruled by passion rather than reason. The fulfillment of the nature of such a person could only take place through serving a master whose possession of reason exempted him from the need to perform manual labor. Barbarians *were* natural slaves, said Aristotle, and thus the Amerindians and the Africans (according to their European subjugators) were born to be slaves and to serve their Spanish masters. Such a theory conveniently overlooked the facts that the conditions of slavery themselves typically created the characteristics which qualified Amerindians and Africans as barbaric, and that advocates of the theory of natural slavery were themselves slavery's beneficiaries. Nevertheless, it was considered that

> it was, in short, in the interests of both the master and the slave that the slave should be deprived of a freedom which was "unnatural" and thus—since it permitted him to continue in the ignorance of his savage ways—harmful to him.[43]

From the Christian as well as the Aristotelian point of view, then, slavery would redound to the benefit of the enslaved, leading to the fulfillment of their humanity. Slavery was "in agreement with both divine and human law."[44]

Countering the argument of natural slavery were the arguments of the influential sixteenth-century legal theorist Francisco de Vitoria, whose *On the Indians Lately Discovered* became a primary source for European theorizing about colonized peoples. Vitoria believed that reason was native to all humans, including the Amerindians, who, as a "free and rational people," had the same inherent rights to property and self-rule as did all other peoples. Rather than to barbarians, Vitoria likened the Amerindians to *children*; they possessed the faculty of reason, but their reason was as yet immature. The king of Spain, therefore, was to be their tutor rather than their master. The papal bulls of donation 1493 which granted ownership of overseas territories to Portugal and Spain were invalid, according to Vitoria: neither the act of discovery nor the need for salvation automatically justified ownership of the New World. In place of these justifications of conquest, Vitoria constructed a system of international natural rights—a Law of Nations—to which all peoples were to be beholden. This law included the Amerindians' rights to *dominium* in their own territories—but it also included the Spaniards' rights of traveling, sojourning, trading and availing themselves of things such as gold or "pearls in the sea" that were believed to be held in common among the Amerindians and therefore were to be shared with strangers. Should the Amerindians deny the Spaniards any of these rights, they would be wronging the Spaniards who then could "enforce against them all the rights of war, despoiling them of their goods, reducing them to captivity, deposing their former lords and setting up new ones."[45]

In 1550 the Spanish crown convened the famous Council of Valladolid, where Las Casas and the humanist Juan Ginés de Sepúlveda were charged with debating the legitimacy of slavery in the New World, focusing on the Spanish subjugation of the indigenous peoples. Sepúlveda argued that it was lawful to enslave the Amerindians because of their purported sins, especially that of idolatry, and because they were natural slaves in the Aristotelian sense. According to Sepúlveda, the Amerindians lacked not only private property but "even vestiges of humanity" and had "barbaric institutions and customs."[46] Conquest and slavery would make Christians of them and would allow the Spaniards to become their protectors, an argument echoed by later advocates of the African slave trade. On the other hand, Las Casas argued his case by demonstrating that the customs of the Amerindian tribes of America were similar to those ancient peoples known to and respected by Europe, such as the Greeks, Romans and Babylonians, and that therefore they ought not to be destroyed or enslaved but respected and led toward Christianity. In so arguing, he created one of the first models of cultural evolution, in which all peoples were seen to possess reason and to be moving along a path of development which would lead through time toward civility and Christianity.[47]

As Robert Williams has shown, the British, as they made their first imperial incursions into the New World, adopted and added to the themes developed by Spanish theorists of the sixteenth century. Newly separated from the Catholic Church and horrified by tales of Spanish cruelty in the Americas, they wished to spread their own true religion among the natives, liberate them from Spain and make them their trading partners. The 1606 Royal Charter for the Virginia Company expressed the hope that the British "may in time bring the Infidels and Savages, living in those parts, to human civility, and to a settled and quiet government."[48] This benign mission quickly gave way, however, to more ruthless colonial aims, and the rhetoric of the Crusades, as well as the theorizing of the Spanish, were at hand to help out. In 1608 Lord Chief Justice Edward Coke pronounced that

> all infidels are in law *perpetui inimici* [perpetual enemies], (for the law presumes not that they will be converted, that being *remota potentia*, a remote possibility), for between them, as with devils, whose subjects they be, and the Christian, there is perpetual hostility, and can be no peace . . . the laws of the infidel are abrogated, for that they be not only against Christianity but against the law of God and of nature, contained in the decalogue.[49]

The English, too, came to see the Amerindians as violating the "laws of God and of nature" and as beings without rationality, and in this way justified their conquest of North America. English writing on the colonization of North America, such as George Peckham's widely read "True Report" on English "discoveries" and possessions in the New World, borrowed liberally from the Spanish Vitoria and his Law of Nations. The English language of colonization, too, argued that the Amerindian was in "violation of natural law and the Law of Nations and possessed no rights that civilized English monarchs or subjects were bound to recognize."[50]

To these religious and natural-law arguments the English added the argument of land use as justification for seizing tribal lands. The prior subjection of Ireland had equipped the English with the theme of under-used land with which to defend dispossession. In 1632 the English Crown denied that the Amerindians were the rightful owners of their lands because their residences were "unsettled and uncertain" and were held "in common."[51] One of the characteristics of the inhabitants of the Americas that struck the earliest explorers was their presumed lack of "*meum et tuum*," their lack of the concepts of "mine and thine": they seemed to hold their property in common and be free, therefore, from the entire structure of law and government necessitated by private holdings. For Rousseau, as for many others, the institution of private property had been the beginning of human injustice and the source of the ills of civilization; it was precisely this lack that made for the inspiring nobility of *l'homme sauvage* (the noble savage). But early colonial settlers saw the holding in common of vast tracts of land used for hunting and gathering as simply an inefficient under-utilization of land. Lands that, by native standards, were in full use were seen as vacant and there for the taking. As Samuel Purchas, the seventeenth-century English compiler of travel literature, wrote in 1625, "stealing in the properest sense it cannot bee, if there be no proprietie [property]."[52]

This perspective was developed systematically by John Locke, who wrote of the "uncultivated waste of America." For Locke, it was man's agricultural labor that made the land he worked his own: "He by his labour does, as it were, enclose it from the common." Such privately held property was "the great and chief end therefore, of men's uniting into commonwealths, and putting themselves under government."[53] Transforming un- or under-used land into private property through agricultural labor was the goal of civilization; land held in common seemed to preclude the possibility of private ownership.[54] Indigenous land usage appeared to be more like that of animals: natives were "as wild beasts in the forest; for they range and wander up and down the country . . . rather than inhabite" their land.[55] The onward march of civilization seemed to demand the requisition of these lands and the supersession of this "primitive" usage by the more advanced practices of tillage and private ownership. The governor of Tennessee stated in 1798 that "no people shall be entitled to more land than they can cultivate."[56] Almost one hundred years later a New Orleans newspaper editorial asserted that Americans should no longer allow the Amerindian "to usurp for the purpose of barbarism, the fertile lands, the products of mines, the broad valleys and wooded mountain slopes, which organized society regards as magazines of those forces which civilization requires for its maintenance and development."[57] The indigenous peoples of the Americas, even as they were held up as paragons of simplicity and liberty, were seen as ripe for dispossession. The primitive nature of both Amerindians and African slaves, like primitive nature itself, was understood to be in need of cultivation.

The invention of the primitive mind

These ideas concerning American "primitives," elaborated through religious, legal and administrative rulings that governed their colonization and enslavement, took on a life of their own as Europeans struggled to include what they were learning about them and other non-Europeans in their understanding of the human condition. Encounters with peoples hitherto unknown to Europe put pressure on traditional mythistorical European self-understandings. The realization that the globe was shared with a plurality of human groups, many of whom exhibited seemingly strange customs and behaviors, was one of a number of challenges to the biblical story of creation that contributed to the Enlightenment preoccupation with the problem of origins. The question of the identity and origin of these peoples was all the more urgent because it was unaccounted for by biblical genealogy. Who were these peoples? Did they descend from Adam, and had they been created by God? If their omission from biblical genealogy cast doubt on traditional religious conceptions, lending credence to growing suspicions of the Judeo-Christian account of creation, what then were the origins of humankind, of religion and of the social institutions of law and ownership? Increasingly European thinkers looked to "primitive peoples" as those whose lives and institutions could explain the origins of their own institutions.

From the fifteenth century on, chronicles and treatises of travelers, trad-
ers and missionaries had been pouring into Europe, where they were widely
read. These accounts of newly colonized and enslaved peoples became the
raw material out of which were fashioned a range of answers to these questions. A wide variety of unrelated peoples apprehended largely in terms
of their lack of European attributes were cast in terms deriving from figures of long standing in the European imagination, filtered through the
imperatives of conquest and colonization. The resulting admixtures were
taken as descriptive of an empirical reality and began to crystallize into
the proto-scientific category of "the primitive." This category was then
put to theoretical use in arguments concerning the origin and development
of the human race and its institutions. Common to many of the theoretical
schemata which included the category of the primitive was the perspective
that contemporary Amerindians were living during the prehistory of the
human race. As John Locke wrote, "in the beginning all the World was
America."[58]

The idea of the Noble Savage had placed the primitive not only outside
civilization but prior to it. The Noble Savage still lived *in the beginning*,
and the first explorers believed that they might have truly discovered that
pre-lapsarian paradise. Even when the mythology of paradise on earth
gave way to more considered accounts of the geography and population
of the Americas, comparisons continued to be made that linked native
Americans with the ancient past: comparisons between the Amerindians
and the ancestors of Europe—ancient Greeks, Hebrews, Scythians and
others—were a principal way of locating Americans on a cultural map.
Las Casas had argued against the subjugation by the Spanish of the
Amerindians by comparing the Amerindians to the Greeks and Romans.
Other early authors of accounts influential in forming European understanding and opinion about the Americas, such as the Spanish Jesuit José
de Acosta, who traveled in what is now Latin America and wrote his
Historia natural y moral de las Indias (*A Natural and Moral History of
the Indies*) in 1590; the French author Marc Lescarbot, who traveled to
Acadia and wrote *l'Histoire de la Nouvelle-France* (*The History of New
France*) in 1609; and Joseph-François Lafitau, the French Jesuit who lived
for a time among the Iroquois in what is now Quebec and wrote *Moeurs
des Sauvages Amériquains, Comparées aux Moeurs des Premiers Temps*
(*Customs of the American Indians Compared to the Customs of Ancient
Times*) in 1724: all framed their texts in terms of the analogy between

the indigenous Americas and the "ancients." This analogy, however, soon
came to be taken as an identity, understood to mean that native Americans
not only were similar to but actually *were* contemporary examples of the
earliest European—and human—ancestors.[59]

In the Americas at the time of early European encounters there were
thousands of cultures with a wide range of mutually unintelligible languages, beliefs and customs.[60] Yet these linguistically and culturally
distinct peoples were considered to be a homogeneous group with common
attributes: Indians. Together with differing peoples in Africa, Australia,
Tasmania and other non-European lands, they were combined into a single
category with European progenitors: they were all primitives. This classification helped consolidate the impression that all non-Europeans were
somehow essentially the same, and that, although living in the same world
at the same time as the Europeans who were writing and thinking about
them, contemporary "primitives" were somehow living in the European
present as preserved texts of the human past. Thus enframed, so-called
primitive peoples seemed to yield empirical evidence for the elaboration of
theories concerning the evolution of the human mind and the origin
of social and cultural institutions. Seen as living embodiments of human
origins, they became grist for a variety of theoretical mills in the ferment
of Enlightenment thinking. Evolutionary theories were developed which,
drawing on travelers' accounts from the colonies, placed primitives at the
beginning of the historical and cultural trajectory that was seen to culminate in European civilization.[61]

At the beginning of the European age of conquest, Christianity had
been the dominant axis along which the difference between Europe and its
others was conceptualized; European dominion was imposed in the cloak
of Christianity. As "Christendom" gave way to "Europe," however, the
standard by which the non-European mind was characterized began to be
articulated in secular terms as well. Various evolutionary theories were
developed defining the nature of the different stages through which, it was
increasingly agreed, all peoples passed in progression. These theories took
advantage of the assumption of the identification of all contemporary non-
western peoples with the ancestors of the human race; and agreed that
there was but one path along which all societies progressed. Varieties of
social and religious practices and beliefs were placed in a purported developmental order along this path, and the development of human capacities
and institutions was traced to what was believed to be their primitive or

natural or original state. In this way, the idea of "the primitive" became the locus of origins: the idea of God as originator of all was supplemented, or at times supplanted, by the idea of the primitive as the origin of all. For some Enlightenment philosophers of history, the standard of differentiation between the primitive and the civilized was economic: the various stages through which humankind had moved were characterized according to their modes of subsistence. Eighteenth-century writers such as Montesquieu, Rousseau, Turgot and Adam Smith based these stages on the modes of subsistence of hunting, grazing, agriculture and commerce. In this scheme, savages were hunters and barbarians were shepherds.[62]

For others, Reason was seen as the flower of human attainment, and therefore stages in the general history of humankind were measured in terms of the progressive development of the capacity for rationality. As Christianity had been counterposed to the ignorance of idolatry, reason was counterposed to superstition. For such philosophers as Pierre Bayle, Charles de Brosses and David Hume, the supposed identity between "primitive peoples" and Europe's ancestors resided in their common belief in superstitious ritual lacking any moral element: primitivity was superstition, and superstition was the dross that was shed with each step in the development of humankind. Where Christianity remained the paramount cultural frame of reference, the inferiority of so-called primitive peoples continued to be ascribed to their idolatrous natures; where secular Enlightenment thought prevailed, their inferiority was seen as the result of superstition and lack of rationality, evidenced most convincingly by their seemingly incomprehensible religious rituals.

In these ways arose the idea of a universal primitive mind as the first stage in the mental evolution of humankind. The indigenous peoples of Europe's colonies, identified with European "ancients," became identified with European children as well, as Vitoria and others had suggested. These linked identities were placed in the service of the analogy between the evolution of humankind and the development of the individual from infancy to adulthood. The European mind was believed to have developed from the primitive childhood of humankind into the maturity of rationality, whereas the primitive mind was still at the infancy of the race, mired in superstition and handicapped by the immaturity of its capacity for reason.[63]

As religious belief increasingly came under Enlightenment suspicion, Christianity became linked, rather than counterposed, to "savage idolatry," and the notion of the primitive as living in the superstitious childhood of humanity was deployed as a covert attack on religion itself. Comparisons were drawn between the religious beliefs and practices of "primitive" peoples on the one hand and those of European Christians on the other, as a way to ridicule and critique Christianity, especially Roman Catholicism. Reviving classical notions of religion as a response to fear, Enlightenment thinkers provided psychological theories according to which the origin of religion was to be found in the response of the earliest humans to the terror of the harshness of nature. English Deists, who believed in a universal natural religion while rejecting revelation, felt that religious truth lay in the rational apprehension of the magnificence of creation. Belief in and worship of supernatural figures were evidence of inferior and unhealthy psychological tendencies. Influenced by seventeenth-century medical reports of possession and witchcraft, Deists considered religious enthusiasm to be a form of madness. By viewing religion as a psychopathology shared by their religious contemporaries, by the ancient pagans who devised the first religions and by savages in non-European lands, the Deists "transposed to aboriginal man the ugly characteristics of the contemporary fanatic personality."[64] Hence primitives were not only superstitious, they were religious fanatics: religious belief was transformed into psychopathology, and madness was set in place as the final element in the triad of savages, children and madmen, which would become the enduring cornerstone of later social evolutionary thought (eventually to emerge in Freud's work).[65]

Contributing to the idea that there was a primitive mind different in kind from the contemporary European one was John Locke, who characterized the primitive mind—shared by savages, children and madmen alike—as simple and concrete, and David Hume, who argued for a conception of consciousness as progressing from a primitive, concrete stage toward an increasing capacity for abstraction.[66] Charles de Brosses borrowed this conception and applied it to the history of religions. He posited a universal, earliest stage of fetishism, the worship of concrete objects said to be characteristic of primitive religions, from which humankind progressed toward rational enlightenment. De Brosses explained that

> since no one is astonished to see children fail to elevate their minds higher than their dolls, believe them alive, and then behave towards them accordingly, why should one be amazed to see peoples who constantly pass their life in an eternal infancy and who are never more than four years old reason incorrectly and act as they reason?[67]

By the late eighteenth century the idea of a distinct primitive mentality shared by human ancestors, contemporary savages, children and madmen had taken shape, a mentality characterized both by its simplicity and concreteness, and by its superstitious and fanatic nature.

Civilization and primitivity

These theories of the primitive mind functioned both as sites of European self-fashioning and fashioning of the other, taking shape in tandem with the development of the modern concept of civilization. That the use of the word *civilization* emerged in Europe in the mid-eighteenth century suggests its role as an expression of European self-appraisal in the face of its encounters with its non-western others. In the words of the historical sociologist Norbert Elias, the concept of civilization "sums up everything in which Western society of the last two or three centuries believes itself superior to earlier societies or 'more primitive' ones."[68]

In his extensive work, *The Civilizing Process*, Elias demonstrates the ways that the development of the idea of "civilization" in Europe was reflected in the successive usages of the terms *courtoisie, civilité* and *civilisation*. The emergence of each of these terms mirrored the gradual process of state formation: from feudal society, with its warring nobility, to the monopolization of power, first by the royal courts and then by the nation-state. The gradual consolidation of power gave rise to changes in interpersonal behaviors originally developed at, and dictated by, court society. These developments in the organization of court society and in the conduct of the ruling classes arose first in the French aristocracy and eventually spread throughout Europe's upper classes. *Courtoisie*, the repertoire of knightly behaviors established at the feudal courts of the Middle Ages, was replaced by the *civilité* of seventeenth-century European royal court society. Civility, with its roots in the Latin *civis*, citizen, and *civilis*, of or belonging to citizens, came to convey the sense of the orderliness necessary for courtly life, where both behaviors and emotions became polite by being polished (*poli*) and policed (*policé*).

The increasing interdependency of members of a nobility subject to an absolute monarch gave rise to a heightened awareness of rank in the social hierarchy and an increased restraint toward others within court society itself. Expressed through intensified regulation of bodily and emotional behaviors, this restraint was reflected in refinements of speech and clothing, in comportment (curtailment of such things as spitting and slurping), in specific uses of table implements (fork, knife and spoon) and in the increasing privatization of bodily functions. The manners that ensued became the marks of distinction by which the aristocratic classes displayed their superiority to those socially below them: the distinction conferred by "civilization" was initially one of class. This regulation of domestic comportment was internalized as a repugnance toward behaviors no longer exercised by the aristocracy but still enjoyed by the peasantry.[69] These distinctions of civilized life were sustained through a sense of shame, the fear of "lapsing into inferiority" of behaviors no longer befitting the upper classes. Built on distinctions between the aristocracy and the other classes, the notions of *courtoisie*, *civilité* and *civilisation* asserted a superior status from their earliest usages.[70]

In the eighteenth century, *civilité* gave way to *civilisation*, the word appearing for the first time in the work of Mirabeau, one of the early leaders of the French revolution. The term *civilisation* was linked with the Enlightenment belief that social institutions could be reformed by increased knowledge: thus the idea of progress, too, was built into its meaning. By the nineteenth century, civilization, considered to have been "completed" by the time of Napoleon, came to convey the idea of progress associated with rationality, order, knowledge, refinement and "the whole modern social process"[71] "especially in contrast with barbarism."[72] The term signified at one and the same time Europe's current social, behavioral and technological arrangements, the process through which it had arrived at them and the status it claimed for having so arrived. The conception of civilization as the march of progress lent itself to the idea of the civilizing mission, as can be seen by the intertwining of themes of religious and civic redemption in the European documents legislating colonial possession. For example, the papal grant of American lands to the Spanish crown instructed the Spaniards both to Christianize and bring civility to the Amerindians, while the Royal Charter for the Virginia Company expressed the hope that the English might bring "human Civility" to the American natives.[73] With the advent of industrialism in Britain, the notion of civilization also came to imply the restraint and delayed gratification necessary to the discipline of work and the accumulation of wealth and political responsibility; primitives, in contrast, lived *in* nature and gave full rein *to* their natures. The meaning of civilization entailed an evolutionary outlook: "Not only the individual advances from infancy to manhood, but the species itself from rudeness to civilization," wrote the Scottish philosopher Adam Ferguson in 1767.[74]

This discourse of civilization represented Europe's conception of itself as the fullest manifestation of the potential of humanity, and included within itself the idea of the primitive as that which civilization was not. Ideas of primitivity and civilization entailed each other, the idea of the primitive functioning as what Hayden White has called a "culturally self-authenticating device"[75]—a term whose purpose is not so much to describe an empirical situation as to sanction, by its contradistinction, the very thing against which it is set in opposition. Primitives—be they Amerindians, Africans or Australians—were "the living embodiment of what [Europeans] must never allow themselves to become."[76] And they were recognizable as such not only by their skin color and clothing but by the fact that they did not organize their lives and conduct themselves according to the behavioral codes originally developed through European courtly and social life.

First developed as a sign of the distinction between the aristocracy and the peasant classes, "civilization" became the distinction between coloniz-ers and colonized, masters and slaves, with Europe becoming "a kind of upper class to large sections of the non-European world."[77] The regimes of personal comportment that had accompanied the emergence of the European nation-state from feudal and monarchical organizations formed the precepts according to which those outside civilization could—up to a point—be molded. In America, as in South Africa, as anthropologists John and Jean Comaroff point out, "bodies and domestic space were vital terrains of colonization"; the civilizing mission was carried out not only in planta-tions, mines, schools and churches but also through the introduction of the implements of civility: "pots, fabrics, soap, tools, clocks, locks and so on."[78]

The racial associations that the distinction between civilization and primitivity were to assume in the nineteenth century were also first worked out in the context of class differences in Europe. In medieval Europe the peasantry were frequently associated with black skin color (because of their exposure to the sun and their nearness to the soil); and their servitude was justified by the same biblical narrative concerning the descendants of the sons of Ham as was used to justify the slave trade from Africa.[79] As Hannah Arendt points out, such codings of the distinction between classes, and later between nation-states, formed the basis of later biologistic racist thinking in the nineteenth century.[80] In his *Inequality of the Human Races* of 1853 (shortly before Darwin's watershed publication), the infamous Count Gobineau was to describe the nobility as a "race of princes"—i.e., the Aryans—and race was to become a way of speaking of a class or a country as a "natural," rather than social or political, "aristocracy destined to rule over all others."[81]

Primitivity and race: biological theories

This racialized understanding of distinctions between classes and cultures became concretized during the nineteenth century through a range of biological theories. Although elements of European colonialist discourse had foreshadowed the biologically deterministic conceptions that were to come, eighteenth-century social theory had conceived of human differences as having to do with differing mental tendencies or differing modes of subsistence. Civilization was seen as a sociocultural achievement rather than a racial inheritance, a goal toward which all peoples, potentially, might aspire. Eighteenth-century thinkers wrote about "peoples" or "nations" rather than about "races." But by the nineteenth century, physical attributes came to be seen as the basis for the differences between human groups.[82]

In the 1780s Linnaeus took the step of classifying humans as animals, placing them among the primates and classifying four types of humans according to skin color and related differences, thereby setting the stage for viewing differences between groups of humans in terms of the anatomical distinctions between humans and animals. Around the same time as Linnaeus, Peter Camper introduced the idea of the "facial angle," the first of what were to be a series of physical measurements used for the comparative ranking of animals and humans along a single scale. The discipline of physical anthropology founded by Paul Broca assumed that physical structure determined the salient differences between human groups. Physical measurement—the size, shape and/or proportions of the skull or brain, and even hair quality—would henceforth "explain" why the primitive mind could not exercise reason and had no aptitude for civilization (and therefore why its owner need not be included in the rights and protections of the civilized). Craniometrists, measuring facial angle and cephalic index, and phrenologists, measuring cranial volume, ranged humans amid a scale that began with apes, orangutans and Africans, and ended with "divers Europeans."[83] Brain weight was measured as well.

Such physically measured arrangements fit in all too readily with the ancient, still flourishing notion of the Great Chain of Being, which ranked all creation along a scale beginning with inanimate objects, moving to animals and humans, then on to the angels, and finally to God. In this Great Chain the African had been placed right after the ape. These new physical measurements gave to the association between Africans and apes, which by the nineteenth century had become a European commonplace, the status of scientific fact.[84]

As the basis for racial classification shifted from social, cultural and religious criteria to biological measurement, civilization came to be seen as a biological, rather than a cultural or political, characteristic, exclusively the "peculiar achievement of certain 'races'"; and the difference between primitive and civilized was increasingly inscribed in a scientifically sanctioned schema of race and skin color. Intelligence and cultural capacity were conceived of as embedded in unalterable biological structures: it was cranial configuration that had fated the white race to become the inevitable and rightful rulers of the world, and cranial configuration was taken to be indexed to skin color.[85] This schema constructed ideal types of racial purity, even though, as the eminent historian of anthropology, George W. Stocking Jr., points out,

> to recreate these types out of the heterogeneity of modern mixed populations . . . produced only an imaginary entity. . . . The fictive individual who embodied all the characteristics of the "pure type" grew in the imagination, obliterating the individual variation of his fellows, until he stood for them all as the living expression of the lost but now recaptured essence of racial purity.[86]

David Hume had anticipated the emphasis on color as a marker on the evolutionary scale when he wrote, in 1748:

> I am apt to suspect the negroes, and in general all the other species of men . . . to be naturally inferior to the whites. There never was a civilized nation of any other complexion than white, nor even any individual eminent either in action or speculation.[87]

A century later biologist Thomas Huxley echoed Hume's sentiment: "The highest places in the hierarchy of civilization will assuredly not be within reach of our dusky cousins, though it is by no means necessary that they should be restricted to the lowest."[88] Primitivity was now recognizable by its color.

Thus a preliminary evolutionary framework that counted humans among the animals and furnished criteria for the hierarchical ordering of animal species and human races was well in place by the time of the publication, in 1859, of Darwin's *Origin of Species*. Proto-evolutionary theories had been around since the earliest accounts of European travelers: Acosta, Las Casas and Lafitau had each fashioned theories concerning the Amerindians that located different societies along a universal historical time line. Evolutionary frameworks had structured the eighteenth-century theories of the development of humankind through various stages of subsistence or stages of the capacity for rationality. By the mid-nineteenth century the evolutionary paradigm was prevalent throughout western Europe, preoccupying many of Darwin's contemporaries, such as the social Darwinist Herbert Spencer, geologist Charles Lyell, polymath and eugenicist Francis Galton, and biologist Thomas Huxley—not to mention Alfred Russell Wallace, who arrived at the theory of natural selection independently of Darwin. Evolutionary considerations were a major part of the never-ending debates about the origins and development of the different peoples of the world and their relationship to the biblical account of creation, as well as their relationship to European civilization.[89]

With the idea of natural selection, Darwin provided a biological explanation for the mechanism of evolution. He proposed that species—including humans—were not immutable entities, each having been created separately by God, but rather were subject to variation and had evolved one from the other. All species had originally descended from common primordial forms, and humankind had evolved from related species in a "community of descent" inclusive of "all other vertebrate animals."[90] Species continuously produced new variations among their members; individuals within each species varied one from the other and from one generation to the next. In the theory of natural selection Darwin united the idea of evolution with the British political economist Thomas Malthus's proposition that, owing to the difference between the rate of propagation of a species and of the resources available to it, each species engaged in a struggle for survival. That every species tended, if unchecked, to produce more individuals than could survive meant that those individuals better adapted to the environment had a better chance of surviving and propagating themselves than the others. Natural selection entailed competition, and the price of failure for "the less improved and intermediate forms of life" was extinction.[91]

In the same year as the *Origin of Species* was published, the discovery was made, at Brixham cave in England, of the *Antiquity of Man*, to borrow the title of pioneering geologist Charles Lyell's account of 1863 that publicized these archaeological findings. Providing the final blow to biblical accounts of the history of humankind, the new fossil evidence of flint implements mixed in with the remains of a mammoth extended human history backward by an "incomprehensibly vast" amount of time.[92] No longer could histories of the world begin with "the ancients." Histories beginning with the Greeks and Hebrews were now understood to be preceded by an extended period of prehistory, and Darwinian evolutionary theory was now on hand to account for the *pre*historic origins of the human race. Faced with the problem of the huge span of time in the fossil records between the emergence of the first ancestors of European civilization on the one hand, and the rest of the animals on the other, Darwinian theory responded by "throw[ing] living savages into the fossil gap."[93] Extending the presumed identity between non-western "savages" and "the ancients" backward in time, evolutionary theory cast contemporary primitives as representatives of those humans who had first evolved out of the animals and from whom Europeans themselves had, in turn, eventually evolved.[94]

The broad arena of nineteenth-century sociocultural evolutionism that came to be associated with Darwin's name both predated and contributed to Darwin's work, and drew great scientific legitimacy from it. It was as much influenced by writers such as Herbert Spencer, Thomas Malthus, the French biologist Lamarck and the German zoologist Ernst Haeckel as it was by Darwin. Darwin himself embedded his more radical proposals within a web of conventional teleological evolutionary beliefs, making it possible for the immensely popular theory associated with his name to be understood in terms of nineteenth-century ideals of human progress rather than in terms of the nonteleological and fortuitous character of natural selection that today is held to be his lasting legacy.[95] For sociocultural evolutionism, whose foremost ideologue was Spencer, the biological laws of which Darwin wrote were responsible not only for the evolution of anatomical structures but also for the evolution of moral capabilities and of social and cultural institutions. Social and cultural differences were understood by Spencer as biological endowments arranged along a racially ordered evolutionary scale that culminated in the moral outlook of the educated Englishman. This sociocultural evolutionism, foundational for the emerging science of anthropology, made use of the figure of the primitive to serve as the locus of the evolutionary origins of humankind and, as such, to define the qualities of civilized Europe by representing their antithesis. As a result, it stressed the negative characteristics of the savage or primitive in what George Stocking has called a "functionalism of the abhorrent";[96] and the status of so-called primitive peoples correspondingly suffered a further debasement in the European view.

Fed by a number of different intellectual currents, nineteenth-century evolutionism encompassed not only the contributions of Darwin and Spencer but also the recapitulation theory propagated by Ernst Haeckel, Darwin's German popularizer, and Jean-Baptiste Lamarck's doctrine of acquired characteristics, taken up by Spencer and Haeckel and acknowledged by Darwin himself.[97] Haeckel, professor at Jena during the last half of the nineteenth century who became known as the German Darwin, applied what he learned from Darwin's *Origin of Species* to cytology and embryology, and synthesized the results with concepts from Lamarck and Spencer to create his recapitulation hypothesis—which was then recycled back into the sociocultural evolutionary mix. Haeckel's recapitulation hypothesis, also known as his biogenetic law, asserted that "ontogeny recapitulates phylogeny"—the individual organism repeats, in its embryological development, the history of the evolution of its phylum or species. Transformed into social theory, this came to be understood not simply in embryological terms but in the greatly expanded terms of the development of the human individual from birth onward: the human child, as he or she would grow up, would recapitulate the history of the human race. The influence of this theory was great, in its popular as well as academic reception: it was "the organizing idea for generations of work in comparative embryology, physiology and morphology."[98]

At the heart of the recapitulation theory lay the twin concepts of (individual) development and evolution (of species), expressed by the same German word, *Entwicklungsgeschichte*. These two concepts converged in the idea of the *primitive*: that which was at the beginning of both the evolutionary history of the species and the developmental history of the individual. The personal beginnings of the human individual recapitulated the beginnings of the human race so that the one could be read as a representation of the other.

The Lamarckian contribution to evolutionism—the theory of the inheritance of acquired characteristics—asserted that evolution took place through the direct inheritance of characteristics acquired by an organism through its response to its environment. Characteristics acquired by an individual during his or her lifetime would be passed down directly to the next generation. Haeckel's theory asserted that each newly acquired characteristic would be added on to, and henceforth preserved in, the ontogenetic development of the next generation. He believed that the Lamarckian thesis was "an indispensable foundation of the theory of evolution" and of his own hypothesis.[99] Taken together, these two theories implied that each generation's response to its environment was immediately biologically (in today's terms, genetically) encoded, and this ever-increasing biological legacy was passed down from one generation to the next.

This meant that each generation recapitulated the sum total of its inheritance, from the childhood of the human race right up to the most recent behavioral additions of its parents. With these contributions, evolutionary theory re-established under the aegis of science that "living savages" were representatives of the earliest stages of the human race: infants recapitulated the earliest stages of savagery, while savages lived in the infancy of the human race. As Spencer wrote, "The intellectual traits of the uncivilized are traits recurring in the children of the civilized."[100] The differences between various peoples were biologized as different stages of human evolution; accordingly, what made so-called primitive races primitive was that their biological endowment did not allow them to ascend very far on the evolutionary ladder.

According to Spencer, adolescence represented the passage from primitive childhood to civilized adulthood. Cranial measurements purported to show that, because of supposed limited brain capacity, the mental development of the uncivilized was limited to the level just prior to that of the adolescence of civilized peoples: savages would never be able to pass through adolescence into adulthood and comprehend the heterogeneous complexity that characterized the attainments of the civilized. They were not capable of the progress that distinguished civilization.[101] In a formulation that would later have psychoanalytic reverberations, Spencer held that the progress of civilization was due to the increased ability to defer gratification, an ability limited to the racial endowment of the higher races. Primitive peoples were impulsive, whereas the repression of immediate impulsive response was the essential mechanism of evolutionary progress in both the intellectual and the moral sphere. . . . Those who were more able to control the forces of nature internal to themselves were also those more able to control the forces of nature that impinged upon them from outside.[102]

The now time-worn identification between children and savages extended to include not only madmen but criminals as well. Cesare Lombroso, founder of criminal anthropology, suggested that criminality was normal behavior for adult savages and European children: criminals bore the marks of the primitive past they had failed to outgrow. Children were little criminals as well as little savages. And if the criminal was "a savage in our midst," the savage was, by dint of his place on the evolutionary scale, a criminal in our midst: "normal behavior in . . . savages" was considered criminal by European standards.[103] In the name of civilizing the Indians, US Indian law codified this perspective, criminalizing many of the customary everyday and ritual practices of native tribes.[104]

The Lamarckian theory stating that acquired characteristics would be passed onto the next generation implied that the responses and adaptations of parents to their environment would account for the behavior and social situation of the children. This allowed Darwin's idea of the struggle of species for survival in nature to be interpreted as the struggle of individuals, within their lifetime, for survival within their social milieux. Parents who had adapted well to the requirements of their social environment would produce children who were well situated in that environment. Survival of the fittest became a question not of random variations and mutations fortuitously contributing to adaptation but of intentional behavioral responses promoting the advancement of an individual in his or her social circumstance and biologically passed on to the next generation. Imbued with the spirit of moral uplift, the Lamarckian perspective reinforced "the belief in both intellectual and moral progress," while blaming poor social standing on the lack of moral rectitude of the preceding generation.[105]

In this way, social inferiority was cast as the result of an innate inadequacy inherited from the parental generation. The process of evolution seemed to be driven by the motor of self-improvement, aiming for the moral perfectibility of humankind.[106] The religious challenge posed by the *Origin of Species*—the seeming absence of God from the drama of human evolution—was met by placing the evolutionary thesis within a teleo-logical structure so that evolution could seem to "embod[y] the creator's purpose by advancing inexorably toward a morally significant goal."[107] Religious and philosophical beliefs in the inherent morality of the world order, seemingly threatened by Darwin, were instead shored up by the absorption of his theory into a social, moral and political framework of progress. Faith in progress took the place of faith in salvation, and the prevailing sociopolitical structure was understood to have triumphed by virtue of its moral superiority.[108]

Through this combination of theories, all biological and social forms were seen to be arranged along a continuum of ever-evolving forms, the highest of which turned out to be the European middle classes. Fitness (as in "survival of the fittest") was the new scientific term that naturalized this racially understood superiority: those who had continued to evolve and survive, biologically, socially and politically, had done so owing to a greater racial fitness for life. Human life was seen as evolving through time (if it was not to be weeded out by extinction) toward its evolution-ary telos, the European, masculine subject. The implication, so important for developments in anthropological, social and eventually psychoanalytic theory, was that deviations from this normative end were represented as *prior in evolutionary time*. Thus savages, children, criminals, peasants and the urban poor, as well as the mentally ill and, of course, women of any social and cultural provenance, were "more primitive," stuck somewhere midway on the evolutionary path.[109]

According to Darwin, defeat in the struggle for survival manifested itself in increased infertility that would eventually result in extinction. Such a biologically inevitable demise would be "promptly determined by the inroads of conquering tribes":[110] even for Darwin, military and eco-nomic strength were signs of superior racial fitness. Those on the wrong side of the imperial battle had simply lost the evolutionary struggle for survival. The fact of conquest itself had demonstrated the superiority of European peoples, and the precipitous decrease of the native populations of places such as the Americas or Tasmania (where the entire indigenous population had perished by 1869) demonstrated the inevitable, if regret-table, inability of the less fit to survive. Their extinction seemed merely to place them "back into the dead prehistoric world where they belonged."[111] Geologist Charles Lyell anticipated Darwin when he wrote, in 1830, of the certain doom of a species less fitted to struggle with some new condition in a region which it previously inhabited, and where it has to contend with a more vigorous species . . . few future events are more certain than the speedy extermination of the Indians of North America and the savages of New Holland in the course of a few centuries, when these tribes will be remembered only in poetry and tradition.[112]

As the historian Victor Kiernan remarks, "From believing [that undeveloped races were bound to die out] to expediting their departure to another world was no great step."[113] Evolutionary triumphalism lent an aura of acceptability and inevitability to colonial policies of expropriation and extermination: an article in the *Popular Magazine of Anthropology* of 1866 stated that "to colonize and to extirpate are synonymous terms."[114] Civilization and colonization became understood as the biologically constituted capacities of a particular race that, by virtue of its superior fitness in the struggle for survival, was bound to overtake the other races.

Evolutionary theory thus provided a full systematization of the relationship between civilization and primitivity and between colonizer and colonized that undergirded the expansion of western colonial policies at the end of the nineteenth century. For example: the relationship between private property and lands held in common was now articulated in specifically evolutionary terms by such writers as Lewis Henry Morgan and Henry Maine. For Morgan, the American anthropologist whose *Ancient Society* (1877) exerted a widespread influence (from Friedrich Engels to American federal Indian policy to Freud), the degree of individual property ownership was the measure of the movement from savagery to barbarism to civilization. The holding of lands in common, which he described as a characteristic of the Iroquois peoples he studied, was the most primitive form of land tenure: primitive communism. Similarly, Henry Maine's *Ancient Law* (1861) suggested that "the linked development of the law of family and of property reflected the central dynamic process in the growth of civilization."[115] Civilization required the development of privately held land, and the person who qualified for civilization—the citizen—was one who owned private property. Expropriation from lands held in common could now be justified in explicitly evolutionary terms. In the last two decades of the nineteenth century, the US government embarked on its policy of allotment, which was to civilize native Americans by dismantling the reservation system and distributing private acreages on which to grow crops. Called by Theodore Roosevelt "a mighty pulverizing engine to break up the tribal mass,"[116] allotment was meant to move American Indians from their primitive stage of communism to the next evolutionary stage of agricultural life on private landholdings.[117]

Evolutionary thought also added to the long history of justifications of forced labor and slavery through its conception of "primitive peoples"—who, by the end of the nineteenth century, were described in terms of "savagery, dark skin, and a small brain and incoherent mind."[118] Since primitive peoples were believed not to be capable of the transition to civilization that European children went through during their adolescence, they remained at a preadolescent level of development and, for this reason, they were believed not yet to have learned the value of discipline and labor.[119] Their unwillingness to be coerced into slavery was supposedly a sign of their laziness, thought to be similar to that of children reluctant to engage in the work of adulthood. The progress of civilization, therefore, required the "internalization of the economic impulse." Where this impulse did not exist, it would be instilled, often through the use of terror. "The objective of conversion to the true religion of civilization . . . was to change the Negro inwardly in such a way that he would lose his prejudice against the value of labour."[120] Colonial policy around the world was often carried out in the name of helping so-called primitive peoples progress to the next evolutionary stage, whether by having them abandon primitive, communistic land usage (thereby giving up their land); by having them internalize the more advanced work ethic by force (thereby becoming enslaved); or by encouraging them to succumb to the inevitable pressures of evolution (thereby becoming extinct).

Meanwhile, in the untroubled calm of the European library, far away from the exotic forests, mines and plantations where bodies were forced by the terror and violence of colonial policies to live out the meanings of these terms, the figure of the primitive continued its abstracted existence, as the theories that enframed it were debated, elaborated and modified, and became absorbed into the foundations of other theoretical schemata—such as psychoanalysis—which took as their topics the origin and structures of society, religion, property, the law and the mind. Ideas concerning indigenous peoples everywhere were pressed into service as "natural reserves for the development of social theory."[121] Arguments concerning savages and infidels were transformed from religious doctrine and philosophical argument into scientific fact; effect was cast as cause, and the imputed characteristics of primitive peoples themselves were understood to allow, if not require, their domination. Relations of colonial domination were reified and naturalized in the figure of the primitive, now cloaked in a purportedly disinterested scientific terminology.

Notes

1 Freud, *Interpretation of Dreams*, SE 5:549.
2 Stephen Greenblatt, *Marvelous Possessions: The Wonder of the New World* (Chicago, IL: University of Chicago Press, 1991), 121.
3 Ronald L. Meek, *Social Science and the Ignoble Savage* (Cambridge: Cambridge University Press, 1976), 57.
4 Anthony Pagden, *The Fall of Natural Man: The American Indian and the Origins of Comparative Ethnology* (Cambridge: Cambridge University Press, 1986), chap. 2, "The Image of the Barbarian," 15–26; Greenblatt, *Marvelous Possessions*, 10. Quote is from *Oxford English Dictionary* (*OED*), 1971 ed., s.v. "barbarian."
5 *OED*, 1971 ed., s.v. "heathen."
6 Ibid., "pagan."
7 Hayden White, "Forms of Wildness: Archaeology of an Idea," in his *Tropics of Discourse: Essays in Cultural Criticism*, 150–82 (Baltimore, MD: The Johns Hopkins University Press, 1978); Lewis Hanke, *Aristotle and the American Indians: A Study in Race Prejudice in the Modern World* (Bloomington, IN: Indiana University Press, 1975), 2–6.
8 White, "Forms of Wildness"; Winthrop D. Jordan, *White over Black: American Attitudes toward the Negro, 1550–1812* (Chapel Hill, NC: University of North Carolina Press, 1968), 17–18; Hanke, *Aristotle and the American Indians*, 4; Pagden, *Fall of Natural Man*, 81. See also Richard Bernheimer, *Wild Men in the Middle Ages: A Study in Art, Sentiment and Demonology* (New York: Octagon, 1970), 7, 11, 12, 47, 76; and Stanley L. Robe, "Wild Men and Spain's Brave New World," in Edward Dudley and M.E. Novak, eds., *The Wild Man Within: An Image in Western Thought from the Renaissance to Romanticism*, 39–53 (Pittsburgh, PA: University of Pittsburgh Press, 1972); and David M. Goldenberg, *The Curse of Ham: Race and Slavery in Early Judaism, Christianity, and Islam* (Princeton, NJ: Princeton University Press, 2003).
9 See Arthur O. Lovejoy and George Boas, *Primitivism and Related Ideas in Antiquity* (Baltimore, MD: The Johns Hopkins University Press, 1935).
10 Hoxie Neale Fairchild, *The Noble Savage* (New York: Columbia University Press, 1928), 6.
11 Lovejoy and Boas, "The Noble Savage in Antiquity," in their *Primitivism*, 287–367; Fairchild, *Noble Savage*, 4–6; Robert F. Berkhofer Jr., *The White Man's Indian: Images of the American Indian from Columbus to the Present* (New York: Random House, 1979), 72.
12 Columbus, quoted in Fairchild, *Noble Savage*, 9.

13 Jacques Cartier, quoted in William Brandon, *New Worlds for Old: Reports from the New World and their Effects on the Development of Social Thought in Europe, 1500–1800* (Athens, OH: Ohio University Press, 1985), 60.

14 Joseph-François Lafitau, *Moeurs des Sauvages Américains Comparées aux Moeurs des Premiers Temps*, 2 vols. (Paris, 1724), 1:103; quoted in Brandon, *New Worlds for Old*, 105–6.

15 From the "Capitulaciones de Santa Fe" (April 17, 1492), one of the documents commissioning Columbus's expedition, cited by Margarita Zamora, *Reading Columbus* (Berkeley, CA: University of California Press, 1993), 27.

16 Greenblatt, *Marvelous Possessions*, 58ff.

17 Robert A. Williams Jr., *The American Indian in Western Legal Thought: The Discourse of Conquest* (New York: Oxford University Press, 1990) especially 13–83. See also Zamora, *Reading Columbus*, 21–38, for a discussion of the move from an economic to a religious justification in the early letters of Columbus; as Greenblatt puts it, the rhetoric of Christian imperialism "[brought] together commodity conversion and spiritual conversion" (*Marvelous Possessions*, 71)

18 Williams, *The American Indian*, quote at 67. Williams traces the interweaving of medieval canon- and natural-law arguments concerning the rights (and lack thereof) of infidels to *dominium*—property and self-rule—which developed as western Christianity consolidated and expanded the temporal foundations of its power. Conquest in the name of Christian husbandry of souls was sometimes predicated on the fact of heathenism itself; at other times, heathens had to be well disposed toward Christianity to justify their being placed under Christian religious and political rule.

19 Tzvetan Todorov, *The Conquest of America* (New York: Harper and Row, 1992), 30, 35–6, 41, 76, 219; Berkhofer, *White Man's Indian*, 5; see also Stephen J. Greenblatt, *Learning to Curse: Essays in Early Modern Culture* (New York: Routledge, 1990), 16ff., 27.

20 Gary B. Nash, "The Image of the Indian in the Southern Colonial Mind," in Dudley and Novak, *The Wild Man Within*, 55–86, quotation at 71. See also Karen Ordahl Kupperman, "Presentment of Civility: English Reading of American Self-Presentation in the Early Years of Colonization," *William and Mary Quarterly 54*, no. 1 (1997), cited in David Brion Davis, *In the Image of God: Religion, Moral Values, and Our Heritage of Slavery* (New Haven, CT: Yale University Press, 2001), 311.

21 The phrase "normative divergence" is Robert Williams's (see Williams, *American Indian*, 13, passim). See also Katherine George, "The Civilized West Looks at Primitive Africa: 1400–1800: A Study in Ethnocentrism," *Isis* 49 (1958): 64; Berkhofer, *White Man's Indian*, 28, 118.

22 Columbus, quoted in Fairchild, *Noble Savage*, 9. See Williams, *American Indian in Western Legal Thought*, 78–85, for a discussion of the justifications for imposing Christian tutelage and slavery in the three bulls of donation issued by Pope Alexander VI.

23 Quoted in Williams, *American Indian in Western Legal Thought*, 92.

24 Ibid., 82–4, 174. In his introduction to the 1992 edition of Las Casas's *Devastation of the Indies*, Bill Donovan reports that "recent studies have produced estimates of pre-Columbian populations and post-conquest declines that support his description of demographic catastrophe." See Bill M. Donovan, introduction to Bartolomé de las Casas, *The Devastation of the Indies: A Brief Account*, trans. Herma Briffault (Baltimore, MD: The Johns Hopkins University Press, 1992), 18.

25 Williams, *American Indian in Western Legal Thought*, 86.

26 Las Casas, *The Devastation of the Indies*, 31, 33, 34, 40, 43, 73, 81, 82, 116, 127.

27 Todorov, *Conquest of America*, 146.

28 C.L.R. James, *The Black Jacobins: Toussaint L'Ouverture and the San Domingo Revolution*, 2nd edition (New York: Vintage Books, 1989 [1963]), in particular chapter 1, "The Property."

29 David Brion Davis, *The Problem of Slavery in Western Culture* (Ithaca, NY: Cornell University Press, 1966), 9, 10, 100, 129; and *In the Image of God*, 207. See *In the Image of God*, chap. 16, "The Benefit of Slavery," 205–16, for a discussion of the role of the slave trade in financing the Industrial Revolution.

30 Genesis 9:22–7. Davis, *The Problem of Slavery*, 41; Davis, *In the Image of God*, 318–21, 329.

31 Columbus, quoted in Fairchild, *Noble Savage*, 9; Davis, *In the Image of God*, 311, citing Kupperman, "Presentment of Civility."

32 As were the peoples of Australia and the Pacific Islands.

33 Thomas Jefferson, *Notes on the State of Virginia* (1787), ed. William Peden (New York: Norton, 1972), 138–40.

34 Jordan, *White over Black*, 28ff., 229; Nancy Stepan, *The Idea of Race In Science: Great Britain, 1800–1960* (Hamden, CT: Archon, 1982), 8.

35 Jordan, *White over Black*, 65, 495.

36 Ibid., 179.

37 Brantlinger, "Victorians and Africans: The Genealogy of the Myth of the Dark Continent," *Critical Inquiry 12* (1985): 175, 181–2; Jordan, *White over Black*, 17–18, 24, 28ff., 56, 65; Victor Kiernan, *The Lords of Human Kind: European Attitudes to Other Cultures in the Imperial Age* (London: Serif, 1995), 203, 242.

38 Davis, *In the Image of God*, 309.

39 Davis, *The Problem of Slavery*, 88, 96.

40 Ibid., 195.

41 Williams, *American Indian in Western Legal Thought*, chap. 2, 59–118; Pagden, *Fall of Natural Man*; Hanke, *Aristotle and the American Indian*, chap. 5, "The Great Debate at Valladolid, 1550–1551: The Application of Aristotle's Theory of Natural Slavery to the American Indian," 44–61.

42 Quoted in Williams, *American Indian in Western Legal Thought*, 83–4.

43 Pagden, *Fall of Natural Man*, chap. 3, "The Theory of Natural Slavery," 27–56, quote at 43.

44 The Spanish "Law of Burgos," quoted in Williams, *American Indian in Western Legal Thought*, 88; Pagden, *Fall of Natural Man*, 34, 35; Hanke, *Aristotle and the American Indian*, 11–13.

45 Williams, *American Indian in Western Legal Thought*, 96–108, quote at 103; Pagden, *Fall of Natural Man*, chap. 4, "From Nature's Slaves to Nature's Children," 57–108.

46 Juan Ginés de Sepúlveda, *Democrates segundo, o de las justas causas de la guerra contra los indios*, quoted in Hanke, *Aristotle and the American Indian*, 47.

47 Donovan, introduction to Las Casas, *Devastation of the Indies*, 9; Davis, *The Problem of Slavery*, 172; Pagden, *Fall of Natural Man*, chaps. 5 and 6, 109–97.

48 Quoted in Williams, *American Indian in Western Legal Thought*, 201.

49 The *Law Reports* of Sir Edward Coke, quoted in ibid., 200.

50 Ibid., 165–72; quote at 221.

51 Ibid.

52 Samuel Purchas, *Purchas his Pilgrimes* (Glasgow: J. MacLehose, 1905–7 [1625]), 16; quoted in Brandon, *New Worlds for Old*, 70.

53 John Locke, "Of Property" and "Of the Ends of Political Society and Government," in Mark Goldie, ed., *Two Treatises of Government* (London: Everyman, 1993 [1924]), 133, 130, 178, quoted in Williams, *American Indian in Western Legal Thought*, 248, 252. See also Thomas de Zengotita, "The Functional Reduction of Kinship in the Social Thought of John Locke," in George W. Stocking Jr., ed., *Functionalism Historicized: Essays on British Social Anthropology*, Vol. 2: *History of Anthropology* (Madison, WI: University of Wisconsin Press, 1984), 10–30.

54 An understanding that was challenged as early as 1920 by Robert Lowie: see Harvey A. Feit, "The Construction of Algonquian Hunting Territories: Private Property as Moral Lesson, Policy Advocacy, and Ethnographic Error," in George W. Stocking, ed., *Colonial Situations: Essays on the Contextualization of Ethnographic Knowledge*, Vol. 7: *History of Anthropology* (Madison, WI: University of Wisconsin Press, 1991), 109, 126. For similar issues concerning Australian aboriginal land use, see Elizabeth A. Povinelli, *Labor's Lot: The Power, History, and Culture of Aboriginal Action* (Chicago, IL: University of Chicago Press, 1993); and, concerning Africa, see Henrika Kuklick, "Contested Monuments: The Politics of Archaeology in Southern Africa" in Stocking, *Colonial Situations*, esp. 163–5.

55 Williams, *American Indian in Western Legal Thought*, 211, 218, 221. Quotation, at 211, is from a sermon delivered by Puritan Preacher Robert Gray in 1609.

56 Quoted in Berkhofer, *White Man's Indian*, 148.
57 Quoted in Frederick E. Hoxie, *A Final Promise: The Campaign to Assimilate the Indians, 1880–1920* (Lincoln, NE: University of Nebraska Press, 1984), 14; see also Berkhofer, *White Man's Indian*, 122.
58 Locke, "Of Property," in Goldie, ed., *Two Treatises of Government*, 139.
59 Todorov, *Conquest of America*, 16; Meek, *Social Science and the Ignoble Savage*, 48, 57; Berkhofer, *White Man's Indian*; Frank E. Manuel, *The Eighteenth Century Confronts the Gods* (New York: Atheneum, 1967), 16ff.; Pagden, *Fall of Natural Man*, 145ff.; Donovan, introduction to Las Casas, *Devastation of the Indies*, 10.
60 Berkhofer, *White Man's Indian*, 2.
61 Meek, *Social Science and the Ignoble Savage*, 33, 71ff.; Manuel, *Eighteenth Century Confronts the Gods*.
62 Meek, *Social Science and the Ignoble Savage*, passim.
63 Manuel, *Eighteenth Century Confronts the Gods*, 10, 11, 44ff.
64 Ibid., 81.
65 As will be seen in the rest of this book. See also Manuel, chap. 2, 57–81.
66 Manuel, 142, 174.
67 Charles de Brosses, *Du Culte des dieux fétiches* (1760), quoted in ibid., 204ff.
68 Norbert Elias, *The Civilizing Process: Sociogenetic and Psychogenetic Investigations*, trans. E. Jephcott (Oxford: Blackwell, 2000 [1939]), 5. See also George W. Stocking's discussion in his *Victorian Anthropology*, chap. 1, "The Idea of Civilization before the Crystal Palace (1750–1850)" (New York: Free Press, 1987), 8–45.
69 Elias, *The Civilizing Process*, 86.
70 Ibid., passim. See also Emile Benveniste, "Civilization: A Contribution to the History of the Word," in *Problems in General Linguistics*, trans. Mary Elizabeth Meek (Coral Gables, FL: University of Miami Press, 1971), 291.
71 Stocking, *Victorian Anthropology*, 11.
72 Raymond Williams, "Civilization," in his *Keywords: A Vocabulary of Culture and Society* (New York: Oxford University Press, 1976).
73 Royal Charter of the Virginia Company, 1606, quoted in Williams, *American Indian in Western Legal Thought*, 201.
74 Quoted in Benveniste, "Civilization," 294. See also "Civilization" in Williams, *Keywords;* Charles Long, "Primitive/Civilized: The Locus of a Problem," in his *Signification: Signs, Symbols, and Images in the Interpretation of Religion* (Philadelphia, PA: Fortress, 1986), 79–96; Stocking, *Victorian Anthropology*, 35.
75 White, "Forms of Wildness," 151.
76 Jordan, *White over Black*, 110.
77 Elias, *Civilizing Process*, 43.
78 John and Jean Comaroff, *Ethnography and the Historical Imagination* (Boulder, CO: Westview Press, 1992), 43, 41.
79 Paul Freedman, *Images of the Medieval Peasant* (Stanford, CA: Stanford University Press, 1999), 89, 139, cited in Davis, *In the Image of God*, 326.

80 Hannah Arendt, *The Origins of Totalitarianism* (San Diego, CA: Harcourt Brace, 1979 [1948]), 173.

81 See Ivan Hannaford, *Race: The History of an Idea in the West* (Baltimore, MD: The Johns Hopkins University Press, 1996), for a detailed intellectual history of the shift in the western concept of civilization from the Greek ideal of participation within a political community ruled by laws, open to all who would enter into its language of law and debate, on the one hand; to the social evolutionist conception of civilization as a quasi-biological organism held together by language and blood, and thus in need of the administration of race hygiene rather than of political institutions, on the other. The origins of the former were located in a political act; the origins of the latter were sought in nature.

82 George W. Stocking Jr., *Race, Culture, and Evolution: Essays in the History of Anthropology* (Chicago, IL: University of Chicago Press, 1982), 35–8.

83 Quoted in Jordan, *White over Black*, 225.

84 A.O. Lovejoy, *The Great Chain of Being: A Study of the History of an Idea* (Cambridge, MA: Harvard University Press, 1961 [1936]); Stocking, "The Dark-Skinned Savage: Primitive Man in Evolutionary Anthropology," in his *Race, Culture, and Evolution*, 110–32; Nancy Stepan, "Race and the Return of the Great Chain of Being, 1800–1850," in her *Idea of Race in Science*, 1–19; Jordan, *White over Black*, 219, 229, 483.

85 Stocking, *Race, Culture, and Evolution*, 35–8; Stephan Jay Gould, *The Mismeasure of Man* (New York: Norton, 1996), 88ff; Stepan, *The Idea of Race in Science*, chaps. 1, 2; Jordan, *White over Black*, 218; John S. Haller Jr., *Outcasts from Evolution: Scientific Attitudes of Racial Inferiority, 1859–1900* (Carbondale, IL: Southern Illinois University Press, 1971), xiv, 4, 7, 38; quote is in Stocking, *Race, Culture, and Evolution*, 36.

86 Stocking, *Race, Culture, and Evolution*, 58–9.

87 David Hume, "Of National Characters," first published in 1748, in his *Essays: Moral, Political and Literary*, ed. T.H. Green and T.H. Grose (London: Longmans, Green, 1875), 1:252; quoted in Jordan, *White over Black*, 253.

88 Thomas Huxley, "Emancipation—Black and White," reprinted in *Lay Sermons, Addresses, and Reviews* (New York: Appleton, 1871), 20–6; quoted in Stepan, *The Idea of Race in Science*, 80.

89 Pagden, *Fall of Natural Man*, 142, 171; Stocking, *Victorian Anthropology*, 14; Meek, *Social Science and the Ignoble Savage*; Anthony Leeds, "Darwin and 'Darwinian' Evolutionism in the Study of Society and Culture," in Thomas Glick, ed., *The Comparative Reception of Darwinism* (Austin, TX: University of Austin Press, 1972), 437–77.

90 Charles Darwin, *The Origin of Species* (New York: Gramercy, 1979 [1859]), 434, 455; idem, *The Descent of Man, and Selection in Relation to Sex* (New York: New York University Press, 1989 [1871]), 29.

91 Darwin, *Origin of Species*, 170. Also see John R. Durant, "The Ascent of Nature in Darwin's *Descent of Man*," in David Kohn, ed., *The Darwinian Heritage*, (Princeton, NJ: Princeton University Press, 1985), 287.

92 Darwin, *Origin of Species*, 293.
93 Stocking, *Victorian Anthropology*, 147.
94 Thomas R. Trautmann, "Of Time and Ethnology," in his *Lewis Henry Morgan and the Invention of Kinship* (Berkeley, CA: University of California Press, 1987); Stepan, *Idea of Race in Science*, 55.
95 Although, as Stephen Jay Gould points out, Darwin's message of the fortuitousness of evolutionary change continues to be disregarded in the popular press even today. See Gould, "Spin Doctoring Darwin," *Natural History* 104, no. 7 (1995): 6–9, 70–1.
96 Stocking, *Victorian Anthropology*, 104.
97 Peter J. Bowler, *Biology and Social Thought, 1850–1914* (Berkeley, CA: University of California Press, 1993), 9; Alfred Kelly, *The Descent of Darwin: The Popularization of Darwinism in Germany, 1860–1914* (Chapel Hill, NC: University of North Carolina Press, 1981), 30.
98 Stephen Jay Gould, *Ontogeny and Phylogeny* (Cambridge, MA: Harvard University Press, 1977), 116.
99 Ibid., 80.
100 Quoted in ibid., 128.
101 Durant, "The Ascent of Nature in Darwin's *Descent of Man*"; Pietro Crose and Paul J. Weindling, "Darwinism in Germany, France, and Italy"; and Robert M. Young, "Darwinism *Is* Social," all in David Kohn, ed., *The Darwinian Heritage* (Princeton, NJ: Princeton University Press, 1985), 283–306, 683–729, 609–38, respectively; Anthony Leeds, "Darwin and 'Darwinian' Evolutionism in the Study of Society and Culture," in Glick, *The Comparative Reception of Darwinism*, 437–85; Haller, *Outcasts from Evolution*, 127. See also Lucille Ritvo, *Darwin's Influence on Freud: A Tale of Two Sciences* (New Haven, CT: Yale University Press, 1990).
102 Stocking, *Victorian Anthropology*, 227–8.
103 Gould, *Ontogeny and Phylogeny*, 120–5; quotes at 120, 123.
104 In the nineteenth century, such traditional native customs as plural marriages, distributing the property of a deceased relative, seeking the help of medicine men and participating in "heathenish dances" were outlawed, as was the refusal to "adopt habits of industry, or to engage in civilized pursuits or employments." See "Extract from the Annual Report of the Secretary of the Interior, November 1, 1883" and "Rules for Indian Courts" of August 27, 1892, in Francis Paul Prucha, *Documents of United States Indian Policy* (Lincoln, NE: University of Nebraska Press, 1990 [1975]), 160–2, 186–9, respectively. Traditional practices such as fishing and hunting and gathering roots, berries and wild rice have often been criminalized at the state and local levels for Indians who participate in them off their designated reservations. See "In Usual and Accustomed Places," in M. Annette Jaimes, ed., *The State of Native America: Genocide, Colonization, and Resistance* (Boston, MA: South End Press, 1992), 217–39. In addition, well into the twentieth century Indian children placed in boarding schools in the United States and

Canada were cruelly punished for, among other things, speaking their native languages. See John Burrows, "Indian Agency: Forming First Nations Law in Canada," in *Political and Legal Anthropology Review* 24, no. 2 (2001): 9–24; and Jorge Noriega, "American Indian Education in the United States: Indoctrination for Subordination to Colonialism," in Jaimes, *State of Native America*, 371–402. I am indebted to Susan Gooding for these references and for familiarizing me with these issues (Gooding, personal communication).

105 Bowler, *Biology and Social Thought*; Greta Jones, *Social Darwinism and English Thought: The Interaction Between Biological and Social Theory* (Brighton, Sussex: Harvester, 1980). Quote is in Stocking, *Victorian Anthropology*, 141.

106 Jones, *Social Darwinism and English Thought*, 152.

107 Bowler, *Biology and Social Thought*, 9, 37.

108 Ibid., 66.

109 Stocking, *Victorian Anthropology*, 228–33.

110 Darwin, *Origin of Species*, part 1, 198.

111 Stocking, *Victorian Anthropology*, 283.

112 Charles Lyell, *Principles of Geology* (1830; repr. 1850), 678; quoted in Marvin Harris, *The Rise of Anthropological Theory* (New York: Columbia University Press, 1968), 113.

113 Kiernan, *Lords of Human Kind*, 276.

114 *Popular Magazine of Anthropology, vol.* 1 (1866), 10–11, quoted in Christine Bolt, *Victorian Attitudes to Race* (London: Routledge and Kegan Paul, 1971), 20.

115 Stocking, *Victorian Anthropology*, 124.

116 Theodore Roosevelt, quoted in Berkhofer, *White Man's Indian*, 175.

117 Feit, "Construction of Algonquian Hunting Territories," 112–13; Hoxie, *Final Promise*, 10, passim; Berkhofer, *White Man's Indian*, 120–3.

118 Stocking, "The Dark-Skinned Savage," 132.

119 Ibid., 126.

120 Jan Breman, "Primitive Racism in a Colonial Setting," in Jan Bremen, ed., *Imperial Monkey Business: Racial Supremacy in Social Darwinist Theory and Colonial Practice*, 89–121 (Amsterdam: Vrije Universiteit Press, 1990), quotation at 110; see also Michael Taussig, *Shamanism, Colonialism, and the Wild Man: A Study in Terror and Healing* (Chicago, IL: University of Chicago Press, 1987), 25.

121 Povinelli, *Labor's Lot*, 66, drawing on Richard White, *Inventing Australia: Images and Identity, 1688–1980* (Sydney: Allen and Unwin, 1981).

Chapter 2

Psychoanalysis and the colonial imagination

Evolutionary thought in Freud's texts

At the dawn of the twentieth century Freud introduced the first works of what would become his towering contribution to western thought. Both a theory of psyche and society and a therapeutic system, his new science of psychoanalysis harbored a host of unsettling propositions concerning the formative role played by infantile sexuality in the constitution of subjectivity, the primacy of the hidden determinants of waking consciousness and the significance of dreams, symptoms and slips of the tongue as inadvertent disguises of unconscious desire. The disturbing implications of Freud's thought eventually came to be set, however, in a larger framework that was influenced by the dominant social ideology of his times, reproducing many of the colonialist assumptions of nineteenth-century anthropology. Psychoanalysis simultaneously dismantled *and* upheld these colonialist assumptions. On the one hand, Freud claimed primitivity to be a universal feature of the psyche of all humankind, rather than a characteristic of savages only, thus sabotaging the presumption of the superiority of the western mind that had been held by the first generation of western anthropologists. This decisively separated him from nineteenth-century anthropology, marking his work as a departure from the Victorian era and an entry into twentieth-century critical thought. But on the other hand, as we shall see, by explaining the primitivity of the contemporary psyche with recourse to the categories and methods of Victorian anthropology, Freud reinstated primitivity as an evolutionarily prior and therefore—by the logic of the evolutionary anthropology from which he borrowed—a racially indexed category. These assumptions did not invalidate the innovations of psychoanalysis, but their presence has continued to lend credence to readings of psychoanalysis that are vulnerable to perpetuating colonialist representations of primitivity with their associated racist implications (in much the same way that psychoanalytic representations of femininity were able to be enlisted for much of the twentieth century as an ally in the subordination of women).

Totem and Taboo is one of the master texts of psychoanalysis that exhibits this evolutionary dimension.[1] Before its publication in 1913, Freud's work had been concerned with developing the insights and techniques of psychoanalysis with regard to the individual, contemporary western subject. In Totem and Taboo Freud joined these investigations to the larger conversation about the origins of human institutions that had been conducted in Europe since the sixteenth century, and linked his descriptions of the constitution of the contemporary psyche to speculations about the primordial beginnings of the psyche and of human society. In so doing, he followed the conventions of this conversation, describing the origins of both psyche and society in terms of the customs of so-called primitive peoples, as they had been reconstructed by European colonialists and anthropologists from the sixteenth through the nineteenth century.

Freud's enlistment of nineteenth-century anthropology via Totem and Taboo and other works brought with it, alongside his groundbreaking insights, problematic implications for psychoanalysis. This chapter traces the specific sources of the anthropological ideas that Freud used, then maps their occurrence and influence in Totem and Taboo and beyond. It goes on to demonstrate how the unconscious came to be seen as primitive, and how the concept of regression came to forge a link between psychopathology and psychoanalysis' raced others.

Freud's anthropologists

Evolutionary theory and its extensions into the sociocultural and anthropological fields pervaded the scientific as well as the popular imagination of the late nineteenth century. Freud had trained in the biological sciences and had studied with leading evolutionists;[2] from his assertion in The Interpretation of Dreams in 1900 that "man's archaic heritage . . . is psychically innate in him" to his summing up, in Moses and Monotheism in 1939, that "the psychical precipitates of the primeval period became inherited property which, in each fresh generation, called not for acquisition but only for awakening," evolutionary assumptions can be found throughout his work.[3] Frank Sulloway has, in my view, overstated things by claiming that "it was precisely this new evolutionary vision that, after the *Project for a Scientific Psychology* (1895), exerted the greatest single and most far-reaching theoretical influence upon Freud's conception of human psychosexual development,"[4] but the influence was nonetheless significant. Freud assimilated evolutionary theory from his medical studies as well as from the temper of the times; but he drew his specific assumptions about the relationship between the structures of the contemporary mind and the prehistory of humankind from the anthropological literature of his day.[5] Through Freud, psychoanalysis borrowed, universalized and helped popularize such exotic terms as *taboo*, *totem*, *fetish* and *mana* as they first appeared in early anthropological discourse.

In the latter half of the nineteenth century, the discipline of anthropology was emerging as a recognizable field of scholarly endeavor in Europe and the United States, with the study of so-called primitive peoples as its special province. The Anthropological Society of London was established in 1863; it reunited with the London Ethnological Society (from which it had previously seceded) to form the Anthropological Institute in 1871. The *Société d'Anthropologie de Paris* was founded in 1859, and the German Anthropological Society in 1869. Edward Burnett Tylor, considered the father of modern Anglo-American anthropology, was appointed as Oxford's first reader in anthropology in 1884. Charged with the task of interpreting data gathered about the non-western and often colonized peoples of the world, the first anthropologists, no less than most other thinkers of their time, breathed the air of evolutionary theory, whose ambassadors to the study of culture they were. Their theorizing was the culmination of the many attempts to order human communities according to a presumed progression from the most primitive to the most civilized according largely to skin color, attempts that had preoccupied European theorists from the sixteenth century onwards, and which fell under the sway of the mighty influence of Darwin in the late nineteenth century. But nineteenth-century evolutionary anthropology took its cues from Herbert Spencer's interpretation of Darwin, which made use of the biologically deterministic theories of Lamarck and Haeckel to explain how *cultural* phenomena became biologically sedimented into *racially* inherited traits. Thus the evolutionary theory they espoused was a form of social Darwinism which cast social and cultural differences as the result of inborn, biological factors. Even Darwin himself, in his *Descent of Man*, at times drifted into a form of social Darwinism when he drew on the writings not only of

Spencer and Haeckel but of the Victorian anthropologists John McLennan, Sir John Lubbock and E.B. Tylor.[6]

These Victorian anthropologists, dubbed "armchair titans" because, with few exceptions, they rarely set foot in any of the lands they wrote about so prolifically, provided questionnaires to be filled out by travelers, missionaries and colonial administrators concerning the indigenous peoples they met, proselytized or governed. These questionnaires inevitably reflected the categories of thought and cultural expectations of those who compiled them.[7] From the answers to these questionnaires, refracted through colonial and evolutionary assumptions and often spiced with liberal doses of imagination,[8] the first generation of anthropologists (who were not yet known as such[9]) compiled their works and constructed their theories. Although they were often at odds with one another over their particular theories of the origins of various social customs and psychological tendencies—Were the first humans originally promiscuous? Was the earliest religion a monotheistic one that degenerated into various forms or a polytheistic one out of which monotheism eventually emerged? Were primitive peoples possessed of the same rational mind as civilized peoples, or were they pre-logical and irrational?—they nevertheless all shared an evolutionary outlook now aligned with the biological sciences, and labored to bring the study of religion and culture into its purview.

Sir James Frazer, author of *The Golden Bough,* first became interested in anthropology through reading E.B. Tylor, and he credited the scholar of religion, William Robertson Smith, with converting him to the field. In his turn, Robertson Smith found Frazer's files to be of great help in the writing of his classic *Lectures on the Religion of the Semites* and was influenced both by Tylor and John McLennan, who invented the word *exogamy* and introduced the concept of totemism to anthropology. Henry Lewis Morgan, a leading American evolutionary anthropologist at the end of the nineteenth century, developed an evolutionary study of kinship systems later taken up by Karl Marx and Friedrich Engels as the basis for their theory of the family and private property.[10] It was from this cadre of nineteenth-century scholars—Frazer, Tylor, Robertson Smith, McLennan, John Lubbock, Morgan and J.J. Atkinson, as well as the noted psychologist Wilhelm Wundt—that Freud assumed the framework, data, methodology and some of the pivotal arguments for *Totem and Taboo.*

Freud read widely in British anthropology, in particular, because it was the English-speaking Ernest Jones who provided him with an anthropological bibliography.[11] (It is interesting to note that Freud was writing *Totem and Taboo* at the same time that Carl Jung was writing his first major work, *Symbols of Transformation*, in which he too made use of the comparative anthropology of the day. The two corresponded with each other as they wrote these works; and the differing theses they each developed out of similar materials were important elements in their final rift.[12]) E.B. Tylor's *Primitive Culture*, first published in 1871, was the foundational work of British anthropology and, as such, exhibits the principles shared to a great degree by this school. *Primitive Culture* applied evolutionary theory to the comparative study of cultures and religions. As the Darwinian project made use of comparative *anatomy* to reconstruct biological evolution, Tylor used the comparison of *cultural* phenomena to reconstruct the cultural evolution of humankind. His use of this anthropological "comparative method" and its associated "doctrine of survivals," together with his conception of animism as the first stage of cultural evolution—all of which have since fallen into disrepute—was widely shared by his colleagues, and adopted by Freud.

The comparative method of anthropology attempted to reconstruct the evolutionary history of humankind by ordering the vast array of colonial data that had been produced by travelers, missionaries and administrators concerning the beliefs and practices of so-called primitive peoples, according to a single, universal scale that began with savagery, moved on to barbarism and culminated in (European) civilization. This scale represented the diversity of human cultures as due to the biological development of the human brain: similarities in cultural phenomena found in different historical eras and geographical locations were believed to be the result of the workings of similar types of brains (which existed in bodies of similar skin color), and therefore were held to signify that the peoples who exhibited them were at the same evolutionary stage. Artifacts from various cultures were compared by arranging them according to their similarities, without regard to their historical eras or cultural contexts, and placed into predetermined evolutionary stages.[13] As Tylor argued in his introduction to *Primitive Culture*,

> little respect need be had in such comparisons for date in history or for place in map; the ancient Swiss lake-dweller may be set beside the mediaeval Aztec, and the Ojibwa of North America beside the Zulu of South Africa.[14]

This was because foreknowledge of the stages of the evolutionary scale told the anthropologist where any particular element from any particular culture would belong. Because "primitive man" was both prehistoric and yet conveniently alive in the colonies, gaps in knowledge concerning the evolution of culture could be filled by examining the appropriate contemporary tribe that was supposed to correspond to a particular evolutionary stage.

Tylor argued for the essential unity of humankind, as against the theorists known as polygenists who saw different races as having had differing evolutionary origins and therefore as having differing capabilities for rationality and civilization. All of humankind, according to Tylor, possessed the same, rational mind. Differences between peoples and cultures merely represented different degrees of rationality, which were correlated with different stages in evolutionary development. Tylor's conception of culture, as the historian of anthropology George Stocking points out, represented Matthew Arnold's definition—"the best which has been thought and said"—mapped onto a social evolutionary scale. This meant that "culture" was ascribed a universal meaning: "people were more or less cultured rather than living in different cultures," and cultural differences were taken as signs of differing stages in evolutionary development.[15] The standard by which such cultural attainment was measured was, of course, the civilized west. As Tylor wrote:

> The educated world of Europe and America practically settles a standard by simply placing its own nation at one end of the social scale and the savage tribes on the other, arranging the rest of mankind within these limits according as they correspond to savage or to cultured life.[16]

In applying an evolutionary scale to the study of human cultures, nineteenth-century anthropologists made use of Lamarck's theory of the inheritance of acquired characteristics and Haeckel's recapitulation theory, both originally formulated to account for the emergence and transmission of *physical* characteristics, to account for differences in *cultural* phenomena. Lamarck's theory of the inheritance of acquired characteristics saw differing cultural behaviors as behavioral adaptations to the environment that became biologically (today we would say genetically) encoded as soon as they were acquired, and then passed on biologically (genetically) to the next generation, thus transforming social and cultural differences into racially inherited differences. Haeckel's recapitulation hypothesis, as we have seen, stated that the contemporary human child would recapitulate the historical evolution of the entire human race as he or she advanced through childhood. The corollary of this theory was that contemporary dark-skinned "savages" were believed to be living in the infancy of the human race, so that the prehistoric origins of contemporary European customs could be sought among them. Both theories adhered to the color-coding of the evolutionary scale: the infancy of the human race was represented by dark-skinned peoples, and the acquisition of desirable cultural characteristics went along with whiter skin.

The comparative method, then, like the social evolutionism of which it was a part, was color-coded: the darker the skin color of the peoples who practiced a particular custom, the lower were both they and it on the evolutionary scale. As Frazer wrote in *Totem and Exogamy*, "savage and barbarous peoples, the lower races as we call them" could be known by their complexion, which "shades off from coal black through dark brown to red"; and "civilization varies on the whole, as it seems to do, directly with complexion."[17] Dark skin was the sign of primitivity, just as white skin was the sign of civilization.

Although Tylor believed in the psychic unity of humankind, his method harbored within it an evolutionary argument for racial inequality. His comparative method seemed to imply that nothing need stand in the way of the complete mental and cultural advancement of any human group: new adaptations could develop and become part of its racial inheritance. But his method assumed that primitive peoples were permanently stuck in their progress along the evolutionary scale. As Stocking writes, the comparative method actually required that dark-skinned savages should not reach the top of the evolutionary ladder: "the evidence of ethnography and history showed that they had not; ethnocentric assumption suggested that they could not and European expansion made it clear that they would not."[18]

Associated with the framework of the anthropological comparative method was the "doctrine of survivals," which was used to account for the persistence of primitive beliefs and customs in evolutionarily advanced cultures. According to Tylor, as a people progressed up the evolutionary ladder, certain traits belonging to earlier stages might be carried along unnecessarily. These "lower" beliefs and behaviors that somehow continued to exist within a "higher" culture were called by Tylor "survivals in culture." Like vestigial organs that had once fulfilled a particular function, they lingered on uselessly, past their appointed hour. By identifying such survivals in contemporary cultures, the anthropologist could retrospectively fill in gaps in the overall historical trajectory of the evolution of culture. Survivals accounted for the persistence of cultural anomalies: elements of contemporary European culture that Tylor judged as outdated were categorized as survivals, vestiges of an earlier time. Through the doctrine of survivals, Tylor continued the Enlightenment use of so-called primitive cultures as foils in the ongoing attack against superstition and Christianity (in particular, Catholicism). By casting the rites of the Catholic Church ("the Roman scheme") as mere survivals of more primitive times, it could be seen that Catholics "more naturally belong[ed] to barbaric culture."[19]

In addition, Tylor introduced the term *animism* to represent the earliest stage in the evolution of religious belief. All people, according to Tylor, had the capacity for reason; but primitive peoples reasoned from false premises and therefore developed mistaken beliefs and peculiar rites. Animism resulted from the combination of reasoning from false premises with the primitive propensity for what he called "mistaking an ideal for a real connexion."[20] Taking mere ideas for actual realities, primitive peoples ascribed to the conjurings of imagination the status of objective reality. Perplexed by the disappearance of activity during sleep and at death, as well as by the appearance of the dead in dreams, primitive peoples, according to Tylor, reasoned that there must be a soul independent of the body. Once having imagined the idea of the soul, they took it to be an external reality which they then made into an object of worship and entreaty. Early humans had been trying to figure out "the profound riddle of the world," as Frazer's biographer has put it;[21] limited by their false premises, they came up with animism and then religion. "It was as though primitive man, in an attempt to create science, had accidentally created religion instead, and mankind had spent the rest of evolutionary time trying to rectify the error."[22]

Tylor's comparative method was shared by Sir James Frazer, a classicist who was considered the greatest anthropologist of his generation. Frazer, too, believed that all humans possessed a fundamentally rational mind and differed only in the development of their capacity to direct this rationality appropriately. It was Frazer to whom Freud turned most frequently in *Totem and Taboo* for information on totemism, exogamy, taboo, kinship and magic. Frazer wrote enormous works in which he applied the evolutionary framework to the study of classical mythology. His twelve-volume *Golden Bough*, whose first edition appeared in 1890, is still in print and alive in the popular imagination, owing in part to T.S. Eliot's citations of it in *The Waste Land*. Like Tylor, Frazer wished to trace the evolution of human culture, and made use of the comparative method to combine his extensive knowledge of the classics with the vast outpourings of colonial ethnographies. Whereas some of the earliest writers on Europe's newly discovered colonies had explained the savages they encountered by comparing them to "the ancients," Frazer inverted this formula and demonstrated what the ancients were really up to by examples culled from nineteenth-century savages around the world. Similar to Tylor's distinction between animism and religion, Frazer distinguished between magic and religion: magic represented the earliest attempts of humankind to coerce nature and the supernatural, whereas religion represented later attempts to propitiate them. According to Frazer, human thought had evolved through the phases of magic and religion to arrive, finally, at science.

In his four-volume work, *Totemism and Exogamy*, which Freud used to great advantage, Frazer gathered together countless descriptions of exogamous practices and totemic beliefs and concluded that although totemism was "a crude superstition," the prohibitions against killing and eating the totem nonetheless represented "an advance in culture," a universal but very early step in the long evolutionary march toward civilization. As such, it was "an institution peculiar to the dark-complexioned and least civilized races of mankind."[23] Freud leaned on Frazer not only for this evolutionary ranking of totemism but also for his descriptions of exogamous practices around the world, and for his contention that the universal prohibition against incest masks an instinctive desire *for* it.

While Freud derived the socioevolutionary framework and comparative methodology of *Totem and Taboo* as well as much of his data concerning so-called savages from Frazer and Tylor (and from associates of theirs such as John McLennan and Sir John Lubbock), the decisive moment of his argument—the description of the primal crime itself—depended on the work of biblical scholar and anthropologist William Robertson Smith, author, editor of the *Encyclopedia Britannica* and an early British advocate of the German school of biblical criticism which studied the Bible as a text of human and plural authorship. Robertson Smith shared most of the evolutionary notions of his time: the use of survivals to reconstruct gaps in the evolution of culture; animism as the earliest evolutionary stage of religion; and the idea that savages mistook imagination for reality: "Savages, we know ... ascribe to all material objects a life analogous to that which their own self-consciousness reveals to them."[24] He took up John McLennan's description of totemism as the social arrangement whereby members of tribes identified themselves with a taboo plant or animal and did not marry others identified with the same totem (that is, they practiced totemic exogamy). To McLennan's conception of totemism and exogamy Robertson Smith linked the idea of the totem sacrifice and meal.[25]

Robertson Smith's Christian beliefs were responsible for the central place held by the question of sacrifice in his scholarly interests: research on the origins of sacrifice could shed light on the prehistory and meaning of the Eucharist. Indeed, although Darwin's discoveries and their associated evolutionary framework are generally thought to have challenged traditional religious beliefs, this was not universally so. The normative ordering and moral progressivism implied by sociocultural evolutionism (although today no longer associated with Darwinian evolution) could also be seen as leading toward Christianity itself. For Robertson Smith and others, evolution, rather than posing a challenge to Christian belief, was a process that culminated in Christianity.[26]

Robertson Smith's classic *Religion of the Semites* (1889) pursued the quest for the origins of religion through an examination of what he believed to be the first religious act, the sacrifice of a totem animal. His use of the comparative method and the doctrine of survivals, applied now to biblical scholarship, allowed him to locate this act in an early evolutionary stage purported to be shared by the ancient Jews with "Phoenicians, Aramaeans, Babylonians, Assyrians" as well as with contemporary Arab Bedouins, and to consider the religious beliefs and practices of these disparate groups "as a whole in its common features."[27] In choosing to study these "Semites," Robertson Smith was adopting the division of peoples into Aryans and Semites that had grown out of European philological studies by the mid-nineteenth century. This classificatory scheme cast members of linguistically related populations as members of the same race, and drew on traditional accounts of the descendants of the three sons of Noah—Ham, Shem and Japheth—to classify the populations of the world according to the three racial categories of most concern to Europeans. As we have seen, the Atlantic slave trade had exploited the notion that the black peoples of Africa were considered descendants of Ham; for the nineteenth-century philology that advertently and inadvertently contributed to the anti-Semitic discourse of Aryanism, Semites were considered descendants of Shem, and Aryans were considered descendants of Japheth.[28] Since Robertson Smith's evolutionary scale culminated in a supposedly Aryan Christianity, "Semitic religion" was considered to be earlier or lower on the evolutionary scale and, as such, could provide materials for understanding the primitive origins of religion.

For Robertson Smith, the group was the fundamental unit of primitive religion; the individual would emerge as the locus of religious life only on the higher end of the evolutionary scale. Rites and ritual—acts, rather than beliefs—were the fundamental and original religious activities. The earliest religion, therefore, was not an affair of an individual's belief in a supernatural god but rather a community's system of rituals which bound its members to one another. Primitive group membership was established by commensality: by virtue of sharing food and drink, the community constituted its bonds of solidarity. The totem animal was considered the ancestor and thus a member of the community, so the community was answerable for its life as well. No one was allowed to kill and eat the totem animal; its sacrifice by the community as a whole was the sacred exception. At the heart of his work on the origins of religion Robertson Smith gave a vivid description of "the oldest known form of Arabian sacrifice": the totem animal, a camel, was wounded and its fresh blood drunk by all; then,

> the whole company fall on the victim with their swords, hacking off pieces of the quivering flesh and devouring them raw with such wild haste that within the day the entire camel is devoured. The victim is devoured before its life had left the still warm blood and flesh. In the most literal way, the community absorbed part of the victim's life into themselves.[29]

In Robertson Smith's view, eating the flesh and drinking the blood of the common ancestor in the form of the totem animal sealed the bond of unity between community members, and between the community and the god. (Here the god was not the totemic victim itself, as Freud would later have it, but was imagined to participate with the community in the sacrificial feast.) This blood bond laid the ethical basis of the community: all members of the community, including the god, were now responsible for each other's lives.

Robertson Smith's narrative of the origins of religion in totemic sacrifice held sway in academic circles for quite some time despite the fact that "evidence for this theory," as the British anthropologist Evans-Pritchard dryly remarked, "is negligible."[30] Evidence turned out to be similarly negligible for many other cherished socioevolutionary conceptions as well. Toward the end of the nineteenth century, even before Freud was making substantial use of them, the assumptions undergirding the anthropological comparative method began to unravel one by one. Missionaries who were Tylor's contemporaries "were uncomfortable with the hypothesis of animism on empirical as well as on theological grounds."[31] Developments in the biological sciences began to discredit the comparative method and the Lamarckian and Haeckelian theories associated with it. Lamarck's theory of the inheritance of acquired characteristics was first challenged in the 1880s by the biologist August Weismann, who demonstrated that acquired characteristics were in fact not inheritable. Weismann showed that only the germ cells (what we would now call the genes) of an organism could transmit hereditary information, while the somatic cells could not. Cutting off the tails of successive generations of mice to illustrate that cut-off tails were not passed on from generation to generation, Weismann proved that the somatic cells of an organism could not affect the germ cells, and thus variations acquired by the organism during its lifetime could not be passed on to its offspring.

The rediscovery of the work of Gregor Mendel at the turn of the century struck a further blow to Lamarckianism by establishing the gene as the unit of inheritance and genetic recombinations and mutations (rather than acquired characteristics) as the source of the variations that are subject to natural selection. Haeckel's recapitulation hypothesis, too, was discredited in the biological sciences by such scientists as Karl Ernst von Baer, who had rejected the idea in the 1820s, and the zoologist William Bateson, a leading proponent of Mendel's work, who rejected Haeckel's idea in the 1890s. Because new genetic combinations or mutations, present from conception, may express change at any stage of an organism's development, one of the implications of the recapitulation theory—that new evolutionary developments are added on to the end point of the previously existing ontogenetic blueprint—could no longer hold. Recapitulation was "abandoned as a universal proposition":[32] contra Haeckel, ontogeny does not necessarily recapitulate phylogeny, and individual development, embryological or after birth, does not recapitulate the evolution of the species.[33]

These new developments in evolutionary science necessarily affected the anthropological theories that had modeled themselves on, and perpetuated, their now discredited predecessors. If physical characteristics acquired during a lifetime could not be biologically inherited, then neither could cultural characteristics. The cultural customs that characterized a people could no longer be seen as having been biologically inherited and racially determined. In the United States, the anthropologist Franz Boas, considered the father of American anthropology, played a key role in working out the implications of these challenges for anthropology, separating the principles of biological heredity from ideas concerning the transmission of cultures.[34]

Boas demonstrated that what had been cast as racial traits by evolutionary anthropology were in fact environmentally determined characteristics. Innate biological structures did not account for the differences between cultures, and contemporary cultural differences did not represent an evolutionary order that moved from savagery to barbarism to civilization. In his 1896 essay, "The Limitations of the Comparative Method in Anthropology," Boas argued that similarities between cultural phenomena from disparate times and places did not indicate a similarity of evolutionary development, but rather arose from "such varied and complex historical, environmental and psychological factors that the similarity of their causes could no longer be assumed."[35] Perceived mental differences between different races were the result of different customs and traditions rather than indications of evolutionary differences. Boas showed that the cultural evolutionary assumption that cultures evolved from the simpler (more primitive) to the more complex was not borne out: the grammatical structure of so-called primitive languages, for instance, could often be shown to be more complex than that of European languages such as English. Impulse control—what Freud would later call the internalization of prohibition—was not the prerogative of the so-called civilized races but was exerted in one form or another by all human groups. Indeed, in an argument that would later be genetically confirmed, Boas asserted that the differences between members of a perceived race were small in comparison to the variations between the members of any one race. The evolutionary premises of the first generation of anthropologists no longer held: by 1917, Boas's student, Alfred Kroeber, was writing that "all men are totally civilized" and that there was "no higher or lower in civilization."[36]

Totem and Taboo

Totem and Taboo was the key site where Freud's earlier description of the psyche as being composed of conscious, preconscious and unconscious elements was placed within a speculative history of both consciousness and of the major institutions of society. Here is where the psychological topography of ego, superego and id began to emerge as a result of the impact of historical events—the primal crime, which eventuated in the superego, on the one hand, and morality, religion and social institutions on the other. *Totem and Taboo* is the origin myth of psychoanalysis (Freud called it his "scientific myth"), and as such, it plays a central role in the structure of Freud's work.

In the study of myth and religion, origin myths are those stories understood as providing narratives of the founding and ordering of the human community; these narratives then serve as models for the elaboration of further social and psychological developments within the community whose founding they describe. *Totem and Taboo* provides a narrative of the inauguration of the social and psychic orders as well as the primitivity that preceded them. Its foundational account is evoked, explicitly and implicitly, whenever the establishment of the agencies of the psyche (such as the superego) or the condition of primitivity is mentioned throughout Freud's oeuvre. And because the details of *Totem and Taboo* lean so heavily on the social evolutionary conceptions of the nineteenth-century anthropology that Freud adopted, whenever its account is referred to, so too is the racial framework to which these anthropological conceptions were indexed. In this way, the colonialist tenets of early anthropological thought continue to circulate throughout psychoanalysis.[37]

More recent critiques of this quest for origins and for the historicity of origin accounts have alerted us to the ideological work done by such myths. As Foucault points out, the quest for origins derives from the belief that they cause and "precede the external world of accident and succession," whereas closer investigation reveals the human construction of origins within that same external, contingent world.[38] By masking their human construction, origin accounts help secure the stability of a particular configuration of the social (and, in this case, psychic) world by concealing the political relations they serve.[39]

Origin accounts that place so-called primitive peoples in a presocial, prediscursive realm conceal the role played by colonial violence in the construction of our conceptions of primitivity, making it seem as though "primitive peoples" are part of nature and outside social processes. This strategy has often been aided by an appeal to science: for the legitimation of his *Totem and Taboo*, Freud turned to the science of anthropology; and those who have gone on to argue for the historical authenticity of Freud's account of the primal crime have often turned to the science of primatology to make their case. But primatology and anthropology, as Donna Haraway and James Clifford have argued respectively, are "in, not above, histori-cal and linguistic processes," and primatology inscribes primates, no less than anthropology inscribes so-called primitive peoples, within a scientific rhetoric which, on examination, reveals particular political assumptions and agendas.[40] With regard to *Totem and Taboo*, the seemingly neutral yet legitimating sciences of anthropology and primatology obscure the violent colonial history that transformed non-white, non-European peoples into prehistoric primitive peoples—Freud's "backwards and miserable . . . sav-ages" of the primal horde.[41]

In *Totem and Taboo*, Freud wove his memorable account of the origins of the superego as well as of society, morality and religion in the primal crime and its aftermath. In preparation, he had read widely and carefully among the anthropologists up to his time, turning to their writings for representations of totemism, taboos and other phenomena of "savage" life. Freud was aware—and warned his readers—of many of the shortcomings with which scholars a century later would assess early anthropological work, pointing out that "those who collect the observations are not the same as those who examine and discuss them," that "the observers are not always acquainted with the native language" and may make use of interpreters or pidgin-English; and that "savages . . . often give false or misleading information for a great vari-ety of motives."[42] Nevertheless, he relied heavily on the data and arguments of evolutionary anthropology, adopting not only its theories of totemism, exogamy and sacrifice but also the comparative method as developed by E.B. Tylor, and its framework of a unilinear progression of humankind from savagery to barbarism to civilization. Although much has been made of his use of Lamarck's doctrine of the inheritance of acquired characteristics, Freud was equally indebted to Haeckel's recapitulation hypothesis.[43]

Both the subtitle of *Totem and Taboo* ("*Some points of Agreement between the Mental Lives of Savages and Neurotics*") and the introduction announce Freud's evolutionary position:

> There are men still living who, as we believe, stand very near to primi-tive man, and whom we therefore regard as his direct heirs and rep-resentatives. Such is our view of those whom we describe as savages or half-savages [*Wilden und halbwilden Völker*]; and their mental life must have a peculiar interest for us if we are right in seeing in it a well-preserved picture of an early stage of our own development.

If that supposition is correct, a comparison between the psychology of primitive peoples [*den Primitiven*], as it is taught by social anthropology, and a psychology of neurotics, as it has been revealed by psychoanalysis, will be bound to show numerous points of agreement and will throw new light upon familiar facts in both sciences.[44]

Totem and Taboo, then, is based on two socioevolutionary axioms: first, that the mental life of contemporary "savages" represents "a well-preserved picture of an early stage of our own development" and therefore can be used to reconstruct the history of present-day western psychological tendencies. Second, it is based on "numerous points of agreement" that purportedly can be found between neurotics and primitive peoples. Both are elaborations of the Haeckelian premise. Since, according to Haeckel's theory, childhood was believed to be the ontogenetic recapitulation of the phylogenetic past, European children were believed to be reliving the earliest historical stages of human development. And in an echo of the correlation between savages, children and madmen which had been established as a cornerstone of evolutionary thought by the Deists,[45] Freud (as will be further discussed below) saw neurosis as a regression to an infantile stage of libidinal development, which in turn was identified with the primitive, raced, past. Thus neurosis was a primitive state of mind. Once it could be taken as established that neurosis = regression to infancy = primitivity, taboos and other cultural expressions of so-called primitive societies could be explained with recourse to data from neurotic patients and children and vice versa, so that anthropological data about primitive peoples and psychoanalytic data concerning children and neurotics could each provide solutions to the questions posed by the other.[46] In *Totem and Taboo*, these "points of agreement" became Freud's somewhat circular methodological principle and the warrant for each of the arguments made on the way to the culminating hypothesis of the primal crime.

Interwoven with this Haeckelian methodology was the notion of a collective mind whose contents, acquired at that momentous time of the primal crime, have continued to be inherited from one generation to the next. As Freud presented it toward the end of *Totem and Taboo*:

I have supposed that the sense of guilt for an action has persisted for many thousands of years and has remained operative in generations which can have had no knowledge of that action. . . . *Unless psychical processes were continued from one generation to the other*, if each generation were obliged to acquire its attitude to life anew, *there would be no progress* in this field *and next to no development* . . . . I shall not pretend that . . . direct communication and tradition . . . are enough to account for the process.[47]

The oedipus complex may develop amid the actual desires and fears of the contemporary child's experience, but its propulsive power derives from inherited psychological processes. As Freud was to write much later in *Civilization and Its Discontents*: "We cannot get away from the assumption that man's sense of guilt springs from the oedipus complex and was acquired at the killing of the father by the brothers banded together."[48] According to Freud, the thought processes of primitive man were and are inherited and recapitulated by each contemporary western child, and arrested at or regressed to in each contemporary case of neurosis.

In *Totem and Taboo* Freud assembled a bricolage of now questionable anthropological materials, held together by evolutionary and psychoanalytic arguments. Following the evolutionary procedure of deducing the origins of contemporary European institutions from the customs of the living peoples considered to be most primitive, Freud focused on the Australian aboriginals because "these poor naked cannibals" were presumed to be representative of the very bottom of the evolutionary ladder.[49] In addition to reviewing the available theories of totemism from McLennan, Frazer and others, he drew on the ethnographies of the two pioneering studies of Australian aboriginals of the time, by Lorimer Fison and William Howitt, and by Baldwin Spencer and F.J. Gillen. Both studies had been organized according to the theoretical directives of European anthropologists: Fison and Howitt followed the lead of Henry Morgan, and Spencer and Gillen took direction from Frazer, who provided them with questions that focused on the issue of totemism so that Frazer could, in his informants' words, "piece together the odd fragments of information" they had acquired to develop his own theories. As with so many other ethnographies of the time, these works framed valuable observations of peoples and practices in evolutionary terms that perpetuated "the most dismal prejudices of [their] time."[50]

Freud adopted Frazer's explanation of prohibition as masked desire ("The law only forbids men to do what their instincts incline them to do")[51] to read the incest taboo as revealing a universal desire for incest. The reported aboriginal aversion to incest was "an infantile feature" whose stringency "reveal[ed] a striking agreement with the mental life of neurotic patients": the taboos of savages were heightened, just like the symptoms of neurosis. Freud then took up psychologist Wilhelm Wundt's suggestion that the totem animal might refer to a forefather of the totem group, and, to confirm this identification of totem animal with father figure, he turned to a child's analysis. In 1909, in the case of "Little Hans," Freud had interpreted a three-year-old boy's fear of horses as a fear of his father.[52] Thanks to the recapitulatory identity between primitivity, childhood and neurosis, Hans's unconscious identification of animal and father could be (and was) taken as proof of the identity between totem animal and patriarchal ancestor. This, in turn, made possible the interpretation of the taboo against killing the totem animal as a prohibition against the desire to kill the father/ancestor of the primitive group. We can see here Freud's transposition of the anthropological comparative method for psychoanalytic use: Freud, like the anthropologists, filled gaps in his knowledge of evolutionary history with data from contemporary "primitive" or "savage" populations. In addition, while the anthropologists turned to contemporary aboriginal peoples to fill gaps in their knowledge about the earliest humans, Freud turned to equally "primitive" children and neurotics to cement his thesis of the totem animal as father figure among the earliest humans.[53]

Freud then placed his readings of the taboos against incest and totemicide within the context of Darwin's view of the original human community as a patriarchal primal horde, adding the conjecture of J.J. Atkinson that patricides were a recurring phenomenon within the horde. To this carefully layered background Freud added his final ingredient, Robertson Smith's vision of the first religious act—the slaying and communal devouring of a totemic camel in a sacrificial feast. Finally, Freud could narrate the celebrated climactic scenario in which "one day, the brothers," frustrated by their leader's sexual monopoly of the females of the horde, murdered and ate their father. Soon overcome with remorse, they found themselves compelled to reinstate and internalize, as the foundational laws of culture and of the psyche, the prohibitions against which they had rebelled.[54] The prohibitions against incest and murder that govern the psyche through the agency of the superego had their origins in this phylogenetic past of human consciousness—as reconstructed by Freud out of disparate elements of nineteenth-century anthropology.

In addition, Freud enlisted three broadly conceived stages of evolutionary development—savagery, barbarism and civilization—to correlate and thereby elaborate his psychoanalytic model of libidinal development. Tylor and Frazer had accorded each of these three stages its characteristic worldview or outlook. Savages believed in animism, according to Tylor, and practiced magic, according to Frazer; barbarians believed in religion—the propitiation, rather than the manipulation, of the gods; and civilized peoples adhered to the principles of science. Freud took over these three categories with their associated worldviews and correlated each of them with one of his three stages of libidinal development. He correlated animism and magic with narcissism; religion with the oedipal stage; and science with the outlook made possible by the dissolution of the oedipal complex.[55] In this way, libidinal development can be seen to recapitulate the evolutionary scale of early anthropology.

For Tylor, animism, the earliest form of belief, was an attribute of savages who were characterized by their tendency to mistake "an ideal for a real connexion."[56] In Freud's hands, this mistaking "an ideal for a real connexion" became the psychoanalytic "omnipotence of thoughts," according to which so-called primitive peoples mistake their hopes and ideals for reality itself, indulging in wishful or magical thinking. Overvaluing their illusory products of their own minds, they ascribed to them an agency and a power of their own, which led to a belief in magic: savages, said Freud, "believe they can alter the external world by mere thinking."[57] But with Freud's Haeckelian correlation of individual libidinal development with the cultural evolution of the human race, the omnipotence of thoughts was seen to typify not only the earliest evolutionary stage of human evolution, i.e. animism, but also the earliest infantile stage of libidinal development, i.e. narcissism. Infants (and others) at the narcissistic level overvalue themselves and the products of their thought processes as Tylor said animists did; primitive peoples, by virtue of their animistic beliefs which were (according to Freud) nothing more than beliefs in their own wishes, demonstrated that they were stuck at the narcissistic stage of human development. Animism and narcissism were two terms, cultural and psychological, respectively, for the mental landscape where belief in wishes reigns supreme. Infants were like animistic savages; savages were like narcissistic children.

For Tylor, Frazer and Freud alike, animism represented the worldview of the earliest evolutionary stage, that of savages, whereas religion was taken to be the worldview of peoples at the second broad stage of evolution, barbarism. For Freud, barbarians, like the oedipal child in thrall to loving and powerful parents, tried to affect the world through the worship and propitiation of gods: Freud correlated religion, the "omnipotence of the gods," with the child's cathexis of the parents during the peak of the oedipal complex. Oedipal children remained unaware of the fallibility of their parents; barbarians, like oedipal children, remained unaware of the fallibility of their gods. Finally, Freud correlated civilization, the culmination of the cultural evolutionary scale of the early anthropologists, with psychosexual maturity. Frazer and Tylor saw civilization as represented by the end of religious belief and the attainment of the scientific perspective; Freud correlated this with the renunciation of oedipal desires. Only those who fully divested themselves of the oedipal illusions of religion and could accept the constraints of the scientific method could lay claim to the (hoped-for) post-oedipal maturity represented by modern civilization.

In this way, Tylor's scale of the evolutionary development of cultures was repositioned by Freud onto a psychological register that charted the universal development of the psyche. As the anthropologist T.O. Beidelman has suggested, "Freud transposed the comparative method—doctrine of survivals and all—from culture to the mind itself."[58] Mapped onto the psychoanalytic model of the development of the psyche, this anthropological evolutionary grid, fortified by its new psychoanalytic alliance, was read back onto the phylogenetic scene to cast savages as narcissists, culturally stuck at this early stage of psychological development.[59] Neurotics, too, were narcissists and, as such, secret animists, worshipping obsessively at the shrines of their perverse gods.

The scaffolding of the evolutionary anthropology that Freud used was a color-coded hierarchy of human races, in which cultural development was presumed to be the result of the evolution of biological structures within the human race, reflected in increased brain size and a progressive lightening of the skin. Thus, by correlating the progression of narcissism, the oedipal stage and maturity with animism (savagery), religion (barbarianism) and science (civilization), Totem and Taboo transposed the racial assumptions of the anthropological evolutionary scale onto the modern psyche. In so doing, Freud inscribed in his model of human development the hidden assumption that, as the individual matures, she or he moves away from narcissism and the associated qualities held to characterize the cultural and psychological worlds of the darker races, and progressively comes to inhabit the psychological world of what Freud elsewhere called "our present-day white Christian civilization" or its hoped-for post-religious successor.[60] The psychoanalytically conceived norm of mature subjectivity was, by virtue of this correlation of libidinal development with the anthropological evolutionary scale, a rationalism whose unstated color was white, just as its unstated gender was male. Through this correlation, the anthropological and psychological conceptions of primitivity in psychoanalysis became sutured together, the one always implicitly signifying the other. This is why whenever we speak of *primitive* psychic urges, we are unwittingly placing the object of our observation within an implicitly racial, as well as psychological, scale.

In Freud's mythic terms, the primal crime—the slaying of the patriarch— inaugurated the institutions of society and the forms of subjectivity made possible by them. It was through primordial violence that subjectivity and the institutions of human society were constituted, Freud seems to say: bodily violence and the subsequent repression of its memory are what secured the reality of socially constituted categories.[61] But the institutions of the modern west were equally constituted by that other primal crime, the murder and subjugation of peoples normatively divergent from Europeans. Indeed, in his reflections on the first encounters between Europeans and the peoples of the New World, Stephen Greenblatt has pointed to the crucial role of violence in securing for Europeans their sense of the reality of this scene of difference. "When the land and its people are intact . . . [they are] strange and ungraspable . . . . Only when it is violated, turned into a charnel house, can it be taken as a reality and appropriated."[62]

If we were to rewrite Freud's primal narrative, then, locating it not in the mists of prehistory but at the inception of the modern age, we could say that the violent subjugation of the west's cultural others and their reinscription as an exploitable racialized primitivity gave rise to the emergence of the modern, civilized subject of psychoanalysis. As the murder of the primal father was, according to Freud, disguised in narratives of religious piety and cultural legitimation, the violent colonial context of the emergence of the modern subject was disguised by inscribing its superseded "primitivity" in the purported neutrality of a scientific myth.

As mentioned earlier, not only the ethnographic data concerning "savages" but the evolutionary theories and methodology on which Freud's argument rested—the theory of the inheritance of acquired characteristics, the recapitulation theory and anthropology's comparative method itself—were already losing ground in biology and anthropology by the turn of the century. The identification of all contemporary non-westerners with the earliest humans, the equation of "savages" with children and neurotics, and the evolutionary speculations concerning the origins of exogamy, sacrifice, totemism and animism were all coming to be seen merely as "projections of ethnocentric concern" even by the time Freud was making use of them.[63] Although some anthropologists have agreed with its themes of the universality of the oedipal complex and the incest taboo,[64] many have criticized *Totem and Taboo*, whether on account of its evolutionary premises, ethnography and methodology; the acceptability of its argument; the question of the historicity of the primal crime; or the universality of the oedipus complex.[65]

In general, psychoanalytic writers have tended to acknowledge the ethnocentrism of *Totem and Taboo* but to minimize its implications, declining to extend criticism of its evolutionary underpinnings to the rest of Freud's work. As Ilse Grubrich-Simitis, the editor of Freud's recently discovered *Phylogenetic Fantasy*, remarks,

> Even in the post-Freudian discussion of metapsychology within psychoanalysis, the antiquated elements in Freud's conceptions of evolutionary biology seem not to have been scrutinized in a similarly thorough manner and not, in the light of new knowledge, to have been revised.[66]

And even with what recognition there has been of the role played by socio-evolutionary theories in *Totem and Taboo* and in others of Freud's works, little attention has been paid to the racial implications of Freud's use of them for the clinical and critical practices of psychoanalysis. Concern with Freud's use of evolutionary theory, where there has been any, has most often been confined to the "antiquated" and/or unsubstantiated nature of these elements of Freud's arguments rather than with the graver issues of their racist implications. To assess *Totem and Taboo* as peripheral to the main concerns of psychoanalysis is to avoid reckoning with its foundational status as the origin myth of psychoanalysis and the resultant paradigmatic status of its narrative for Freud's work as a whole; and it is thus to avoid reckoning with the implications of the racial assumptions of *Totem and Taboo* for all of psychoanalysis.

Beyond *Totem and Taboo*

Although *Totem and Taboo* presented the full evolutionary framework of his thought, Freud had been making use of evolutionary theories from the time of *The Interpretation of Dreams*. And even though the biological and anthropological theses on which he drew were losing credibility in their own disciplinary territory around the turn of the century, Freud continued to make use of them throughout his work, laying the ground for the role played by psychoanalysis in helping to keep these assumptions alive long past their scientific discreditation. The evolutionary premises and thesis of *Totem and Taboo* are picked up again and again in many of his other texts, both cultural and metapsychological, where he continued to stress the inherited and recapitulatory nature of the psyche. Not only did Freud adopt the theories of Lamarck and Haeckel and the methods and data of Tylor and Frazer, he believed that psychoanalysis was the newest science to carry on their evolutionary work.

We find an early statement of the recapitulation thesis, and a claim for the role of psychoanalysis as furthering the anthropological comparative method, in *The Interpretation of Dreams* (1900) where Freud writes:

> Behind this childhood of the individual we are promised a picture of a phylogenetic childhood—a picture of the development of the human race, of which the individual's development is in fact an abbreviated recapitulation influenced by the chance circumstances of life.... [W]e may expect that the analysis of dreams will lead us to a knowledge of man's archaic heritage, of what is psychically innate in him. Dreams and neuroses seem to have preserved more mental antiquities than we could have imagined possible; so that psycho-analysis may claim a high place among the sciences which are concerned with the reconstruction of the earliest and most obscure periods of the beginnings of the human race.[67]

Since dreaming revives the impulses that dominated childhood, and since childhood recapitulates the evolutionary development of humankind, dreams can reveal to us the "mental antiquities" of the human race. This is the recapitulatory crux of the evolutionary matter. In the introduction to the *Three Essays on the Theory of Sexuality* (1905)—a strikingly recapitulationist work—Freud put it this way:

The phylogenetic disposition can be seen at work behind the ontogenetic process . . . disposition is ultimately the precipitate of earlier
experience of the species to which the more recent experience of the
individual, as the sum of accidental factors, is super-added.[68]

In 1911 he concluded the Schreber case by stating:

"In dreams and neuroses," so our thesis has run, "we come once more
upon the *child* and the peculiarities which characterize his modes
of thought and his emotional life." "And we come upon the *savage*
[*den Wilden*] too," we may now add, "upon the *primitive* man [*den
primitiven Menschen*], as he stands revealed to us in the light of the
researches of archaeology and of ethnology."[69]

Freud's adherence to recapitulation theory is further demonstrated in his
Introductory Lectures (1916–17), where he writes that "each individual
somehow recapitulates in an abbreviated form the entire development of
the human race" and tells us that both the ego instincts and the sexual
instincts "are at bottom heritages, abbreviated recapitulations of the development which all mankind has passed through from its primaeval days
over long periods of time."[70] In their experiences of anxiety,

children would merely be repeating . . . the behaviours of prehistoric
men and of modern primitive peoples who as a result of their ignorance and helplessness are afraid of every novelty and of many familiar things which no longer cause us any anxiety today.[71]

And in the essay "A Child Is Being Beaten" (1919) we read further that
"children . . . are compelled to recapitulate from the history of mankind
the repression of an incestuous object-choice."[72]

The correlation of the psychological stage of narcissism with the evolutionary stage of animism in *Totem and Taboo* was evoked when Freud
formulated his theory of narcissism in the 1914 paper of that name. This
new extension of his theory, he wrote,

receives reinforcement from . . . our observations and views on the
mental life of children and primitive peoples. In the latter we find
characteristics which, if they occurred singly, might be put down to

megalomania: an overestimation of the power of their wishes and mental acts, the "omnipotence of thoughts," a belief in the thaumaturgic force of words, and a technique for dealing with the external world—"magic"—which appears to be a logical application of these grandiose premises.[73]

And in "The Uncanny" (1919) he wrote of "the primary narcissism which dominates the mind of the child and of primitive man."[74] When, further on in the essay "On Narcissism," he refers to "the primitive feeling of omnipotence,"[75] it is not possible to disentangle the ontogenetic meaning (developmental history of the contemporary subject) from the phylogenetic meaning (evolutionary development of the species), the psychological from the anthropological: the phylogenetic is sedimented in the ontogenetic such that the two are inseparable. This is why, even when the idea of primitivity in psychoanalysis is taken to signify exclusively the earliest levels of the individual psyche and the anthropological dimension is disregarded entirely, the former ends up signifying the latter. The very way in which the idea of "primitive levels of the psyche" were first psychoanalytically imagined was in the terms of their phylogenetic origins; the idea itself carries with it the imprint of the evolutionary premises with their racial entailments. Freud never abandoned his position that the infantile levels of development which have a lasting influence on the personality and continue to exert their force on the individual throughout the course of life are a recapitulation of the events of early human history as recounted in *Totem and Taboo*. As he would later write in *Civilization and Its Discontents* (1930):

> When a child reacts to his first great instinctual frustrations with excessively strong aggressiveness and with a correspondingly severe superego, he is following a phylogenetic model and is going beyond the response that would be currently justified; for the father of prehistoric times was undoubtedly terrible, and an extreme amount of aggressiveness may be attributed to him.[76]

Freud gave free rein to his psychoanalytic Lamarckianism in the recently discovered *Phylogenetic Fantasy*, which was to have been the last of the series of metapsychological papers he wrote between 1911 and 1915. In this remarkable paper, a "playful comparison" that developed out of an exchange of ideas between Freud and his colleague Sándor Ferenczi, Freud carried the Lamarckian dimension of psychoanalysis to new speculative heights, correlating specific neuroses to evolutionary stages by seeking to demonstrate that what are now neuroses "bear witness to the history of the mental development of mankind."[77] In this essay we are told that anxiety first arose as an adaptive response to the deprivations of the Ice Age: the need to limit offspring to newly limited food supplies resulted in the need to curb sexual intercourse, which in turn produced hysteria. Obsessional neurosis recapitulated the advent of language, which brought with it the omnipotence of thoughts and the magical worldview of animism together with the arrogation by the head male of the exclusive sexual favors of the women. In an elaboration Freud retained and reiterated toward the end of his life, the earlier thesis of *Totem and Taboo*, that the patriarch drove out the sons from the horde as they came of age, was replaced by the assertion that the father actually castrated them,[78] "after which they are able to stay in the horde as harmless laborers," a stage supposedly corresponding to dementia praecox. Those sons who could fled and lived together: hence the historical emergence of homosexual feelings, the sublimations of which gave rise to the social feelings which became "the basis for every later society."[79] Paranoia, the defense against homosexuality, recapitulated this stage of evolution. And, finally, "melancholia-and-mania" (manic depression, now called bipolar disorder) recapitulated the elation followed by regret occasioned by the fateful slaying of the primal father. As in *Totem and Taboo*, the narrative features fathers and sons; the experience of women is referred to only in the single enigmatic remark that it is "obvious to everyone" that the neuroses of "the second generation"—that is, of the sons rather than of the fathers (anxiety hysteria, conversion hysteria and obsessional neurosis)—"can only be acquired by men (as sons); whereas dementia praecox, paranoia, and melancholia can just as well be produced by women."[80]

Two years later, in a letter to Karl Abraham describing the evolutionary ideas he was developing with Ferenczi, Freud suggested that he wanted

> to put Lamarck entirely on our ground and to show that the "necessity" that according to him creates and transforms organs is nothing but the power of unconscious ideas over one's own body, of which we see remnants in hysteria, in short the "omnipotence of thoughts." This would actually supply a psycho-analytic explanation of adaptation; it would put the coping stone on psycho-analysis.[81]

Freud declined, it seems, to stand by the evolutionary excursions of *A Phylogenetic Fantasy*, in itself a logical extension of the animism/ narcissism correspondences of *Totem and Taboo*, since he kept it from publication.[82] However, it was the extent of the elaboration of evolutionary mapping he drew back from rather than the principle itself, which he continued to use and defend to the very end. In *Analysis Terminable and Interminable* (1937) we are informed that "analytic experience has forced on us a conviction that even particular psychic contents, such as symbolism, have no other sources than hereditary transmission."[83] In *Moses and Monotheism* (1939), he stated that "the archaic heritage of human beings comprises not only dispositions but also subject matter—memory traces of the experience of earlier generations,"[84] and in his final summation, the posthumously published *Outline of Psychoanalysis* (1940), he wrote of

> the archaic heritage which a child brings with him into the world, before any experience of his own, influenced by the experiences of his ancestors. We find the counterpart of this phylogenetic material in the earliest human legends and in surviving customs.[85]

Not only do Freud's writings demonstrate a strong adherence to the recapitulation theory and to the Lamarckian theory of inheritance; Freud believed that the phylogenetic inheritance of each individual subject— which for him included specific desires and fantasies—wields its influence regardless of whether the subject has had any exposure to the particular experience at issue. In *Three Essays on the Theory of Sexuality* (1905), speaking of the latency period, he stated that "this development is organically determined and fixed by heredity, and it can occur without any help at all from education."[86] Later, in the *Introductory Lectures* (1916–17), he explained why the infantile sexual fantasies of seduction and castration which engender neurosis have such a force even though they "are not true in the majority of cases":

> I believe these primal phantasies, . . . are a phylogenetic endowment. In them the individual reaches beyond his own experience into primaeval experience at points where his own experience has been too rudimentary. It seems to me quite possible that all the things that are told to us to-day in analysis as phantasy—the seduction of children, the inflaming of sexual excitement by observing parental intercourse,

the threat of castration (or rather castration itself)—were once real occurrences in the primaeval times of the human family, and that *children in their phantasies are simply filling in the gaps in individual truth with prehistoric truth*. I have repeatedly been led to suspect that the psychology of the neuroses has stored up in it more of the antiquities of human development than any other source.[87]

Freud filled in the gaps in individual truth with the received wisdom of nineteenth-century anthropology in the same way that E.B. Tylor filled in the gaps in the evolutionary development of culture with data from contemporary "primitive people." Again in the *Outline of Psychoanalysis*, we find a final statement of the psychoanalytic transposition of the anthropological comparative method: once one assumes the evolutionary sequence, one can fill in the gaps in a particular case of contemporary development even without any actual evidence:

> In all this the phylogenetic foundation has so much the upper hand over personal accidental experience that it makes no difference whether a child has really sucked at the breast or has been brought up on the bottle and never enjoyed the tenderness of a mother's care. In both cases the child's development takes the same path.[88]

The phylogenetic events that took place at the time of origins are seen to have a paradigmatic or archetypal status, structuring contemporary ontogenetic experience regardless of the actual content or contexts of that experience.

The primitive unconscious

Although he mapped his models of libidinal development onto the evolutionary scale of late nineteenth-century anthropologists, there was a critical difference: Freud did not agree with the anthropologists' notion that, with the exception of survivals, each successive stage of cultural evolution cast off the characteristics of previous stages. For Freud, characteristics of earlier evolutionary stages remained part of a universal human inheritance: the differences between "savages" and Europeans were not absolute, as his anthropological precursors had made them out to be. Primitive stages along the developmental trajectory of the mind did not disappear as they were superseded, but endured in the unconscious, capable of resurfacing at any moment in dreams or symptoms and threatening to disturb the achievements of the civilized psyche. "Every earlier stage of development persists alongside the later stage which has arisen from it; here succession also involve[s] co-existence."[89]

The passage from childhood to adolescence had commonly been seen by socioevolutionists as the passage of the western child out of the mental processes of primitivity and into civilized adulthood. But for Freud, what the child left behind (magical thinking, the peremptoriness of desire) as she or he hazarded the journey toward western adulthood found its place in the underworld of the unconscious. As the conscious, secondary processes of the civilized subject developed, primitive mental formations were deposited, so to speak, in the unconscious: the unconscious became the "imperishable"[90] repository of phylogenetic inheritance. "The man of prehistoric times survives unchanged in our unconscious," he wrote;[91] and throughout his texts the unconscious and the id are commonly described in terms of the primitive or prehistoric mind. In his essay, "The Unconscious," Freud states:

> The content of the *Ucs.* may be compared with an aboriginal population in the mind [*Den Inhalt des Ubw. kann man einer psychischen Urbevolkerung vergleichen*]. If inherited mental formations exist in the human being—something analogous to instinct in animals—these constitute the nucleus of the *Ucs.* Later there is added to them what is discarded during childhood development as unserviceable; and this need not differ in its nature from what is inherited.[92]

Freud's retention of the characteristics of primitivity as part of a universally conceived psyche cut both ways: his descriptions of the unconscious (in his first topography of consciousness, the preconscious and the unconscious) and of the id (in his later topography of ego, superego and id) often reproduced the comparison, if not the identification, of the unconscious with "primitive man." Freud described the unconscious—as Columbus had described the indigenous Americans he encountered—in terms of lack: the unconscious exhibits a lack of rationality, a lack of relationship to reality, an inability to represent itself in words, a lack of restraint, sexual and otherwise, a lack of morality and a lack of the sense of time. It is capable neither of negation nor of "mutual contradiction," logical operations that make rationality possible. The unconscious lacks the capacity to make the distinctions on which the secondary processes of consciousness depend. Like the mind of animistic man, the unconscious "consists of wishful impulses,"[93] not having capitulated to the reality principle. The indiscriminate nature of its wishes points to the immorality of the unconscious: the id is nonmoral. Like savages, who were "the hapless children of the moment,"[94] the unconscious is timeless; its processes "have no reference to time at all."[95] The primitive mind is close to nature, expressive of the promptings of the body's instincts. Indeed, Freud sees the unconscious as a nature preserve in the midst of the civilizing requirements of the conscious mind.[96]

But if the unconscious *is* the mind of primitive man, the question then arises: did primitive humans have an unconscious? In *The Ego and the Id* (1923) Freud muses:

> Which was it, the ego of primitive man or his id, that acquired religion and morality in those early days out of the father-complex? If it was his ego, why do we not speak simply of these things being inherited by the ego? If it was the id, how does that agree with the character of the id? Or are we wrong in carrying the differentiation between ego, superego, and id back into such early times?

And he answers with recourse to the theories of Lamarck and Haeckel:

> The question whether it was the ego or the id that experienced and acquired these things soon comes to nothing . . . no external vicissitudes can be experienced or undergone by the id, except by way of the ego, which is the representative of the external world to the id . . . . The experiences of the ego seem at first to be lost for inheritance; but, when they have been repeated often enough and with sufficient strength in many individuals in successive generations, they transform themselves, so to say, into experiences of the id, the impressions of which are preserved by heredity. Thus in the id, which is capable of being inherited, are harboured residues of the existences of countless egos; and, when the ego forms its super-ego out of the id, it may perhaps only be reviving shapes of former egos and be bringing them to resurrection.[97]

It was the ego of primitive man which experienced the oedipus complex; through its repetition in successive generations, it became sedimented into the id of today. In other words, the ego of primitive man has become the unconscious of contemporary man. The figure of the primitive, forged through centuries of colonialist discourse, comes to represent the unconscious ground of European consciousness.

Not only does Freud tell us that the id and/or the unconscious is primitive, but, through the workings of his recapitulationist logic, he tells us that the mental formations of those peoples called primitive are limited to what in civilized peoples is found in the unconscious. "In the adult human being," wrote Freud in "The Unconscious" (1915), "the system *Ucs.* operates, strictly speaking, only as a preliminary stage of the higher organization."[98] While the modern civilized subject adds to this unconscious system the elaborate repertoire of the secondary processes, the psychic realms of so-called primitive peoples are held to be limited to the "inherited mental formations" of the human race: "primitive man" has only a "primitive psyche." By contrast to the unconscious as primitive and defined by lack, consciousness in psychoanalysis becomes the locus of the valued and defining qualities of the modern west: history, rationality and autonomy. The characteristics of modern western subjectivity become the universally prescribed form of psychological maturity, contributing to what the South Asian social theorist Ashis Nandy has called "the second form of colonialization" which "helps generalize the concept of the modern West from a geographical and temporal entity to a psychological category."[99]

The "timeless" quality of the unconscious comes to mean outside of and *prior to* the "time" of the development of consciousness. The timelessness of the unconscious—that is, the continuing presence of unconscious contents over the course of a lifetime—becomes represented as *the past*, signified by the figure of the primitive.

Regression, survivals and symptoms

The relationship between consciousness and the timeless unconscious, together with the relationship between the modern subject and the primitive past, has been constructed in psychoanalysis through the concept of regression. The developmental lines of psychoanalysis—from narcissism to object choice to oedipal renunciation, from orality to anality to genitality, from external to internal authority, from polymorphous perversity to monogamous heterosexuality—actually trace a two-way path, traveled along in one direction through the maturation process, traveled along in the reverse direction through regression. As infants develop, they are held to recapitulate the primitive stages of human evolution; as they mature, the condition of primitivity—infantile, prehistoric, ethnographic—endures in the unconscious. But through regression, the modern, civilized subject may become reimmersed in primitivity. The content of dreams, the symptoms of neurosis, the phenomena of perversions and the behaviors that take place under conditions of group formation (as discussed in Chapter 3) were all considered by Freud to be part of the repertoire of primitivity; and regression was the mechanism that accounted for the manner in which the civilized subject could come under their sway.

The developmental lines of psychoanalysis represent the progress of the secondary processes of consciousness as they increasingly come to instantiate the particular aims or ideals of the psychoanalytic model. While growth generally involves the unfolding of new capacities and abilities, any standardized developmental scale represents a temporal arrangement of normative social behaviors and practices. Development is envisioned as the sequential accumulation of experiences creating the capacities for these normative behaviors, an accumulation that culminates in a culturally syntonic subject. At the apex of a developmental scale reside our paramount cultural ideals; at its originating point, everything we wish to exclude. The individual subject may be in conflict with the normative requirements of any particular stage; but the scale prescribes the culturally syntonic possibilities for resolving the conflict.[100] As the social historian Norbert Elias has written,

> The specific psychological process of "growing up" in Western societies . . . is nothing other than the individual civilizing process to which each young person, as a result of the social civilizing process over many centuries, is automatically subjected from earliest childhood.[101]

Developmental models, like evolutionary ones, need ways of accounting for those phenomena that seem not to belong to the stage at which they are seen to occur. For E.B. Tylor and the evolutionary anthropologists, cultural anomalies were cast as survivals: seemingly anachronistic beliefs and behaviors found in civilized cultures were seen as remnants of evolutionary stages (which should have been) long since discarded.

As Philip Rieff and Edwin Wallace have noted, neurotic symptoms occupy the same place in Freud's scheme that survivals occupied in Tylor's.[102] For Freud, psychopathology, legible in neurotic symptoms, was a return to remnants of past developmental stages that had been repressed in the unconscious. Dreams, too, were psychological survivals: because of the motor inhibition of sleep, libido was forced in a backward direction toward a revival of the dreamer's childhood, a revival "of the instinctual impulses which dominated it and of the methods of expression which were then available to him."[103] The correspondence between evolutionary survivals, on the one hand, and dreams and neurotic symptoms, on the other, was noted by Freud, who characterized the neurotic constitution as "an atavistic vestige,"[104] and explained that,

> What once dominated waking life, when the mind was still young and incompetent, seems now to have been banished into the night—just as the primitive weapons, the bows and arrows, that have been abandoned by adult men, turn up once more in the nursery.[105]

Cultural vestiges—abandoned artifacts of a superseded past—wound up as survivals in the games of children, while psychological vestiges—elements of superseded levels of the development of consciousness—wound up in the unconscious, from where they could emerge in dreams and symptoms. Not only neurotic symptoms and dreams, however, but perversions, and any other psychological phenomena that did not conform to the culmination of the psychoanalytic conception of libidinal development, were accounted for by being placed earlier in the developmental trajectory: they all tended toward the primitive. Regression to primitivity was the mechanism that accounted for psychological anomaly.

In *The Interpretation of Dreams* Freud had established three dimensions to his notion of regression: the topographical, the temporal and the formal.[106] The topographical dimension configured the movement from consciousness to the realms of the unconscious in spatial terms. At the same time, however, regression was temporal: it was a "harking back to older psychical structures," backward in time to the childhood of the dreamer, still intact in the unconscious. And in a synthesis of these two it was "formal," in that, in regression, the older, more primitive modes of expression, i.e. the sensory and imaginal, replaced the more advanced forms, i.e. rational thought. When neural excitation "moves in a backward direction" it regresses to the sensory end of the mental apparatus where thoughts are "transformed into images."[107] During the motor inhibition of sleep, or during the life course when libido is frustrated in its forward movement by external obstacles, it regresses to an earlier stage of its organization, where it attempts to find satisfaction in a previously outgrown and repressed libidinal position, to which it gains access through the processes of fantasy. Like dreams, psychopathology, in the form of neurosis, represents a regression to these repressed, early stages.[108]

Freud saw perversions, too, as regressions to or arrests at earlier stages of development. Regression in neurosis was in conflict with consciousness: neurotics were caught between their perverse desires and their wish to conform to the dictates of the civilized ego. But if the regressive search for libidinal satisfaction was *not* opposed by the ego, the subject could find satisfaction in regressive, non-normal perversions. "Neuroses are, so to say, the negative of perversions."[109] Homosexuality—which Freud personally did not castigate as pathology, although he believed it to be "produced by a certain arrest of sexual development"[110]—was classified among the perversions, demonstrating again how deviations from social norms were displaced backward in time. "In inverted [homosexual] types, a predominance of archaic constitutions and primitive psychical mechanisms is regularly to be found."[111]

Freud had broken with the conventional thought of his time which considered reproductive heterosexuality to be the intrinsic biological aim of human sexuality. In the *Three Essays on the Theory of Sexuality*, he uncoupled sexual instinct from sexual aim: the aims of the sexual instincts were not biologically ordained, but rather, the two (aims and instincts) became "soldered together" through the ongoing development of subjectivity. Whereas the European physiology of the time claimed that disrupting the "normal and intrinsic" reproductive aim of sexuality could lead to exhaustion and death,[112] Freud held the more tolerant view that the non-reproductive "perversions" were not necessarily threatening to the biological health of the individual. However, by placing the "soldering together" of sexual aim and instinct along a developmental scale, Freud reinstated on a psychological register what he had abandoned on the biological one: he categorized perversions as regressions or arrests at a lesser stage of development, and thus, by definition, a *per-version* of the developmental process; that is, development "turned the wrong way."[113]

Regression was the reverse of development, the path from the present to the past, from consciousness to the unconscious, from psychological well-being to psychopathology. But because the developmental trajectory in psychoanalysis was itself mapped onto an evolutionary trajectory, regression was believed to retrace not only the steps of individual development but also of human evolution: regression always moves (backward) along an ontogenetic *and* a phylogenetic path at one and the same time. Deviations from social norms were cast as relics of the past, of insufficiently mastered developmental stages keyed to evolutionary stages. The greater the difference from the normative ideal, the greater the regression and the greater the "primitivity." Regression was the mechanism that returned neurotics to an earlier stage of human development as well as to an earlier stage of human evolution, where, like savages, they became narcissistic, prey to the omnipotence of thoughts and to the animistic belief that "they can alter the external world by mere thinking" and by obsessive, ritual acts. "With neurotics it is as though we were in a prehistoric landscape—for instance, in the Jurassic. The great saurians are still running around; the horsetails grow as high as palms."[114]

In sum, not only psychological difference (as in neurosis) and behavioral difference (as in homosexuality) but also racial difference (assumed to be lower on the evolutionary scale) were positioned as primitive, as regressions to and/or arrests at an earlier developmental and evolutionary time. And because pathology and perversion, too, were defined as regressions to or arrests at earlier stages on the developmental scale, racial difference became psychoanalytically legible as perversion or pathology. The racial other, by virtue of his or her divergence from western norms, could only be more primitive. When one regresses, one becomes more primitive: one goes back in evolutionary time; one "goes native," "goes instinctual," "goes black."[115]

Smuggled into psychoanalysis through the evolutionary premises of Freud's thought, the recapitulatory identity between the infantile past of the individual subject and the evolutionary past of the human race endured in psychoanalytic theory through the first half of the twentieth century and beyond. Its lessons were not lost on the new practitioners of the fledgling discipline. In 1914 a number of articles concerning "the Negro" appeared in the early volumes of the *Psychoanalytic Quarterly* in which the authors, basing their contentions on the belief that "the individual in his development relives the history of the race," arranged their clinical material to demonstrate that black peoples regressed more quickly and easily to psychosis because of their lower position on the sociocultural evolutionary scale. These articles repeated the argument that black psychological development became arrested at adolescence (an argument later psychoanalytically elaborated in terms of the supposed inability of blacks to complete the separation-individuation phase of development), and featured remarks that characterized Africans as "the raw material of civilization"; "submission to despots" as their "racial characteristic"; and, in an echo of sixteenth-century Christian and Aristotelian arguments which saw the fulfillment of the "natural" slave as taking place through serving a master, commended slavery as "the most wonderful thing" because it had introduced the Negro to the ability to engage in sustained work and to the ideals of Christianity.[116]

As late as 1949 Claude Lévi-Strauss pointed to the continuing role of recapitulationism in psychoanalysis by addressing its "tempting" but spurious identity between "primitive" and "infantile" mentalities, a correlation he dubbed the "archaic illusion." Lévi-Strauss argued that, within any given culture, those who do not approximate its norms seem childish: "civilized" adults may appear to so-called primitive peoples as childish, as may the latter to the former. The child represents the plasticity of human possibilities that in time will become limited to the specific repertoire in which the child becomes enculturated. What Freud called a regression to infantile stages of development is a move to cultural expressions excluded from normative conceptions of the aims of adult development, but it "is not a return to an archaic 'stage' in the intellectual development of the individual or species."[117] But in spite of this and other disavowals of Freud's endorsements of evolutionary theory, we find this recapitulatory "archaic illusion" taken as axiomatic by twentieth-century psychoanalysts as diverse as Melanie Klein, Michael Balint, Sandor Ferenczi, Otto Fenichel and Geza Róheim[118] (the list could go on); in general, it has continued within the general corpus of psychoanalytic thought to this very day.

Freud's discourse of psychoanalysis both subverted and sustained the cultural evolutionary theses he inherited from late nineteenth-century anthropology. His stress on the overriding importance of the unconscious in mental life was, in his view, the third of three humbling blows that science dealt to the European self-concept (after those of Copernicus, who taught that the earth was not the center of the universe, and of Darwin, who taught that humans are part of, rather than superior to, the animal world): psychoanalysis taught that "the ego is not master in its own house," and dethroned the imperial European subject, "his majesty the ego," who had sat at the apex of the evolutionary scale of Freud's anthropological mentors. For Freud, unlike the evolutionary anthropologists, the colonial subject—the primitive—was not wholly Other to the civilized individual: both civilized and primitive shared an underlying psychism, which civilized humans would never transcend once and for all. This affirmation of a universal, shared stratum of the mind was of critical importance in that it negated the gulf between western and non-western, white and non-white, minds. Freud repatriated, so to speak, the figure of the primitive from the exotic antipodes back to the domestic western mind.

Indeed, in Freud's hands the signifiers of primitivity—animism, totemism, fetishism—became concepts that would undermine the presumption of superiority of the civilization championed by the evolutionary framework out of which they had arisen. For Freud, these supposedly primitive behaviors were seen to lurk not only in the pathological and in the past but in the everyday customs and the great cultural institutions of modern European civilized public and private life. In the end, we are all more or less neurotic; we are all more or less primitive; we are all saurians among the horsetails.

Yet an underlying ambiguity remains. In the very act of bridging the great divide between civilized and primitive as seen by colonial anthropology, by enlisting the figure of the primitive to represent a universal stratum of the mind, Freud placed this figure at the beginning and/or in the unconscious of a developmentally ordered model of the mind, representing the primitive as both constituting, yet partially excluded from, modern civilized subjectivity. By adopting and holding on to Lamarckian and recapitulation theories, he guaranteed that psychoanalytic conceptions of development would remain tethered to evolutionary conceptions of culture long after these conceptions had been renounced by the mainstream of anthropological thought. By casting difference as deviation and accounting for anomaly by regression, thereby consigning difference to the past, he insured that psychoanalysis would conflate racial difference with pathology and see both as evolutionarily and developmentally prior to white western norms. By mapping his representation of libidinal development onto the socioevolutionary scale of Tylor and Frazer, he produced a racially coded model of development in which maturity was measured as a movement away from primitivity: a movement toward the qualities that (according to the evolutionary anthropologists) characterized whiteness and away from the qualities held to characterize the cultural/psychological worlds of the "darker races."

Notes

1 Freud, *Totem and Taboo*, *SE* 13:1–164.
2 Frank J. Sulloway, *Freud: Biologist of the Mind* (New York: Basic Books, 1979); Ritvo, *Darwin's Influence on Freud*; Edwin R. Wallace IV, *Freud and Anthropology* (New York: International Universities Press, 1983). See also Ilse Grubrich-Simitis, "Metapsychology and Metabiology" in Sigmund Freud, *A Phylogenetic Fantasy: An Overview of the Transference Neuroses*, ed. Ilse Grubrich-Simitis, trans. Axel Hoffer and Peter T. Hoffer, 102–3 (Cambridge, MA: Harvard University Press, 1987 [1915]).
3 Freud, *The Interpretation of Dreams*, *SE* 5:549; *Moses and Monotheism*, *SE* 23:132.
4 Sulloway, *Biologist of the Mind*, 237.
5 As a glance at the footnotes to *Totem and Taboo* reveals. See Wallace, *Freud and Anthropology*, 57 and passim. Philip Rieff gives a thorough elucidation of Freud's anthropological, evolutionary sources in his *Mind of the Moralist*, chap. 6, 205–40.
6 J.W. Burrow, *Evolution and Society: A Study in Victorian Social Theory* (London: Cambridge University Press, 1966), 120–7; Stocking, *Victorian Anthropology*, 128, 169, 179, 224–6, 235, 245–57, 286; and Stocking, "The Dark-Skinned Savage," in his *Race, Culture and Evolution*, 113ff.; Bowler, *Biology and Social Thought*, 7.
7 George W. Stocking, "The Ethnographers' Magic: Fieldwork in British Anthropology from Tylor to Malinowski," in *Observers Observed: Essays on Ethnographic Fieldwork*, Vol. I: *History of Anthropology* (Madison, WI: University of Wisconsin Press, 1983), 71ff.; Stocking, *Victorian Anthropology*, 258–61.
8 See Jonathan Z. Smith, "When the Bough Breaks," in his *Map Is Not Territory: Studies in the History of Religion* (Chicago, IL: University of Chicago Press, 1978), for a devastating deconstruction of the flights of imagination by which James Frazer arrived at his (non)thesis in *The Golden Bough*; see also E.E. Evans-Pritchard, *Theories of Primitive Religion* (Oxford: Clarendon, 1965), 6–11.
9 The first scholars in the field that was coming to be known as anthropology were ethnologists, folklorists, archaeologists, classicists, philologists, colonial administrators and other Victorian polymaths.
10 Stocking, *Victorian Anthropology*, 166, 296, 258; Robert Ackerman, *J. G. Frazer: His Life and Work* (Cambridge: Cambridge University Press, 1987), 53; Robert Alun Jones, "Robertson Smith and James Frazer on Religion: Two Traditions in British Social Anthropology," in George W. Stocking, ed., *Functionalism Historicized: Essays on British Social Anthropology*, Vol. 2: *History of Anthropology* (Madison, WI: University of Wisconsin Press, 1984), 31–58.
11 Wallace, *Freud and Anthropology*, 57.
12 These developments can be followed fairly clearly in their correspondence: see William McGuire, ed., *The Freud/Jung Letters: The Correspondence between Sigmund Freud and C. G. Jung* (abridged version), translated

by R.F.C. Hull and Ralph Mannheim (Princeton, NJ: Princeton University Press, 1974/94).

13 Stocking, "Matthew Arnold, E. B. Tylor, and the Uses of Invention," in Stocking, *Race, Culture and Evolution*, 69–90, esp. 80–1.

14 Edward B. Tylor, *Primitive Culture: Researches into the Development of Mythology, Philosophy, Religion, Language, Art, and Custom* (New York: Brentano's, 1924 [1871]), 6.

15 Stocking, "Matthew Arnold, E. B. Tylor, and the Uses of Invention," 87.

16 Tylor, *Primitive Culture*, 26.

17 James George Frazer, *Totemism and Exogamy: A Treatise on Certain Early Forms of Superstition and Society*, 4 vols., Vol 4: *Summary and Conclusion* (London: Macmillan, 1910), 14.

18 Stocking, *Victorian Anthropology*, 177.

19 Tylor, *Primitive Culture*, 450. See also Stocking, *Victorian Anthropology*, 190–1; Evans-Pritchard, *Theories of Primitive Religion*, 15.

20 Tylor, *Primitive Culture*, 114.

21 Ackerman, *J. G. Frazer: His Life and Work*, 83.

22 Stocking, *Victorian Anthropology*, 192.

23 Frazer, *Totemism and Exogamy*, 4, 8, 14.

24 William Robertson Smith, *Lectures on the Religion of the Semites*, ed. T.O. Beidelman (Chicago, IL: University of Chicago Press, 1974 [1894]), 85–6.

25 Ibid.; Stocking, *Victorian Anthropology*, 166–7, 297; T.O. Beidelman, *W. Robertson Smith and the Sociological Study of Religion* (Chicago, IL: University of Chicago Press, 1974), 30.

26 Beidelman, *W. Robertson Smith*, 29, 38, 53, 57; Robert Young, *Darwin's Metaphor: Nature's Place in Victorian Culture* (Cambridge: Cambridge University Press, 1985).

27 Robertson Smith, *Religion of the Semites*, 2.

28 The division of races into Aryan and Semite had begun with the recognition of a systematic relationship between all Indo-European languages (including Sanskrit, Greek, Latin, Persian and German) as distinct from Semitic languages; and the positing of their common linguistic ancestry in a proto-Indo-European language. The idea of a common linguistic ancestry was quickly extended to indicate a common racial ancestry, even though such a connection had been challenged by physical anthropologists as early as the 1850s; see Stocking, *Victorian Anthropology*, 75. "Aryan" became the name for the "race" of peoples who spoke Indo-European languages, as "Semite" became the name for the "race" of peoples who spoke Semitic languages. Although Jesus had been Jewish, it was argued that it was the genius of the Aryans that had saved his message by creating Christianity. See Maurice Olender, *The Languages of Paradise: Race, Religion and Philology in the Nineteenth Century*, trans. Arthur Goldhammer (Cambridge, MA: Harvard University Press, 1992); Léon Poliakov, *The Aryan Myth: A History of Racist and Nationalist Ideas in Europe*, trans. Edmund Howard (New York: Barnes and Noble, 1971), esp. 188ff.; Stefan Arvidsson, "Aryan Mythology

as Science and Ideology," *Journal of the American Academy of Religion* 67, no. 2 (1999): 327–54; Bruce Lincoln, *Theorizing Myth: Narrative, Ideology, and Scholarship* (Chicago, IL: University of Chicago Press, 1999), 47–101.

29 Smith, *Religion of the Semites*, 338.

30 Evans-Pritchard, *Theories of Primitive Religion*, 52; Beidelman, *W. Robertson Smith*, 35–55.

31 Stocking, *Victorian Anthropology*, 235; see also Wallace, *Freud and Anthropology*, 52, 113.

32 Gould, *Ontogeny and Phylogeny*, 206.

33 Stocking, "Lamarckianism in American Social Science," in his *Race, Culture, and Evolution*, chap. 10, 234–69; Ernst Mayr, *The Growth of Biological Thought: Diversity, Evolution, and Inheritance* (Cambridge, MA: Harvard University Press, 1982), 698–707, 710–76, 790–4; Peter J. Bowler, *Evolution: The History of an Idea*, 237–9; Robert C. Olby, "Mendel, Mendelism and Genetics", 1997, at www.mendelweb.org/MWolby.html; Gould, *Ontogeny and Phylogeny*, 167–206.

34 During his trip to the United States in 1909, Freud attended a lecture given by Boas at Clark University entitled "Psychological Problems in Anthropology," but Boas does not seem to have influenced Freud's work. See George Stocking Jr., ed., *The Shaping of American Anthropology, 1883–1911: A Franz Boas Reader* (New York: Basic Books, 1974), 220–1.

35 Franz Boas, "The Limitations of the Comparative Method in Anthropology," in his *Race, Language, and Culture* (New York: Free Press, 1966), 270–3; Stocking, "Franz Boas and the Culture Concept," in his *Race, Culture and Evolution*, chap. 9, 195–233, 209–210; Wallace, *Freud and Anthropology*, 117–18.

36 Stocking, *Race, Culture, and Evolution*, chaps. 8, 9 and 10, 161–269; quote from Kroeber is at 267.

37 The phylogenetic dimension of *Totem and Taboo* has been mentioned by Kalpana Seshadri-Crooks in "The Primitive as Analyst," *Cultural Critique*, 28 (1994): 194, who has also suggested that we see "race and whiteness at the heart of Freudian theories of subjectivity" in "The Comedy of Domination," in *The Psychoanalysis of Race*, ed. Christopher Lane (New York: Columbia University Press, 1998), 354. Similarly, Daniel Boyarin has pointed to the "colonialist racism . . . found in Freud's developmental theories and especially as encoded in his acceptance of the principle that 'ontogeny recapitulates phylogeny'," in Boyarin, "Epater l'embourgeoisement," *Diacritics* 24, no. 1 (1994): 32.

38 Michel Foucault, "Nietzsche, Genealogy, History," in Paul Rabinow, ed., *The Foucault Reader* (New York: Pantheon, 1984), 76–100, quote at 78. See also Bruce Lincoln, who discusses the ideological dimensions of myths, arguing that they "packag[e] a specific, contingent system of discrimination in a particularly attractive and memorable form" (Lincoln, *Theorizing Myth*, 145–9).

39 See Judith Butler, *Gender Trouble: Feminism and the Subversion of Identity* (New York: Routledge, 1990), 7, 25, 30, 36, 93; and Michelle Rosaldo,

"The Use and Abuse of Anthropology: Reflections on Feminism and Cross-Cultural Understanding," *Signs: Journal of Women in Culture and Society* 5, no. 3 (1980): 389–417, for arguments about how naturalizing gender and racial/cultural differences conceals the political relations which construct the way we understand these differences.

40 Donna Haraway, *Primate Visions: Gender, Race, and Nature in the World of Modern Science* (New York: Routledge, 1989); James Clifford; "Introduction: Partial Truths," in James Clifford and George Marcus, eds., *Writing Culture: The Poetics and Politics of Ethnography* (Berkeley, CA: University of California Press, 1986), 1–26, quote at 2. Haraway has demonstrated how the portrayal of primate groups has varied over the twentieth century according to the eras and agendas of particular researchers. Early visions of heroic Man the Hunter gave way in mid-century to descriptions of cooperative scavenger-gatherers: the image of the primate horde led by its male leader, which was popular during Darwin's and Freud's time, was replaced by a focus on mother-centered groups in chimpanzee communities. By the 1970s a recognition of the centrality of female reproductive strategies for the development of culture emerged: whereas tools and weapons (fashioned by male hunters) had long been considered the first cultural inventions, more recently it has been suggested that food containers and baby slings (fashioned by mothers) may have been the first tools of culture.

41 Freud, *Totem and Taboo*, SE 13:1.

42 Ibid., *SE* 13:102.

43 Gould, in *Ontogeny and Phylogeny*, 155–66, stresses the under-acknowledged role of the recapitulation theory in Freud's work.

44 Freud, *Totem and Taboo*, SE 13:1; *GW* 9:5.

45 See Chapter 1, notes 65 and 66.

46 Paul Ricoeur has referred to this arrangement in *Totem and Taboo* as "a huge vicious circle." See Ricoeur, *Freud and Philosophy: An Essay on Interpretation* (New Haven: Yale University Press, 1970), 208.

47 *Totem and Taboo*, SE 13:157–8 (my emphasis). It is interesting that in this passage, Freud asserts the presence of a collective unconscious, the stipulation of which is often understood to be one of the major dividing issues between Jungian and Freudian psychologies (Jung pro, Freud contra). Again in *Moses and Monotheism*, Freud states that although not much is to be gained by the concept, "the content of the unconscious, indeed, is in any case a collective, universal property of mankind" (*SE* 23:132).

48 Freud, *Civilization and Its Discontents*, SE 21:131. Writing in *The Ego and the Id* of the outcome of the oedipus complex—that is, the formation of the superego or ego ideal—Freud tells us that "owing to the way in which the ego ideal is formed; it has the most abundant links with the phylogenetic acquisition of each individual—his archaic heritage" (*SE* 19:36).

49 *Totem and Taboo, SE* 13:2. Sociologist Emile Durkheim, too, chose Australian society as the laboratory in which to discover the elementary forms of religious life, since only in "societies as slightly evolved as possible" was it possible to find "the most primitive and simple religion." Emile Durkheim,

The Elementary Forms of the Religious Life, trans. Joseph Ward Stain (New York: Free Press, 1965 [1915]), 115.

50 Lorimer Fison and A.W. Howitt, *Kamilaroi and Kurnai: Group-Marriage and Relationship, and Marriage by Elopement Drawn Chiefly from the Usage of the Australian Aborigines; also, The Kurnai Tribe, Their Customs in Peace and War* (Canberra, Australia: Aboriginal Studies Press, 1991; orig. Melbourne: G. Robertson, 1880); Baldwin Spencer and Frank. J. Gillen, *The Native Tribes of Central Australia* (London: Macmillan, 1899). See Adam Kuper, *The Invention of Primitive Society: Transformation of an Illusion* (London: Routledge, 1988), chap. 5, "Australian Totemism," 92–104. Kuper quotes Baldwin Spencer writing to Frazer: "The knowledge that there is someone like you, who can piece together the odd fragments of information which isolated workers can acquire is a great stimulant" (102). Second quote is from D.J. Mulvaney and J. Calaby, *So Much That Is New: Baldwin Spencer, 1860–1929* (Melbourne: Melbourne University Press, 1985), cited in Timothy Mason, "The Anthropologist's Bagmen: Frazer, Spencer and Gillen and the Primitive in Australia," http:// perso.club-internet.fr/tmason/WebPages/Publications/Spencer_Gillen.htm.

51 The quote is from Frazer, *Totemism and Exogamy*, 4:97; see, in particular, Wallace, *Freud and Anthropology*, 59–112, for a presentation of the sources of *Totem and Taboo*, who cites this quote of Frazer's on 68. This idea actually goes back to St. Paul, who is said to have stated in Romans 7:7, "I had not known sin, but by the law: for I had not known lust, except the law had said, Thou shalt not covet."

52 "Analysis of a Phobia in a Five-year-old Boy," *SE* 10:3–149.

53 Freud, *Totem and Taboo*, *SE*, 13:106–9.

54 As has often been noticed, women barely figure in this narrative, and then only as passive by-standers and objects of male lust and exchange. For a counterexample that inverts this gender dynamic, one might consider the story told by the Ona Selk'nam people of Tierra del Fuego about the origins of their social institutions, related by Michael Taussig: Originally, say the Ona Selk'nam, the secret lodge of the men had belonged exclusively to the women, who "practiced and passed on to the younger women the secrets of magic and sorcery of which the men were ignorant. Frightened, the men banded together and massacred the adult women. They married the young ones, and, so as to prevent them from reconstituting the link between the feminine and magical power, made their own secret society" (Michael Taussig, "Maleficium: State Fetishism," in Emily Apter and William Pietz, eds., *Fetishism as Cultural Discourse* (Ithaca, NY: Cornell University Press, 1993), 238–9.

55 Freud, *Totem and Taboo*, *SE* 13:88–90.

56 Tylor, *Primitive Culture*, 114.

57 Freud, *Totem and Taboo*, *SE* 13:87.

58 Beidelman, *W. Robertson Smith*, 50.

59 In the field of psychological anthropology there is a considerable literature debating whether the shaman is psychotic or schizophrenic (contemporary categories that have come to signify many of the elements intended by

Freud's term *narcissism*) based on derivatives of this argument. A partial bibliography is provided by G. Obeyesekere in *The Work of Culture: Symbolic Transformation in Psychoanalysis and Anthropology* (Chicago, IL: University of Chicago Press, 1990), 297 n. 71.

60 *Future of an Illusion, SE* 21:20.

61 See Elaine Scarry, *The Body in Pain: The Making and Unmaking of the World* (New York: Oxford University Press, 1985), for a sustained meditation on the role of bodily violence in consolidating the institutions of political power.

62 Greenblatt, *Marvelous Possessions*, 134.

63 Stocking, *Victorian Anthropology*, 315.

64 Jones cites anthropologist Clyde Kluckhohn saying that Freud "depicted with astonishing correctness many central themes in motivational life which are universal" (Ernest Jones, *The Life and Work of Sigmund Freud* (New York: Basic Books, 1957), 3:332).

65 See Wallace, *Freud and Anthropology*, 129–72. The question of the universality of the oedipus complex has received much critical treatment and is far from settled. The first major argument against it was Malinowski's *Sex and Repression in Savage Society*, heatedly rebutted by Ernest Jones in 1932, and more recently by Melford Spiro in *Oedipus in the Trobriands* (Chicago, IL: University of Chicago Press, 1982). (One can, of course, accept the universality of the oedipus complex without subscribing to the hypothesis of *Totem and Taboo*.) Since the oedipal drama of *Totem and Taboo* inscribes only males as its protagonists, the universality of the oedipus complex has implications for gender as well as racial difference, as will be discussed more fully in Chapter 3. The implications of oedipal universality and of the "law" established by it have been challenged by Judith Butler, who criticizes Slavoj Žižek's "invocation of a preideological 'law,' . . . that works invariantly throughout all history" as "preempt[ing] the specific social and historical analysis that is required" in Butler, *Bodies That Matter: On the Discursive Limits of "Sex"* (New York: Routledge, 1993), 206–7.

66 Grubrich-Simitis, "Metapsychology and Metabiology," 102–3.

67 Freud, *Interpretation of Dreams, SE* 5:548–9.

68 Freud, *Three Essays on the Theory of Sexuality, SE* 7:131.

69 Freud, "Psycho-analytic Notes on an Autobiographical Account of a Case of Paranoia" (The Schreber Case), *SE* 12:82, *GW* 8:316.

70 Freud, *Introductory Lectures on Psychoanalysis*, Lecture 22, "Development and Regression," *SE* 16:354.

71 Ibid., Lecture 25, "Anxiety," *SE* 16:406.

72 Freud, "A Child Is Being Beaten," *SE* 17:188.

73 Freud, "On Narcissism," *SE* 14:75.

74 Freud, "The Uncanny," *SE* 17:235.

75 Freud, "On Narcissism," *SE* 14:98.

76 Freud, *Civilization and Its Discontents, SE* 21:131.

77 Freud, *A Phylogenetic Fantasy*, 11. *A Phylogenetic Fantasy* is the name, given by the editor, of a manuscript of Freud's discovered in draft form by Ilse Grubrich-Simitis in 1983 among the papers of Sándor Ferenczi. It seems

to have been the twelfth of the metapsychological papers, of which only five, until 1983, had come down to us in published form. Along with six other metapsychological papers, it had been presumed to have been destroyed by Freud himself. Quotes are at 19 and 79.

78 "It is our suspicion that during the human family's primaeval period castration used actually to be carried out by a jealous and cruel father upon growing boys" (Freud, *New Introductory Lectures*, SE 22:86–7; "Outline of Psychoanalysis," *SE* 22:190 n. 1).

79 Freud, *Phylogenetic Fantasy*, 17, 18.

80 Ibid., 19. See Chapter 3 for more about Freud's treatment of the psychology of femininity.

81 *A Psycho-Analytic Dialogue: The Letters of Sigmund Freud and Karl Abraham, 1907–1926*, ed. Hilda C. Abraham and Ernst L. Freud, trans. Bernard Marsh and Hilda C. Abraham (New York: Basic Books, 1965), 261–2.

82 An even more exuberant development of these ideas was given expression by Sándor Ferenczi in his *Thalassa: A Theory of Genitality*, trans. Henry Alden Bunker (Albany, NY: *Psychoanalytic Quarterly*, 1938).

83 Freud, "Analysis Terminable and Interminable," *SE* 23:240.

84 Freud, *Moses and Monotheism*, SE 23:99.

85 Freud, *Outline of Psychoanalysis*, SE 23:167.

86 Freud, *Three Essays on the Theory of Sexuality*, SE 7:177.

87 Freud, *Introductory Lectures*, Lecture 23, "The Paths to Symptom Formation," *SE* 16:371 (my emphasis).

88 Freud, *Outline of Psychoanalysis*, SE 23:188–9.

89 Freud, "Thoughts for the Times on War and Death," *SE* 14:285.

90 Ibid., 14:286.

91 Ibid., 14:296.

92 Freud, "The Unconscious," *SE* 14:195; *GW* 10:294.

93 Freud, "The Unconscious," *SE* 14:186.

94 Freud, *Three Essays on the Theory of Sexuality*, SE 7:242.

95 Freud, "The Unconscious," *SE* 14:187.

96 Freud, *Introductory Lectures*, Lecture 23, *SE* 16:372.

97 *The Ego and the Id*, SE 19:38.

98 Freud, "The Unconscious," *SE* 14:189.

99 Ashis Nandy, *The Intimate Enemy: Loss and Recovery of Self under Colonialism* (Oxford: Oxford University Press, 1983), xi.

100 Erik Erikson's is one of the most thoroughly worked out and well known of such psychoanalytic scales; he defines each stage of life in terms of its cardinal conflict and desired resolution. See Erik H. Erikson, *Identity and the Life Cycle* (New York: Norton, 1980 [1959]), 51–107, 178–9.

101 Elias, *The Civilizing Process*, xi.

102 Rieff, *Mind of the Moralist*, 222; Wallace, *Freud and Anthropology*, 25.

103 Freud, *Interpretation of Dreams*, SE 5:548.

104 Freud, *Totem and Taboo*, SE 13:66.

105 Freud, *Interpretation of Dreams*, SE 5:567.

106 Sulloway and others have demonstrated Freud's indebtedness to the English neurologist John Hughlings Jackson (1835–1911) and, through him, to Herbert Spencer, for the development of his idea of regression. Jackson had envisaged an evolutionary development in which the higher, voluntary functions of the mind came to supersede the lower, involuntary ones, a development that took place within the individual as well as in the history of the human race. He believed that this process could be reversed, as Freud was to describe, and that the lower levels of the mind expressed themselves during dreams. Sulloway, *Biologist of the Mind*, 270.

107 See the section on "Regression" in Chapter 7, "The Psychology of the Dream Processes," Freud, *Interpretation of Dreams*, SE 5:533–49. Quotes are at 542, 544, 548.

108 Freud, *Introductory Lectures*, Lecture 23, *SE* 16:358–77.

109 Freud, *Three Essays on the Theory of Sexuality*, *SE* 7:135–43.

110 See his letter to "a despairing mother in America" concerning her homosexual son, reproduced in Jones, *Life and Work*, 3:195.

111 Freud, *Three Essays on the Theory of Sexuality*, *SE* 7:146 n. 1.

112 See Robert A. Nye, "Medical Origins of Sexual Fetishism," in *Fetishism as Cultural Discourse*, ed. Emily Apter and William Pietz (Ithaca, NY: Cornell University Press, 1993), 13–30.

113 *OED* definition of perversion.

114 Freud, *Totem and Taboo*, *SE* 13:87; "Findings, Ideas, Problems," *SE* 23:299.

115 Michael Vannoy Adams helpfully pairs these terms in his *Multicultural Imagination: "Race," Color and the Unconscious* (London: Routledge, 1996), 51–2.

116 A.B. Evarts, "Dementia Praecox in the Colored Race," *Psychoanalytic Review* 1 (1913–14): 388, 396, 393; John E. Lind, "Phylogenetic Elements in the Psychoses of the Negro," *Psychoanalytic Review* 4 (1917): 331; see also John E. Lind, "The Ontogenetic Against the Phylogenetic Elements in the Psychoses of the Colored Race," *Psychoanalytic Review* 3 (1916): 272–87. See Chapter 1, 28–30, to compare with the Christian and Aristotelian arguments offered to justify Spain's treatment of Amerindians in the years following Columbus's arrival in the New World.

117 Claude Lévi-Strauss, "The Archaic Illusion," in *The Elementary Structures of Kinship*, trans. J.H. Bell, R. von Sturmer and Rodney Needham (Boston, MA: Beacon, 1969 [1949]), 84–97; quote is at 97.

118 Melanie Klein, *The Psychoanalysis of Children*, trans. Alix Strachey (London: Hogarth, 1932; rev. ed. 1975), 188, 196; Michael Balint, "Psychosexual Parallels to the Fundamental Law of Biogenetics," in *Primary Love of Psycho-Analytic Technique* (New York: Liveright, 1953); Ferenczi, *Thalassa*; Otto Fenichel, *The Psychoanalytic Theory of Neurosis* (New York: Norton, 1945), 421, 46ff.; Geza Róheim, *Psychoanalysis and Anthropology: Culture, Personality and the Unconscious* (New York: International, 1950).

Chapter 3

Race and gender, primitivity and femininity
Psychologies of enthrallment

Group psychology and the analysis of the ego

In *Totem and Taboo* Freud gave an account of the origins of psyche and society that cast contemporary psychological development as a recapitulation of a racially conceived evolutionary trajectory of culture. This conception of the genealogy of modern subjectivity made its way into the foundations of Freud's metapsychological theories; and its assumptions emerged, among other places, in his descriptions of the unconscious, characterized as the sedimentation of earlier stages of developmental/evolutionary growth. Because of this characterization, regression could be seen to pave a road not only between the subject's current experience and infantile past, consciousness and the unconscious, well-being and psychopathology; but also between the present and the evolutionary past, so that pathology became linked to the "primitive" psychologies of supposedly culturally superseded races.

In *Group Psychology and the Analysis of the Ego*,[1] Freud develops his theory of how modern subjectivity arose out of primitive groups or communities. In so doing, he provides us with his implicit psychology of primitivity, demonstrating the ways in which the psychic configurations of members of "primitive" groups differ from those of the modern individual subject. This chapter follows the argument of *Group Psychology* to search out the logic internal to its configuration of primitivity and goes on to examine the relationship between race and gender as found in Freud's configurations of primitivity and femininity, exploring the psychologies of enthrallment with male power by which he characterized them both. These raced and gendered characterizations are then traced back to the psychoanalytic premise of separation or exclusion as the operation necessary to the constitution of subjectivity; and toward the end, the chapter turns to an investigation of this premise and suggests a possible alternative.

Group Psychology and the Analysis of the Ego, written in 1921, presents a disconcerting mix: an acute analysis of the psychology of mass move-ments and of the psychological dynamics that fuel their authoritarianism, placed within an evolutionary framework in which mass psychology is a feature of the psychology of primitive peoples from which the modern individual is held to have emerged. This work synthesizes the assump-tions of *Totem and Taboo*, as they were worked through Freud's following metapsychological works on narcissism and on the unconscious, together with the classic early last-century work on mass psychology, *The Crowd*, by Gustave LeBon.[2] LeBon, whose *The Crowd* is still in print today, was the author of a number of books notable for their racist, anti-Semitic and antidemocratic intent, including the extremely popular *Les Lois psychologiques de l'évolution des peuples*, the "locus classicus" of the evolutionary justification for the subjugation of members of "primitive" races.[3] In his works LeBon elaborated theories about the inborn inequality of races and of classes, and warned against the dangers of racial mixing and popular uprisings. As Philip Rieff has pointed out, the English trans-lation of "group" for the German "Massen" in the title of Freud's work obscures the reactionary resonances the latter had in the European political literature of the turn of the century,[4] as is illustrated by LeBon's introduc-tion to *The Crowd*:

> The claims of the masses . . . amount to nothing less than a determina-tion to utterly destroy society as it now exists, with a view to making it hark back to that primitive communism which was the normal condi-tion of all human groups before the dawn of civilization.[5]

Freud borrowed generously from LeBon's appraisal of crowds but turned his analysis against the antidemocratic purposes in whose service LeBon used it, maintaining his categories but reversing their intent. If we con-sider the distinction Hannah Arendt made between popular uprisings that are struggles for political representation, on the one hand, and mobs that "shout for the 'strong man' and the 'great leader'," on the other, LeBon wrote about crowds to condemn the former whereas Freud wrote about group psychology to condemn the latter.[6]

While LeBon saw traditional religious and state institutions as necessary constraints against the power of the masses who threatened to overwhelm the status quo and rise up against it as had the French revolutionaries of 1789, Freud saw those same religious and state institutions (the church and army, the two examples with which he demonstrates his argument in *Group Psychology*) as the very embodiment of the dangers of mass psychology. As remarks in his letters indicate, "the masses" represented for Freud the anti-Semitic mob, backed by state and clerical powers.[7] The Catholic Church was a traditional seat of political influence in Freud's Austria, and it was under the banner of Christian Socialism that the notorious Karl Lueger popularized and institutionalized anti-Semitism during his tenure as mayor of Vienna at the turn of the century. Anti-Semitic forces found official representation in the church and the army—institutions that supported, rather than threatened, a civilized European state. *Group Psychology* is thus an overt critique of so-called civilized institutions, revealing their "primitive" underpinnings, and a veiled critique of the forces at work in the popular mass anti-Semitism of the era. It is a prescient analysis of the psychology of the totalitarianism that was to come, providing an explanation of how a lack of internal psychological structures of moral agency allows for the powerful ties that bind populations to tyrants, creating "the means of dominating and terrorizing human beings from within" that Arendt saw as the chief characteristic of totalitarianism.[8]

All the more troubling, then, that this critique is clothed in a rhetoric which makes use of the colonialist construct of primitivity and sustains its racial overtones. Freud's subversion of the political implications of LeBon's text furnishes the crucial ideological orientation of his essay. By demonstrating the human susceptibility to domination within contemporary organizations, he demonstrated how very alive this susceptibility remains at all times, requiring only the right conditions to emerge anew. But by the same token, his usage placed this susceptibility in an evolutionary framework, according to which it was the characteristic of (racially marked) primitive peoples: the behavior of groups exhibited "a regression of mental activity to an earlier stage such as we are not surprised to find among savages or children."[9] Freud retained LeBon's use of the category of the primitive as the critical term of opprobrium against which the desirable state of a modern, emancipated subjectivity could be measured. In so doing, he located the dangers of the unrestrained dynamics of power both in the "primitive unconscious" of the contemporary subject and among evolutionarily prior "primitive peoples." As is shown below, this essay exhibits a mixed discourse in which primitivity is seen to be a characteristic of primitive races at the same time that it is seen to be produced by relationships of domination and submission.

Freud leaned heavily on LeBon for the basic premises of *Group Psychology*, laying the foundation for his own book by devoting the entire first chapter to an exposition of *The Crowd*. Freud begins with LeBon's contention that the collective mind of the group lacks the distinctive qualities of individual consciousness. Although LeBon had not developed the conception of repression, which, for Freud, was constitutive of the unconscious, he nonetheless shared Freud's sense of both the importance and the inheritable nature of the unconscious. According to LeBon, once submerged in a crowd, the individual loses the capacity for reason, and "the racial unconscious emerges."[10] The collective mind of the crowd is none other than the unconscious mind of all its members; and this unconscious mind, held in common by all, is itself the sedimentation of earlier evolutionary stages of mental development. Once in a crowd, the individual "descends several rungs in the ladder of civilization . . . he is a barbarian" who has all the qualities of "primitive beings."[11] Freud commended LeBon for demonstrating "how well justified is the identification of the group mind with the mind of primitive people,"[12] and found further confirmation of this thesis from William McDougall, a leading and prolific psychologist who concurred that groups demonstrated an "intensification of affects and inhibition of intellect" and that their behavior resembled "that of an unruly child or an untutored passionate savage."[13] Echoing his own descriptions of animism and narcissism in *Totem and Taboo*, Freud cites LeBon's contentions that, like savages, groups cannot brook delay and have "a sense of omnipotence"; further, they "demand illusions, and cannot do without them. They constantly give what is unreal precedence over what is real." Groups are "extraordinarily credulous" and "inclined . . . to extremes"; they are "intolerant [and] obedient to authority."[14]

Freud also turned to the work of sociologist Wilfred Trotter who, in his work on *The Herd Instinct in Peace and War*, had developed and popularized the idea that humans, like other animals (such as sheep and bees), exhibit a gregarious "herd" instinct.[15] Freud agreed with this idea, which Trotter had developed in the face of the millions of lives lost during the First World War, but argued, as he did with LeBon, for a greater importance of the role of the leader: the sociability or gregariousness of group members was in actuality a "horde" instinct. Every group reenacted the dynamics of a primitive community whose prototype was the primal horde with its male leader. The collective mind of a group, then, was the primitive mind found in the primal horde of prehistory, among contemporary "primitive peoples," and constituted the unconscious mind of civilized populations.[16] The corollary was that individuality did not exist in this collective primitive mind.

For Freud, as for so many others before and after him, nothing akin to the rise of the western individual, associated with the European Enlightenment, was believed to have taken place in non-European societies. Indeed, the idea that the autonomous individual is peculiar to the west, although challenged by many anthropologists, persists as part of the received narrative of western intellectual history, whose claims seem to indicate, according to the distinguished anthropologists John and Jean Comaroff, that its imagined "absence elsewhere impl[ies] a deficit, a failure, a measure of incivility on the part of non-Europeans." The Comaroffs go on to say that "*pace* the conventions of Western knowledge, the antinomy between Euroindividualism and African communitarianism, past and present, is profoundly misleading . . . Nowhere in Africa were ideas of individuality ever absent."[17] The Comaroffs' claims about Africa could be echoed by others who have written about so-called primitive communities elsewhere: the lack of individuality among "primitive people" turns out to be an artifact of the colonizing gaze. It was useful to colonial policy to hold that individuality was the mark of civilization whereas collectivity was the mark of primitivity. As Albert Memmi later wrote: "The colonized is never characterized in an individual manner; he is entitled only to drown in an anonymous collectivity."[18] Unsurprisingly, most European anthropological writers upon whose work Freud drew, including not only LeBon but also Robertson Smith, McLennan and others, held that "primitive peoples" innately lacked the capacity for individuality.[19] In *Group Psychology*, the group mind is presented as the same as the unconscious mind, which in turn is the same as the mind of members of so-called primitive communities. Modern individuality is seen by Freud to have emerged out of the primitive mind at a certain point in evolutionary history; but it can become resubmerged in primitivity when in the presence of a crowd. Through this identification of primitivity with the crowd and with the unconscious, the primitive—the west's racial other—is once again shown to represent the past of modern, civilized society, a past that is still present in the unconscious as in the colonies, always threatening to overcome modern European civilization should the members of the latter let down their rational guard.

This, then, is the framework within which Freud worked out his theory of the dynamics of group/mass/mob psychology. Freud followed LeBon's indication that the collective mind of the group communicated itself from one group member to another through the same kind of suggestion that operates in hypnosis. This suggestibility held groups together, and Freud contended that it worked via hypnotic bonds forged between group members and their leaders. (We should remember that Freud was well familiar with the workings of hypnosis. At the beginning of his career he had studied with the French hypnotists Jean-Martin Charcot and Hippolyte Bernheim, and his early *Studies on Hysteria* show him experimenting on his earliest patients with the techniques of hypnosis.) Freud saw the group member as similar to someone under hypnosis. Compelled to do whatever the hypnotist suggests, the group member "wants to be ruled and oppressed"[20] and exhibits "an extreme passion for authority."[21]

How does the group member come to be under such sway? Freud assays a number of distinctions and explanations, finally focusing on the role of external authority, which occupies a different relation to the primitive mind of group members than it does to that of the civilized subject. Here, as in *The Ego and the Id*, Freud describes the processes by which the psychic structures of an individualized subjectivity arise through attachment to and subsequent loss of significant others, known in psychoanalytic terminology as "objects." As beloved objects are lost or abandoned, their representations are internalized to form both ego and ego ideal (later to be called the superego): in Freud's words, "the character of the ego is a precipitate of abandoned object-cathexes."[22] Internal psychological structures arise out of and substitute for lost external relationships, in a development central to the formation of the agencies of the modern, civilized mind. In tune with conventional evolutionary beliefs, Freud saw the shift from external to internal control as the backbone of the development of civilization out of primitivity. Herbert Spencer had argued that the repression of immediate impulses was the motor of evolutionary development: the ability to control one's inner nature went hand in hand with the development of the ability to control the forces of external nature which characterized civilizational progress.[23] Freud contended that this civilized ability to repress immediate impulses depended on the internalization of prohibitions previously imposed by external others. But primitive man identified with and was controlled by the external authority of the leader, and thus lacked the capacity to control his appetites on his own.

As Freud had explained in *Totem and Taboo*, the crucial step from primitivity to the beginnings of civilized culture and morality had been made possible by violent rebellion against external patriarchal authority. The murdered patriarch represented the first lost object, and the remorse for this act led to the internalization of the paternal object in the form of the superego. This momentous step in the development of a civilized subjectivity, the loss of the father and the internalization of his law in the form of the superego, would be recapitulated by each contemporary (male) child with (his) dissolution of the oedipus complex. The shift from external object to internal structure was the crucial step from a primitive to a civilized psyche. It would make its first ontogenetic appearance with the dissolution of the oedipus complex but would take place again and again over the course of a lifetime:

> Throughout an individual's life there is a constant replacement of external by internal compulsion . . . every internal compulsion which makes itself felt in the development of human beings was originally— that is, in the *history of mankind*—only an external one.[24]

These constant replacements take the form of identification: not only the superego but also "the ego is formed to a great extent out of identifications which take the place of abandoned cathexes by the id."[25] As Diana Fuss has written, "subjectivity can be most concisely understood as the history of one's identifications."[26]

Although this is the manner in which the psychoanalytic concept of identification is most commonly understood, Freud tells us there are two other forms of identification as well: the identification felt between those who share something of value, as with members of groups who share the same leader; and the earliest emotional tie itself, a form of identification that developmentally precedes, rather than follows, object love. In *The Ego and the Id*, we are told that identification with the parents "is apparently not in the first instance the consequence or outcome of an object-cathexis; it is a direct and immediate identification and takes place earlier than any object-cathexis."[27] There is therefore both a primary form of identification that precedes object love, and a secondary form that follows upon its loss. The oedipus complex results from the "confluence" of this primary form of identification with object love.[28]

Members of groups exhibit this same confluence of primary identification with object love; but, unlike modern subjects, they do not exhibit the secondary form of identification that grows out of object loss. Like the members of the primal horde before the primal crime, the primitive group member does not rebel against authority and so does not suffer the loss of object cathexis that initiates internalization, secondary identification and the shift from external to internal compulsion. Because of this, the primitive group member never develops a superego: he never internalizes the prohibitions that give rise to an inner sense of conscience. The psychology of the primitive group member corresponds to the psychology of the son who fails to resolve the oedipus complex "in an ideal manner" and who therefore "remains all his life bowed beneath his father's authority."[29] Rather than internalizing an identification with the leader, the group member "hypercathects" him: the leader is retained as an idealized, *external* object, and the ego ideal or superego (Freud had not yet distinguished between these two terms in *Group Psychology*) is not constituted. Instead, the group leader functions *in the place* of the group member's ego ideal. This is the explanation of the inflated power of the leader or demagogue: the psychic agency through which the individual might exercise moral independence does not exist in members of collectivities, its place being entirely taken up by the external object. The leader himself occupies the inner psychic space that otherwise would be taken up by the superego.

Freud aligns the relationship of group member to leader with that of the subject of hypnosis to the hypnotist: like the hypnotized subject, the group member hypercathects the external object, entering a relationship of sexually inhibited love or enthrallment with the external object. On the one hand, Freud tells us, such aim-inhibited relationships are ideally suited to create enduring group ties precisely because they are not sexually consummated. On the other hand, however, they impoverish rather than strengthen psychic structure: they come "at the ego's expense" and contribute to the "sapping of the subject's own initiative."[30] This impoverishment is a result of the lack of the psychological structure that would otherwise emerge if the external object were lost rather than retained. And since the psychic processes prior to those made possible by object loss are, in the final analysis, the processes of narcissism, Freud has arrived here at the same conclusion he reached in *Totem and Taboo*: the psychology of primitivity is the psychology of narcissism. "Primitive peoples," the paradigmatic group members, are seen to be immersed in social formations characterized by group psychology which in turn is conceived in terms of immature relationships with external objects. Such people are in thrall to external authority, lacking the psychological agency necessary to the moral, intellectual and sexual autonomy of modern subjectivity.

Recalling the primal horde and its patriarchal leader, Freud saw primitive psychology as a polarization of two extremes: the unrestricted power, authority and sexuality of the patriarch/group leader/father/hypnotist, and the subjugation of the sons/group members/hypnotized subjects, who lacked the capacity for independent thought and sexuality. (Again, the members of Freud's exemplary primitive group were implicitly male—women and girls existing only as objects of desire, never as proto-historical subjects.) The group leader gave full rein to his appetites, having no internalized principle that would lead him to renounce any of his prerogatives, while the group members complied with the restrictions he imposed, having no internalized moral principle that would allow them to resist. The leader's power was directly imposed on the members through the confluence of their cathexis and their "direct and immediate"[31] primary identification with him. Thus the primitive group relationship was a relationship unmediated by psychological structures or by political institutions. Primitivity was the psychology of unmediated power: of dominating fathers and subjugated sons, of patriarchal leaders and group members, of totalitarian demagogues and their masses.[32] Like Hegel, Freud saw the earliest stage of the development of human consciousness in terms of a relationship of lordship and bondage.[33]

While *Group Psychology* outlined the changes required for the transition from primitive group member to modern, civilized subject, Freud found the model for the transitions required of the primitive patriarch in the figure of Moses, with whom he had a life-long fascination and sense of identification. In *The Moses of Michaelangelo* and *Moses and Monotheism* Moses emerges as the model of a patriarchal renunciation necessary for the progress of civilization. Through his examination, in *The Moses of Michaelangelo*, of the details of Michaelangelo's *Moses* at St. Pietro di Vincoli in Rome, Freud demonstrated how the patriarch renounced his unrestrained libido, aggression and domination. The conventional interpretations of Freud's time saw this statue as a straightforward depiction of Moses' anger when confronted with the idolatry of his moblike people, just prior to his smashing the tables of the law. For our purposes, this uninhibited expression of rage and vengeance would be a mark of the primitive group leader; and the biblical Moses would indeed be an exemplar of a primitive patriarch. But Freud argued against this conventional interpretation, seeing in Michaelangelo's depiction of Moses an improvement on the biblical narrative, and Moses himself as a civilizing advance over primitive patriarchal power. With his subtle visual analysis, Freud contended that rather than giving in to his desires and breaking the tables, Michaelangelo's Moses was actually *restraining* himself from acting on these desires. It was this restraint and renunciation of desire in the service of a higher ideal that characterized the transformation of primitive leadership into the qualities necessary for civilized subjectivity. Freud saw in this Moses "the highest mental achievement that is possible in a man, that of struggling successfully against an inward passion for the sake of a cause to which he has devoted himself."[34] A leader of a group or community, who starts out as free to express his desires, violence and power, must renounce his prerogatives and subject his passions to restraint to make the transition out of primitivity.

Members of primitive groups, on the other hand, must free themselves from their compliance with subjugation; they must dare to rebel, to aspire to the violence of the father and only then to renounce it. As in Hegel's metaphor of the master-slave dialectic, which required that the slave risk death by rebelling against the master's lordship to assume his full humanity, rebellion—the desire for patricide—is a preliminary and necessary step on the way to the renunciation of instinct, the exemplary civilizing act that inaugurates an internal and therefore "higher" sense of guilt. In *Civilization and Its Discontents* Freud wrote that small children, who "are following a phylogenetic model,"[35] exhibit a lower sense of guilt in their simple compliance with external authority, because it is born out of the fear of loss of parental love. Renunciation of instinct *before* the emergence of the desire for rebellion is indistinguishable from mere adherence to the will of the father, who forbids his children the exercise of their instincts: it is simply the fear of external authority. In the higher stage of guilt, this external paternal authority has been rebelled against, "murdered" in the life of fantasy and "lost" as a revered external object. Only then can he be internalized as the superego, the psychological ambassador of civilization which, having conquered the primitive mind, sets up its internal "garrison" in the mind.[36] Taboo is transgressed, only to be replaced by renunciation.

Freud's ideal of the modern civilized (masculine) subject combines the rebellion of the primitive son together with the renunciation of the Moses-like patriarch: the successful resolution of the oedipal complex represents this intergenerational compromise of rebellious desire and its renunciation. Neither total subjection nor unrestrained power, these extremes are now mediated within the subject by the institution of inner conscience, and between members of civilized societies by institutions of political representation. Lacan's designation of the superego as the phallic bearer of the "law" of patriarchal society which governs subjectivity through the use of language usefully demonstrates the links in Freud's thought between inner psychic structure and the capacity for political participation and representation. For Freud, the institution of inner conscience goes hand in hand with an individual's ability to participate in the institutions of political representation; for Lacan, the ability to represent oneself through language makes possible the ability to represent oneself in society and politics.

In its discussion of primitive psychology, *Group Psychology* makes claims on both the ontogenetic (individual) and phylogenetic (evolutionary) registers. On the ontogenetic register, participation in crowds is seen to lead contemporary subjects to regress to a primitive level of mind characterized by a greater susceptibility to domination. On the phylogenetic register, this susceptibility to domination is seen as a characteristic of evolutionarily "primitive" communities among whom individuality is held to have not yet developed. Relational affiliations in social formations are conceived of as forms of enthrallment with authority and are racially marked through their categorization as primitive. It is from immersion in such "primitive" relationships that the autonomous (white, male) subject has evolved, independent in the exercise of his moral, intellectual and sexual capacities. The poor ego who was not master in his own house was considered, nonetheless, an evolutionary advance over the primitive psychical organization where the ego had not yet even managed to emerge from group (un)consciousness.

But this evolutionary narrative is, importantly, embedded in a mixed discourse that includes a secondary, alternative account according to which primitivity is seen to be socially produced as an effect of power. This alternative account is not as fully fleshed out as what has been described above. Nevertheless, in it Freud gives voice to a view of primitivity as the result of the imposition of domination, rather than as a characteristic of early, less-evolved races whose mentality lives on in the unconscious of the civilized. Although Freud tells us that the primitive sons "want[ed] to be ruled and oppressed," he also tells us that they were "*persecuted* by the primal father, and *feared* him equally."[37] In these elements of this text, the narcissistic processes of primitivity are not described as inborn among primitive group members; instead, they are seen to have been elicited by the group leader. It was the primal father, Freud tells us, who "forced [his sons] . . . into group psychology" by compelling their sexual abstinence. This abstinence, in turn, locked them into the psychological processes that precede the loss of object cathexis, producing the narcissistic ties characteristic of primitivity that excluded the possibility of independent desire, thought, morality and action.[38] As mentioned previously, Freud even went so far as to suggest, in the unpublished *Phylogenetic Fantasy*, in Lecture 32 of *New Introductory Lectures*, and in the final summation of *An Outline of Psychoanalysis*, that in an act anticipating circumcision, the primal father actually castrated his sons, the better to ensure their slavelike submission.[39] The familiar colonial tale of the primitive as a member of the evolutionarily prior, darker races, who lives in a hordelike community, desires his own oppression and lives in subjection to the leader of the community, is supplemented by a view of primitivity as determined by the unrestrained exercise of or compliance with authority. Here we find a theory of the political production of primitivity: primitivity is the psychology of domination and subordination. It is social and political arrangements of domination that produce enthrallment: the imposition of authority becomes inscribed on the psyche as desire, and primitivity is revealed as an erotics of authority and subjugation.

Group Psychology cautions that the church and the army, institutions of twentieth-century civilized Europe, are themselves exemplars of group psychology and hence of the primitive group mind. The dangers of primitivity are not long gone and consigned to the archaic past; they continue on in the heart of contemporary European psyches and institutions. What is primitive, then, is the structural deficiency that inhibits the expression of an independent conscience, thus allowing for unmediated relationships of oppression. From this perspective, a psychological configuration is "primitive" not by virtue of its priority in human history but rather by virtue of its contradistinction from the Freudian ideal of civilization whose hallmarks are individual moral freedom and freedom of thought, coupled with moral restraint. This is why the church and the army—and totalitarian movements and dictatorships—are primitive: their leaders usurp the psychic space of their followers where the agency for intellectual and moral independence and responsibility might otherwise flourish.

Nonetheless, the Freudian ideal of moral freedom and restraint is expressed in a rhetoric which assumes that a racially inflected evolutionary priority in human history *is*, by definition, the measure of the distance from that ideal. "Primitivity" signifies evolutionary priority and the desire for domination enduring in, and at times emerging from, the unconscious. However, Freud's mixed discourse allows for the ever-present possibility of slippage between, on the one hand, an understanding of primitivity as a psychology that is the effect of unmediated relations of domination, a condition that can take place anytime, anywhere; and, on the other hand, an understanding of primitivity as a racial category, where relations of domination are evolutionarily ordained and racially indexed characteristics.

Race and gender: primitivity and femininity

The psychoanalytic category of the primitive is to the question of race what its category of the feminine is to the question of gender: both are psychologized categories of difference configured as positions structurally inferior and developmentally prior to the fully developed subject. Both are correlated with the "natural" origins of the subject (phylogenetic origins in the case of primitivity and ontogenetic origins in the case of maternal femininity); and both are indexed to particular groups of people—representatives of racial and gender difference from the white, male norm—whose psychology is said to be limited to the inferior psychological structures represented by these categories.

In her influential article on "The Traffic in Women," Gayle Rubin placed the psychoanalytic account of subjectivity within the framework of the theory of culture put forth by Lévi-Strauss in his *Elementary Structures of Kinship*: culture is instituted by the exchange of women by men to establish communication and ties of reciprocity between various kinship groups. In Rubin's reading, Freud's psychology of femininity describes those who are used within cultures as objects of exchange ("women on the market" in the words of Luce Irigaray).[40] The conventions of the principles of kinship exchange which have founded each society—who exchanges whom—are inscribed within the psyche of each subject, coming to seem both natural and inevitable. Rubin recasts the traditional psychoanalytic difference between male and female—to have the phallus or to be castrated—as the Lévi-Straussian difference between exchanger and exchanged, reading the psychoanalytic conception of sexual difference as an economic relationship between dominator and dominated, exploiter and exploited. In this way, kinship structures are shown to construct the inferiority of femininity through the positioning of women as objects of exchange, as commodities within the economy of kinship. While, according to Lévi-Strauss, rules of exogamy insured that women would be exchanged in marriage outside the family group, avoiding incest to insure sociality, Judith Butler and Jean Walton have pointed out that traditional kinship principles have also functioned to coordinate exogamy with the rules of endogamy (marriage within a racial/ethnic group), ensuring that communities would avoid miscegenation; that is, to maintain racial purity.[41] The oedipus complex, that critical historical/ developmental moment in which the prohibitions of society are internalized as the superego and become represented by the phallus, coordinates both exogamy and endogamy: the oedipus complex coordinates both the prohibition against incest and the prohibition against marrying outside the ethnic/racial group, and thus establishes both sexual *and* racial norms.

Rubin's view leads to my contention that primitivity in psychoanalysis is the psychology of those who are positioned as objects of exchange: within a society (women) or between societies (colonized and/or enslaved others). Primitivity is the psychology of those whose land, bodies and labor contribute to the support of a social order to whose symbolic and political institutions they themselves have no direct access, a society in which they have no rights or protection, a society in which they have no representation, discursively or politically speaking. Those people outside the European ethnos who themselves became commodified to support an incipiently modern, global economy were, like European women, considered a part of the nature that would make possible the continued sustenance and expansion of that economy, without themselves being counted among its members. The phallus is therefore not only "the embodiment of the male status," nor only "an expression of the transmission of male dominance,"[42] a symbol of *intracultural* dominance, understood as gender. It is also the symbol of the transmission of *intercultural* dominance, the dominance of one cultural group over another, inscribed in terms of race. Not only is the phallus male, it is also white.[43] Those forced into the position of objects of exchange are seen, by the cultural system which so coerces them, as lacking the phallus, or, in Freudian terminology, lacking the superego that the phallus symbolizes. The superego/phallus represents the agency born of the internalization of the norms of modern, civilized subjectivity. Primitivity is the condition of lacking the superego/phallus, coded as racial difference.

This points to the ways in which the classical psychoanalytic figuration of normative subjectivity is itself keyed into a political economy that necessitates the exclusion and repression of qualities marked as primitive and feminine. The effects of these exclusions turn up in psychoanalytic characterizations of primitivity and femininity as incomplete and subordinate psychologies, characterizations inscribed in a mixed discourse where they appear sometimes as biologically, and other times as socially, produced.

Psychoanalytic notions of primitivity and femininity as inferior others are overlapping and mutually implicating, in a continuation of the age-old homology linking women and so-called primitives with nature. Identified with the timeless rhythms of nature, both the primitive and the feminine have, in the history of western thought, been seen as standing outside historical and social forces. The rhetoric of colonialization took up the conflation of these terms, characterizing Europe's new worlds as uncultivated nature, alluringly and submissively awaiting European possession and cultural inscription.[44] Primitivity and femininity formed "a powerful scientific analogy . . . that occupied a strategic place in scientific theorizing about human variation in the nineteenth and twentieth centuries."[45] Freud took up this analogy, epitomized in his well-known reference to female sexuality as the "dark continent" of psychoanalysis, invoking the familiar evolutionary characterization of Africa as primitive and dark. His comment is emblematic of the reciprocal implications of race and gender in psychoanalysis, where primitivity and femininity each came to signify the other in a network of evolutionary correspondences.

Evidence of a mixed discourse concerning femininity can readily be found in Freud's writings on gender, on sexuality and on women. On the one hand, Freud counseled his readers to abjure sexual stereotypes, writing of "the constitutional bisexuality of each individual" and asserting that femininity and masculinity were not identical with biological male and female genders.[46] He contended that "Man" has "an unmistakably bisexual disposition . . . For psychology the contrast between the sexes fades away into one between activity and passivity, in which we far too readily identify activity with maleness and passivity with femaleness."[47] According to his views in his essays on women, women are made, not born, as Simone de Beauvoir remarked:[48] it is only by a "very circuitous path" that the female child arrives at the "ultimate normal feminine attitude," defined as "taking her father as love-object."[49] Although his writings do not clearly disentangle sexuality from gender, his early views that sexuality arises independently from sexual object, that "the sexual instinct and the sexual object are merely soldered together,"[50] form the basis for the more recent view of gender and sexual orientation as culturally constituted rather than given by nature.

On the other hand, Freud's writings include a biologistic-essentialist dimension, positing femininity as a psychological configuration that arises from the biological particularities of women. Freud, famously citing the cliché *anatomy is destiny*, placed considerable weight on sexual anatomy as that which impels psychosexual development: "anatomical distinctions" have specific "psychological consequences," as the title of his 1925 essay suggests. In his essays on femininity and on female sexuality, femininity is cited as determined by two factors related to biology: the female "lack" of external genitalia and the female condition of being of the same sex— sharing the same anatomy—as the first object, the mother. The normative feminine position results from these two factors: the "turning point" in female development is "the discovery that she is castrated"; and "the most important step in the little girl's development" is "the turning-away from the mother."[51] Although Freud argues that activity and passivity are not necessarily the concomitants of masculinity and femininity, a woman who does not successfully repress her "active strivings" is seen as phallic: her activity can only be represented as masculine. Only masculinity is "completely ego-syntonic"[52] and only masculinity is expressive of a full-fledged subjectivity that is morally and intellectually capable. This masculinity, too, is both a psychological and biological condition: "Maleness combines [the factors of] subject, activity and the possession of a penis; femaleness takes over [those of] object, and passivity."[53] As de Beauvoir put it: "It is among the psychoanalysts in particular that man is defined as a human being and woman as a female—whenever she behaves as a human being she is said to imitate the male."[54] Development is to culminate in the coincidence of activity with masculinity and femininity with passivity; masculinity is revealed as the biological and psychological form in which the human subject is fully incarnated.[55]

And, as mentioned above, Freud deploys a similarly ambiguous mixed discourse in his figuration of the relationship between psychological primitivity and "primitive" peoples. In a manner corresponding to his warning against a too-easy identification of masculinity with activity and femininity with passivity, he prefaces his use of the ethnographies of his time with the caveat that

> primitive races are not young races but are in fact as old as civilized races . . . . The determination of the original state of things thus inevitably remains a matter of construction . . . . We misunderstand primitive men just as easily as we do children, and are always apt to interpret their actions and feelings according to our own mental constellations.[56]

Freud's argument for the universality of the primitive psyche, found in primitive and civilized people alike, provided a crucial antidote to the biologically conceived racial distinction drawn by evolutionary anthropology between civilized and primitive minds. But however cautious in his appropriation of anthropological materials, Freud could not help but press into service the available colonialist constructions concerning the "primitive peoples" of his day, and, as a result, the psychoanalytic universality of primitivity, like its universal bisexuality, masks a hierarchy of particularities. As the civilized subject is supposed to overcome an initial polymorphous sexuality in favor of a fixed adult psychosexual position (heterosexual or homosexual), this same subject is to overcome its primitive tendencies through its transformation of external authority into the internalized superego. The primitive psyche is, on its own, sufficient only for primitive races; for the civilized races it represents "a preliminary stage of the higher organization" of which it is only a part.[57] Thus, in the case of both femininity and primitivity, Freud reproduces the very stereotypes he cautions against. He begins by providing an inclusive discourse—we all have active and passive (masculine and feminine) components within us, the primitive mind is part of us all—which is then superseded by a particular normative position that repudiates the previously included categories of femininity and primitivity by casting them as developmentally and evolutionarily inferior. With racial as with sexual difference, the promised revolution "end[s] up with a restoration of the monarchy."[58]

As mentioned earlier, although primitivity entailed both submission of the sons and domination by the father, Freud's theory of primitivity was construed largely in terms of the sons. It was the phylogenetic drama of the primitive sons that provided the oedipal model of rebellion and remorse and that is recapitulated in the ontogenetic trajectory of the contemporary subject and his negotiation of the oedipus complex. And since regression involved a tracing backward of the path already followed, the primitivity to which the modern subject was said under certain circumstances to regress, like the primitivity out of which he had developed, was the primitivity of the son. Thus it is the primitivity of the son which becomes central in the comparison between primitivity and femininity.

Freud's key characteristics of femininity—passivity, submissiveness, narcissism and masochism; lack of intellectual, moral and rational development; excessive emotional ambivalence; and a difficult or restricted sexuality—are all shared by the primitivity of the son. The psychological dynamics of both the primitive and the feminine are organized around the wish for fulfillment characteristic of narcissism. Women are said to be narcissists: they overvalue themselves as a compensation for their reputed organ deficiency; their primary need is to be loved rather than to love.[59] Primitive peoples, too, as we have seen, are said to live in a state of narcissism, which entails not only the omnipotence of thoughts and belief in animism but a psychic organization lacking the psychic agencies of their evolutionary superiors. The primitive is said to desire oppression as the feminine is said to be masochistic. Both the feminine and the primitive, like the neurotic,[60] are characterized by a greater sense of ambivalence. It is only the civilized boy who is capable of successfully negotiating ambivalence by projecting his hostility completely onto his father and leaving his mother as the unalloyed recipient of his love. This allows the psychic consequences of his hostility to emerge, setting into motion the internalization of the superego.[61] (Of course, this is a somewhat simplified description: the boy presents both an active and passive relationship to his father and, in the passive oedipal position, desires his father's love. However, this passive position *is*, psychoanalytically speaking, femininity, located for the moment in the passive homosexual male rather than in the female.) Finally, femininity and primitivity are both characterized by an impaired sexuality. According to Freud, the primitive son is restricted in his sexuality because of the relegation of sexual prerogative to the primitive leader or patriarch. As his writings on femininity make clear, Freud believed that women are restricted in their sexuality because of the convoluted course of their development: the complications of the psychological development of a girl "often enough" have as their outcome that "a considerable portion of her sexual trends in general is permanently injured too."[62]

The similarity between femininity and primitivity in psychoanalysis is reinforced by its common identification of the feminine with the maternal. In Freud's conception of the "final normal feminine attitude,"[63] female sexuality and female psychology are seen to be in the service of reproduction, and femininity is aligned with maternity: mature femininity finds its fulfillment by replacing the desire for the penis with the desire for a child. But the maternal woman, the apex of mature femininity, is also the most "primitive" object from the position of the male subject whose gaze organizes the psychoanalytic field. (Maternity viewed from the mother's perspective would present a rather different picture indeed.) In *Civilization and Its Discontents* Freud stated that "an infant at the breast does not as yet distinguish his ego from the external world as the source of the sensations flowing in upon him" and described the earliest pre-oedipal relationship in terms of the sensation of immersion in oceanic oneness.[64] Drawing on these formulations, the various psychoanalytic renditions of the earliest stages of life describe the mother–infant dyad as the undifferentiated unit from which the infant begins to emerge (as in object relations theory) or as the prediscursive unit whose disruption by the paternal member of the family institutes language and subjectivity (as in Lacanian theory). As subjectivity develops, it is the mother who continues to represent the subject's memory of the merged consciousness of the earliest stage of life. For this reason the mother, seen retrospectively as the site of a dreaded but enthralling fusion of subject and object, remains the very definition of psychoanalytic primitivity, representing the site of ontogenetic origins just as the primitive represents the site of phylogenetic origins. The development of subjectivity is held to depend on achieving a critical distance from or repudiation of the merged relationship with the mother: maturity becomes defined in terms of distance from primitive maternity. For Freud, the primitive position to which neurosis is a regression "always has a 'feminine' character."[65]

As mentioned earlier, both the primitive and the feminine are represented by psychoanalysis as compromised in their ability to fully develop a superego. As we have seen, the primitive psyche is the psyche without a superego: neither the primitive father with his unlimited powers nor the primitive sons, slavishly restricted in their exercise of libido and rationality, are able to perform the psychological task of the internalization of prohibition in the form of the superego, an internalization which founds both civilization and subjectivity. The primitive languishes at the narcissistic level of cultural development, in bondage to authority tempered only by the illusory consolations of animism, lacking access to the possibilities of civilized culture. The Lacanian trope of the phallus, representing as it does the patriarchal law inherent in language and culture into which the subject is inducted through the dissolution of the oedipal complex, effectively highlights the identification of the superego and the introjection of the law of the father with the capacity for self-representation in the symbolic and political structures of civilization. Like the unconscious he is held to represent, the "primitive" lacks the capacity for cultural self-representation. Thus, in Gayatri Spivak's words, within the discourse of psychoanalysis the subaltern cannot speak.[66]

Because her developmental trajectory diverges from that of civilized masculinity, the woman of psychoanalytic theory, like the primitive, is also unable to internalize a complete superego. The prototypical—male— oedipus complex is constellated around the intensification of the boy's love for his mother and the projection of his hostility onto his father. The dissolution of this complex and the resulting installation of the superego is catalyzed by his discovery of sexual difference and his interpretation of it as the threat of castration. But girls' recognition of sexual difference is cast by Freud as the acknowledgment—rather than the fear—of a castration that has already taken place. This acknowledgment causes girls to turn away in hatred from their mothers and in love toward their fathers; girls' recognition of sexual difference *begins* their oedipus complex (love of the parent of the opposite sex) rather than ending it, as with boys. Because she has already undergone the tragedy of castration rather than living in terrified anticipation of it, the young girl lacks the incentive that would cause her, like her brother, to renounce her oedipal feelings and develop an internalized, prohibitory superego. The woman is "inimical" to civilization since she has had nothing to lose that would set her on its renunciatory path. (To the culturally capable woman Freud contends: "This doesn't apply to *you*. You're the exception: on this point you're more masculine than feminine."[67])

Women, like primitives, never reach the threshold of rebellion/renunciation necessary for modern subjectivity. Never wishing to rebel against paternal authority, their oedipal complex guiding them in love toward the father rather than in hostility toward him, they never have to fully rebel against the father and internalize his prohibitions completely: they remain psychologically like children. (We might parenthetically point out, however, that the opposition between feminine submission and masculine rebellion/renunciation is contradicted in places by Freud himself. After all, the psychoanalytic representation of femininity requires the *renunciation* of activity for passivity. A girl must renounce her clitoral sexuality "as a necessary pre-condition for the development of femininity"; she must renounce her desire for the phallus and replace it with a desire for a baby—renunciations which, if we were to accept this account, seem no less onerous or potentially less psychically productive than the renunciations necessary to masculinity. And even with all the ministrations of psychoanalytic treatment, a woman's "phallic" desires—the only adjective available within the psychoanalytic lexicon to represent her desires for an active subjectivity—are not so easily dispensed with. They stubbornly endure, for they are, by Freud's own admission, the bedrock of her personality. In this arena, "nothing can be done to help her" to become truly feminine; that is, subordinate and passive. Her feminine identity, it seems, is not actually within her reach, but is rather the dream of the culture that attempts to impose it on her.[68])

Both femininity and primitivity, then, are constellated around the lack of a complete superego, resulting in an underdeveloped seat of conscience and morality. Like the primitive group member whose conscience is merely fear of external authority, a woman's conscience is largely "the result of upbringing and of intimidation *from the outside* which threatens her with a loss of love."[69] Women, in Freud's famous words, "show less sense of justice than men, are less ready to submit to the great necessities of life, and are far more often influenced in their judgments by feelings of affection or hostility"; they are "weaker in their social instincts and [have] less capacity for sublimating their instincts."[70]

In these gendered differences of subjectivity we can see the recapitulation of the primordial conditions set out in *Totem and Taboo*, where the primal father possessed all the girls and women whom he denied to the sons. Contemporary masculine development repeats the original unavailability to the sons of their mothers who were the exclusive sexual property of the primal father, while feminine experience repeats the ready availability of the girls of the horde to their fathers. On both phylogenetic and ontogenetic registers Freud sees the male as needing to rebel against the obstacle of patriarchal power. Phylogenetically, the father kept the son from sexual activity; ontogenetically, the father stands in the way of the son's desire for his mother. For the female, however, paternal power is not the obstacle to, but the object of, her desire. Phylogenetically, she was not deprived of sexuality, forced though it might have been;[71] nor, onto-genetically, is she deprived of her father's love. Only the male children of civilization wish to rebel against patriarchal power, which they will then inherit through internalization. Since in Freud's view it is only through this rebellion and internalization that the subject gains access to full membership in the cultural, moral and civic dimensions of modern civilized life, both the primitive and the feminine live outside the gates of civilized culture. In Lacanian terms, both the primitive and the feminine remain outside the structures of representation that govern them; again, the phallus, never feminine, is always white.

According to this perspective, those who do not have completely formed superegos cannot take up full-fledged positions in language, culture and the social polity, and are thus excluded from the rights and protections that civilization promises. This in turn suggests their need for the guardianship by those who purportedly have no such lack. Read in this way, psychoanalytic theory reproduces notions of the need for "tutelage" by the European male citizen on behalf of his gendered and racial/cultural others, suggesting that those without a complete superego need, for their completion as human beings, to be bound to those who have such a superego. We are returned to the words of Aristotle and his fifteenth-century Spanish disciple, Sepúlveda, according to whom it was only through becoming enslaved that the American "savage" could gain access to the reason which, on his own, he did not possess. As Sepúlveda wrote, such primitive people

> require, by their own nature and in their own interests, to be placed under the authority of civilized and virtuous princes or nations, so that they may learn, from the might, wisdom and law of their conquerors, to practice better morals, worthier customs and a more civilized way of life.[72]

Such a perspective persisted in the writings of major Enlightenment theorists, as Charles Mills points out: Kant, for example, in his essay, "The Different Races of Mankind," correlated variation in skin color with a hierarchy of "innate talent"; John Stuart Mill argued that barbarians "need European colonial despotism"; and Hegel "suggested that blacks were morally improved through being enslaved."[73] The psychoanalytic figuration of the raced primitive as not in possession of a complete superego lends additional support to the claim that the subaltern is suited, by virtue of his or her primitive psychology, for colonialization and slavery, and unfit for the responsibilities and privileges of civil society. It has also lent support to a psychiatric corollary to this claim common until sometime into the twentieth century: if freed, slaves and colonized peoples would be prone to mental disturbance. Lacking a superego, the argument went, they were without the psychological resources to cope with freedom.[74] The French psychoanalyst, Octave Mannoni, suggested an updated version of this psychoanalytic thesis in his *Prospero and Caliban* (1950), postulating a "dependency complex" among colonized peoples such as the Malagasy of Madagascar, who "must have parent figures if they are not to go insane."[75] (After having directed the information services of the French colony of Madagascar, Mannoni went on to become an associate of Lacan's.)

Similarly, on the axis of gender, Freud's psychoanalytic conception of femininity implied that only by becoming married could a woman gain vicarious access to a superego and thus become eligible, through her husband, for the protections and privileges of civil society. This view was in accordance with the law of coverture, brought by English colonists to North America, according to which women could not have a separate legal or civil identity apart from their husbands. Owing to the law of coverture, up until various points in the nineteenth and twentieth centuries, women were excluded from the right to vote, to own property, to file law suits and to have their labor protected.[76]

However: within the psychoanalytic map, the two categories of femininity and primitivity—of gender and race—differ critically. As Seshadri-Crooks has pointed out, alongside its essentialist assertions, psychoanalysis does offer a theory of how woman "came into being," whereas the only representation offered of the primitive is that he "merely 'is'."[77] This is because, for psychoanalysis, femininity is a *diverted* masculinity, whereas primitivity is a *proto*-masculinity. As Freud puts it, originally the little girl is "a little man." She must divert herself from an original masculinity, divert the site of her sexuality from clitoris to vagina, divert her relational longings from her mother to her father, and divert her originally active, outward strivings toward a narcissistic passivity. Primitivity, on the other hand, is not a diversion of civilized energies: the primitive has *not yet* achieved the masculinity that the female must renounce. Nonetheless, the "primitive" submission and dependency which the modern subject has left behind turns up as the normative position of a civilized femininity. Freud's theory of femininity inscribes the domesticated trace of a racialized primitivity in the gendered discourse of civilized modernity.

That the feminine in psychoanalytic theory is the reinscription of primitivity within civilization points to the fact that a "primitive feminine" position—the position of the non-white woman—does not appear at all on the discursive map of psychoanalysis. The psychoanalytic understanding of femininity derives from and is limited to the condition of the white European woman who shares some basic psychosocial givens with her male counterpart (she is, after all, "within civilization") even though the imperatives of her sexual development lead her to a position subordinate to his, whereas it seems the racial other is always already primitive. As the work of critics Spivak and Butler might suggest, it is the "subaltern feminine" on whose exclusion the entire psychoanalytic system of representation rests.[78]

In writing of the connection between norms of gender and the bodies which live them out, Judith Butler has written that the "exclusionary matrix by which subjects are formed . . . requires the simultaneous production of a domain of abject beings, those who are not yet 'subjects,' but who form the constitutive outside to the domain of the subject."[79] Normative subjectivity within psychoanalysis is suffused not only with the implicit assumptions about gender that are entailed in its portrait of femininity but also with the implicit racial assumptions that are entailed in its portrait of primitivity. The formation of the psychoanalytic subject requires the psychological exclusion of qualities associated with primitivity and femininity, which are then projected onto classes of subordinated—raced and gendered—peoples, whose psychologies are held up as "natural" exemplifications of these excluded qualities. In the same way that femininity is fundamental to masculine subjectivity as its excluded yet constitutive other, primitivity is fundamental to civilized subjectivity as *its* excluded yet constitutive other.

Enthrallment and domination

Freud's theory of primitivity suggests that relationships of authority are impressed on the psyche as desire. Not only power and the exercise of authority but the obedience and subservience which they inspire or coerce are described as erotic. The term *enthrallment*—Freud uses the word

Hörtigkeit, enthrallment or bondage, when describing the effects of the external object taking the place of the ego ideal[80]—points to this erotics of authority, this blend of desire and domination which, in psychoanalytic theory, characterizes primitivity and femininity. Freud wrote that the desire for paternal authority is never entirely extinguished in women, just as the primitive is defined by his desire for domination.

Postcolonial critics have acknowledged the vexed issue of the desire of the colonized for the (status of the) colonizer; they have seen it as an effect of domination, of the "perverse mutuality" of the colonizing relationship.[81] They have pointed to the seductions of colonizing power: its civilizing mission with its promise of "development" and of a superior humanity; the wealth and privilege of regimes that have governed subaltern populations while excluding them from access to the material and symbolic resources made possible by their servitude. Ashis Nandy has written how many in British India "saw their salvation in becoming more like the British"[82] and Frantz Fanon has written eloquently about how he did not even know that he was neither white nor French until he left Martinique and arrived in France.[83] Colonized peoples, especially the elites, often came to adopt and identify with the values and institutions (and cultural formations, including, occasionally, psychoanalysis) that construed them as mentally and culturally inferior. These values were sometimes turned back on the west to criticize it, but, as often as not, they produced an "identification with the aggressor" that transmuted colonizing contempt into self-hatred and cultural disavowal. Fanon wrote of the desire of the colonized to be recognized as human by the Other in a racial economy in which whiteness alone signifies humanness: this urgent yet frustrated desire for recognition of one's humanity finally drives the black person to declare, "I will quite simply try to make myself white."[84] The impossible situation of living within a social order that withholds recognition as well as social and cultural possibilities from its indigenous inhabitants/racial others creates a desire for that recognition and those possibilities, and creates a desire for the power identified with them, that of the colonizer. As James Baldwin wrote, "How can one . . . dream of power in any other terms than in the symbols of power?"[85]

When Freud wrote that the primitive desires domination, however, he was talking about the effects of power as well as about what he cast as a naturalized desire inherent in so-called primitive races. *Group Psychology* (not to mention the history of the twentieth century) demonstrated that contemporary institutions can be as barbaric as anything evolutionary history might have to show us; but its evolutionary language described a desire for domination as part of the intrinsic psychological structure of "primitive man," Europe's forebear and cultural/racial other. How and why does the psychoanalytic construction of subjectivity enlist and reproduce an understanding of racial alterity as an enthrallment with authority arising from its intrinsic psychological structure? How and why does psychoanalysis continue to reproduce primitivity, like femininity, as the exclusion that makes normative subjectivity possible? Since it is feminist/gender theorists who recently have most urgently interrogated psychoanalysis concerning issues of domination and exclusion, I turn now to these theorists to pursue these questions.

Feminist psychoanalytic theorizing can be seen to have developed (roughly speaking) along two differing lines: on the one hand, those influenced by Lacan, who give pride of place to the intransigence and determinacy of the symbolic law of patriarchal culture; and, on the other hand, Anglo-American theorists who favor particular historical, social and familial structures as the critical mechanisms that reproduce and enforce particular configurations of desire. Both schools, along with Freud, tend to figure development in terms of a separation from embeddedness within the maternal relation that makes possible a differentiated subjectivity. For the first, Lacanian-influenced school, subjectivity consists of the inauguration of a consciousness alienated by the very workings of the language through which it expresses itself. A preliminary developmental stage of undifferentiation is followed by the mirror stage in which the infant, a bundle of contradictory drives and fragments, models its sense of self on the misleadingly coherent image encountered in the mirror. This stage, in turn, is followed by the oedipal complex in which the subject takes up his or her position in language, culture and society through the internalization of the paternal prohibitions encoded in the superego. Lacan identifies oedipal prohibitions with the "name of the father": the resolution of the oedipus complex is the intrapsychic, intergenerational transmission of patriarchal law. The disruption of the mother/child dyad by the paternal function makes possible the acquisition of language, but simultaneously creates an irreparable rupture with undifferentiated being. Meaning, made possible by the representational structures of language, seems retrospectively to have displaced being, creating an existential lack at the heart of a representable identity. In the oedipal moment which effects the fateful rupture of the pre-oedipal infant/mother dyad by language, recognition of sexual difference codes the phallus as the master signifier of the economy of representation into which the subject is enculturated, whereas the female "lack" of external genitalia comes to signify the lack of being at the core of identity. The "being" from which the speaking subject is excluded is the infantile, undifferentiated union with the mother; the paternal and civilizational regime of language and meaning comes to dominate the primitive, maternal domain of being.[86] This school has been criticized for the lack of agency conceded to the subject, who seems to have no choice but to be passively inducted into these discursive regimes; and especially to women, who become fixed in the position of femininity as necessarily outside the system of structures of signification altogether.

The Anglo-American feminist school has generally looked more to the socially situated gendering of social and familial structures—especially those of parenting and work—for explanations of the inscription of desire along the lines of domination and subordination. Drawing much of its inspiration from the object relations school of psychoanalysis, it privileges relationship with others as the primary desire of the child, and tends to see the acquisition of language as an incremental and nontraumatic event in the service of increased relationality. This in turn decreases the critical weight of the oedipal complex by focusing on the complexities of pre-oedipal life. Lack and loss tend to be seen as contingent rather than constitutive qualities of the speaking subject; necessary rupture and conflict are accompanied, if not displaced, by the potential for recognition and coherence. This school has inherited the language of separation and autonomy developed by American ego psychology (which was excoriated by Lacan for its adaptive propensities), and often focuses on the differences in the ways sons and daughters fantasize about and relate to fathers and mothers. It has been criticized for its notions of unitary selves (although more recently theories of multiple selves have been developed) and for its tendency to ignore the coercive dimension of the cultural regimes which condition familial and social structures.[87]

Julia Kristeva has extended the Lacanian scenario by positing the *abject* as the uttermost position of subordination,[88] a realm prior to the demarcation of subject and object out of which both are carved. The abject is the domain of infantile experience in which repression has not yet managed fully to exclude the contents of the unconscious. Not fully delineated or distinct from the subject as an object would be, the abject is a relationship of immediacy with the maternal that powerfully promises and threatens to re-encompass the emerging subject, exerting both fascination and dread. The social and symbolic orders are constituted, as is the subject, over and against this abject immediacy with the maternal. The processes of separation from the mother become paradigmatic of the series of repudiations necessary to subjectivity and to the social order; such additional repudiations (of filth, for instance) are "in the last analysis relat[ed] to fusion with the mother,"[89] continuing the identification of femininity with maternity and of maternity with the undifferentiated matrix out of which both subject and object are formed. Kristeva identifies the abject not with feminine desire but as the position psychologically and culturally ascribed to women through their association with maternity. From this perspective, the biological separation of the child from the mother's womb is the template for the constitution of the subject and of the social and symbolic order out of the undifferentiated abject: Kristeva implies that the discursive position of femininity as subordinate is due to the tension between becoming a subject and being "of woman born."

In the Freudian, Lacanian/feminist and Kristevan perspectives, then, subjectivity develops through separation and differentiation from, and repudiation and repression of, embeddedness in the maternal surround, whether this separation is conceived of as a single, oedipal moment or as a series of movements over time. Disgust is associated with this repression and helps maintain it as a defense against regression to undifferentiation. Enthrallment describes the desire and fear of the ever-beckoning lure of repressed undifferentiation, imagined retrospectively as femininity and primitivity. Judith Butler, bringing together Lacan and Kristeva with Foucault, gives a more dynamic account of subjectivity as in continuous production through the repeated performance of the exclusionary norms that govern it, also arguing that exclusion and repression are the foundational moves necessary to the institution of subjectivity.[90]

But a subjectivity (psychoanalytically conceived of as) emerging through separation and exclusion always produces an excluded remainder—the primitive/maternal as the matrix of undifferentiated being—that becomes identified with actual gendered and raced others who are held to be both psychologically and socially inferior. Lacanian, Kristeva and object relations perspectives all posit subjectivity as founded through separations, exclusions and repressions, which in turn presuppose an initial stage of infancy in which the infant cannot distinguish between self and other, between self and surround: they all posit a period of undifferentiated immersion in the natural and maternal relationship from which the subject must separate. To this we may juxtapose Freud's contention that the historical/evolutionary emergence of individual subjectivity was effected by separation from sub-mergence in the social ties of primary identification and enthrallment that held primitive communities together, constituting a "group psychology" in which members lacked individuality, i.e. they were undifferentiated from one another. In both cases, what is separated from or excluded becomes repressed so the modern subject can emerge; yet what has been excluded continues to threaten the subject through a potential regression to primitive/ maternal undifferentiation. Theories that see the subject as formed through separation and exclusion require the prior hypothesis of this pre-existing undifferentiation, which is identified with the maternal in a developmental register, and with the primitive in an evolutionary register. Development is then conceived in terms of the distance effected by separation from, and repudiation of, a relationship of undifferentiation with mother/nature/prim-itivity, through the mediation of the father/civilizing law. Particularly in the Lacanian-derived accounts, repudiation is figured as *the* crucial operation necessary to the attainment of cultural legibility; it is figured as inevitable, universal and ahistoric. As Butler writes, from this perspective it seems

> that there is no possibility of speaking, of taking a position in language outside of differentiating moves, not only through a differentiation from the maternal which is said to install a speaker in language for the first time, but [through] further differentiations among speakers positioned within kinship.[91]

The laws of language and subjectivity appear to be part of an unavoidable prison of gender and racial asymmetry: if one tries to escape the repudia-tion of the primitive/maternal, one refuses the possibility of speaking, of being heard, of becoming a subject at all.

However, it is possible—and necessary—to see these laws themselves as historically and culturally located. As Ashis Nandy reminds us, in Europe it was only since around the seventeenth century that

> the hyper-masculine over-socialized aspects of European personality had been gradually supplanting the cultural traits which had become identified with femininity, childhood, and later on, "primitivism." As

> part of a peasant cosmology, these traits had been valued aspects of a culture not wedded to achievement and productivity. Now they had to be rejected as alien to mainstream European civilization and projected on to . . . the new cultures European civilization encountered.[92]

In other words, the processes of separation from and exclusion of the maternal/primitive underwrite the formation of a culturally and historically specific form of subjectivity. The subjectivity that emerges from the exclusion of the maternal/primitive allows us to speak, but allows us to speak only one language: the language of a colonizing modernity. To take up one's place in this language is to take up the rules of representability demanded by the grand narratives of modernity, themselves predicated on the abjection of the primitive and the feminine. The subaltern cannot speak because the subaltern—the primitive—is that which had to be seen as excluded from a full humanity for the modern world to come into being.

Recently various resources have emerged that allow us to propose an alternative to the psychoanalytic figuration of subjectivity as predicated on an abjected and excluded maternal/primitive. Both the evolutionary and developmental implications of such representations of subjectivity have come under question, as have the ideas of an originary state of undifferentiation or a prediscursive past that would precede such constitutive exclusions. Anthropological studies from the middle of this century on have discredited the assumption of a fixed, historical sequence of cultural development moving from psychological undifferentiation toward an ever greater differentiation; and they have discredited the "archaic illusion" that sustained the Haeckelian identity between this purported evolutionary schema and its ontogenetic counterpart. Postcolonial critic Homi Bhabha has pointed out how "the impossible desire for a pure, undifferentiated origin" (i.e. the maternal/ primitive) has been implicated in "'official knowledges' of colonialism."[93]

On the ontogenetic side, American infancy research has challenged the idea that the earliest infantile experiences are exclusively those of merged undifferentiation with the mother. The work of Daniel Stern, Beatrice Beebe, Joseph Jaffe and Frank L. Lachmann, among others, has demonstrated that infants are never actually in a state of complete symbiosis with their mothers but rather, from birth on, are sensitive to movements and changes in their parents' expression. They are capable of distinguishing themselves from their environment, alternating "an absorption in internal rhythms" with an interest in externality. They engage with their primary parental figures in ongoing preverbal communication and mutual regulation of such things as sleep, wake and feeding cycles from the outset.[94] Across the board, the earliest psychological state can no longer be assumed to be a state of undifferentiated oneness with mother/nature.

In her analysis of gender and domination in *The Bonds of Love*, Jessica Benjamin has taken up the work of Stern, Beebe et al together with that of the British psychoanalyst D.W. Winnicott to offer an alternative account of the inauguration of subjectivity in which recognition plays as salient a role as separation. Once undifferentiation loses its status as the privileged condition of origins and the capacity for differentiation is seen to coexist with undifferentiation from the very beginning, the defining act inaugurating subjectivity can no longer be figured exclusively as a progressive separation from oneness. Instead, the development of subjectivity also becomes a question of "how we connect to and recognize others."[95] Benjamin builds on the work of Winnicott, who proposed an alternative (or perhaps an addition) to Lacan's understanding of the mirror stage. Rather than through the distorted image of a coherent self seen in a mirror, Winnicott suggests that it is the loving gaze ("mirroring") of the parent through which the child gains a sense of subjectivity. We first discover ourselves not in a mirror (to which, one must imagine, not all infants have access), but in the communicative eyes of the loved ones who have brought us into this world.

It is the parents' gaze, and later on its trace or remembrance, that endows us with confidence in our sense of subjecthood. This loving gaze endows the child with the confidence to play in the presence, and eventually in the absence, of the parents. For Winnicott, play is neither exclusively subjective (an intrapsychic fantasy) nor exclusively objective (an external reality), but takes place in a transitional zone in between the two. It is only through this kind of creative play, says Winnicott, undirected and unconstrained yet supported by benign parental presence, that "the individual discovers the self."[96] In other words, Winnicott propounded the notion that it is *within* the context of dependence on our earliest parental relationships, rather than through separation from them, that a sense of subjectivity is able to develop. From this perspective, meaning does not rupture the fabric of being and displace it forever, relegating being to the site of irreducibly lost and therefore "primitive" origins, no longer accessible in the present. Rather, meaning emerges from and lives in a dynamic relationship *with* being. Thus subjectivity need not be understood as resulting solely from the separation from and repression of bonds with earliest others but can be thought of as elaborated *in relation* to these others. As Michael Eigen, also drawing on the British school of object relations, writes, "There is no reason to suppose that our sense of separateness and connectedness do not arise together and make each other possible."[97]

Benjamin echoes Winnicott's view on the role of the parental gaze, contending that the earliest desire is for recognition by the other, and that this recognition is what confirms a sense of independent subjectivity. Since an independent subjectivity is dependent on the recognition conferred by another, it is the desire for recognition that makes us susceptible to interpellation into familial and social domains. According to Benjamin and Winnicott, the recognition necessary for the confirmation of subjectivity still requires a form of repudiation of the other. But, critically, this other must not remain repudiated: the other must survive repudiation to come to be real to the infant.[98] Winnicott discussed the crucial role of this psychic survival in his essay, "The Use of an Object and Relating through Identifications,"[99] where he described the role played by aggression in the emergence of the infant's recognition of reality. The infant expresses innate aggression through fantasies of the destroying the parent. (We can see here Winnicott's modification, via Melanie Klein, of the Freudian concept of oedipal rage.) When the parental other can be seen to remain alive and unharmed in spite of these fantasies, the infant is able to recognize the other as truly existing in the outer world and not merely as an inner object of fantasy. That the parental object survives this fantasied destruction confirms her or his reality "outside the area of the subject's omnipotent control."[100] And only a "real" object, who exists outside of fantasy, can confer the gaze and the recognition that confirms subjectivity.

Benjamin emphasizes the crucial suggestion that to survive in this way, the one who confers a sense of subjectivity through recognition must herself be an independent center of subjectivity, perceived by the infant as objectively real. Only someone who is seen to be an active and acting subject in the world is capable of surviving the infant's destructive energies and therefore of appearing real enough to offer effective recognition. "Only someone who fully achieves subjectivity can survive destruction and permit full differentiation."[101] The mother cannot merely be a sea of undifferentiation to confer the necessary recognition, but an independent entity in her own right. The earliest relationship is thus not a sea of undifferentiated consciousness, but the scene of dynamic interchanges characterized by both recognition *and* destruction or repudiation. And thus the maternal/primitive—and the actual beings associated with these terms—rather than being exclusively separated from and repudiated as the constituent exclusions of subjectivity, are seen to remain active and competent co-inhabitants of the world.

For Benjamin, domination by and subordination to parental and other figures are caused by inevitable failures in the ongoing mutuality of recognition that gives rise to and sustains subjectivity. She argues that when the desire for recognition is thwarted, it devolves into the polarized desires for domination of or submission to the other. If the parents are unable, in the infant's view, to survive the infant's rage, they are not effectively able to provide the recognition on which subjectivity can be founded. Then the difference *within* the primary relationship cannot be recognized, and the desire for recognition collapses into a submission to parental enthrallment (the desire to be dominated, in Freud's terms) or into a parental repudiation (the desire to dominate). When the differences within the primary relationship cannot be recognized, the child splits feelings of dependency and independence, either desiring to assimilate the other completely, i.e. domination; or desiring the other's recognition at any cost, i.e. submission. Difference splits along the axis of independence/dependency, which become distorted into domination and subordination; and at the oedipal stage, according to Benjamin, each of these are projected onto different genders. Femininity, via motherhood, comes to represent dependence and merger; masculinity, via the father, comes to be seen as the avatar of the separateness necessary for independence. Domination replaces recognition as the result of the "inability to sustain the tension of paradox" with which difference and recognition present us. Domination and submission are the denial, rather than the necessary entailment, of difference.

The paternal authority that undergirds Freud's notions both of primitivity and its oedipal resolution is itself seen by Benjamin as a defense against the fear of the dangerous immersion in the abjection-threatening maternal relationship. Freud indirectly acknowledged this when he likened the pre-oedipal arena to "the Minoan-Mycenaean civilization behind that of Greece" and associated both with the "dread of being killed (devoured?) by the mother."[102] In other words, behind the oedipal truce lurks the dread of the pre-oedipal mother. In traditional psychoanalytic perspectives, the father intervenes in the "natural" dyad of mother and child as the "cultural" representative of society, saving the child from dangerous immersion in maternal undifferentiation and leading the child into the world of language and culture. As Benjamin suggests, this classical understanding of the oedipus complex resolves the question of sexual difference that inaugurated it by repudiating the position of dependency on the mother and replacing it with submission toward the father. The civilizing, oedipal solution to the paternal domination and filial submission of primitivity itself has been attained through a transformation of a feared primitive/maternal domination into a disdained primitive/feminine submission, and thus continues to reproduce rather than solve the problem of domination.

Benjamin's model suggests that rather than sexual difference per se, it is difference itself that poses the fundamental question of identity, that provides the first testing-ground of aggression and that can grant the recognition that confirms subjectivity. It is the breakdown of the recognition of difference that results in the rigid binaries that organize the multiple tensions of dependency and independence along hierarchically ordered axes of gender and racial difference. The breakdown of recognition—a breakdown that always takes place to some degree, since difference always exceeds our capacity fully to encounter and represent it—enlists the reigning cultural vocabulary and social arrangements in its service. The available cultural codes concerning the foundational relationships of kinship, exogamy and endogamy, gender and race, (over)determine the forms of binarism into which the contradictions of otherness will separate. Difference splits into dependency and independence, subordination and domination; dependency and subordination become seen as an abject submission to the maternal and primitive; and submission to the maternal and primitive is repudiated in the desire for a subjectivity that will, omnipotently, be sufficient unto itself.

Benjamin replaces the traditional psychoanalytic narrative that progresses from originary maternal merger to a subjectivity based on separations from the maternal, with a narrative that proceeds from mutual recognition to the breakdown of recognition. However, the developmental assumption itself must be questioned here (the question of the temporal framework of psychoanalysis in which its developmental accounts are embedded will be addressed more fully in Chapter 4). Even though this narrative favors recognition rather than repression of the early and the excluded, a developmental model always posits a scenario of beginnings or origins which is necessarily imagined retrospectively from the apex of its scale, in comparison with which beginnings are necessarily immature, inferior and incomplete. But recognition and repudiation, rather than sequential moments along a developmental line, are both continuously available possibilities. The relationship of mutual recognition that Benjamin places at the beginning of her developmental narrative, like the intergenerational truce between domination and submission that Freud placed at the end of a complex evolution/development, are both possible at all times, as are their rupture or breakdown. Neither separation nor repudiation nor the possibility of mutual recognition should be exclusively identified with beginnings or endings, phylogenetic or ontogenetic.

A similar position is arrived at by Charles Shepherdson in his considerations of the relation of psychoanalysis to questions of nature and culture.[103] Shepherdson reads Lacan and Kristeva within the context of a broadly represented French psychoanalytic feminism engaged in the clinical domain. He argues that the intent of psychoanalysis, contrary to its reception in so many places, is to offer neither an essentialist *nor* a social-constructivist notion of gender but to refuse the opposition of nature and culture altogether. He demonstrates that our readings of Freud, Lacan and Kristeva need not—indeed, should not—reinforce this opposition with all that it implies. Rather, the body, its drives and anatomy—in short, human biological nature—is always inscribed within cultural orders of representation. Its meanings for us are always mediated by the relationships through which we come to know ourselves, relationships with others who are themselves subjects, hence representatives of the cultural order into which they induct us. The relationship with the mother is never a "natural dyad," in the sense of a relationship between two people outside the cultural order. Thus neither the maternal nor the "primitive nature" that the maternal represents exist outside, or prior to, the symbolizing cultural order.

Shepherdson arrives at his conclusions through his readings of various post-Lacanian French feminists; here I focus on his discussion of Kristeva's use of the categories of the symbolic and the semiotic. Kristeva's *semiotic* designates a presymbolic yet signifying mode of the body and its drives that expresses itself in the rhythmic pulsations of poetry and music. Her use of the term *symbolic*, on the other hand, designates the arena where subjectivity fully arises—both as agency and as subjection to the codes of culture, expressed in linear narrative and lawful rationality, and associated with the father, the phallus and the patriarchal imperative. In a not uncommon reception of Kristeva's work, the semiotic and the symbolic are understood as developmentally ordered and linked to gender in a way corresponding to the domains of the pre-oedipal and the oedipal. The semiotic, like the pre-oedipal, is taken as a pre-cultural phase governed by the relationship with the mother; in the symbolic/oedipal stage, the infant becomes subject to the codes and prohibitions that make culture possible via the mediation of the father's intervention in the mother/child relation.

Shepherdson challenges the characterization of Kristeva's categories of the semiotic and the symbolic as developmentally indexed to maternal and paternal domains, respectively; by implication, he resists the conception of subjectivity as arising through successive separations from the abjected maternal/primitive surround which I have described earlier as intrinsic to her discussion of the abject. Rather, the semiotic and the symbolic are "mutually constitutive and equiprimordial."[104] According to this reading the maternal does not exist outside, or prior to, the symbolizing cultural order because the maternal is itself a symbolizing rather than a presymbolic domain. The mother's desire is directed both toward the child and elsewhere. This "elsewhere" of her desire creates the critical lack or absence within the child that opens up the possibility of symbolic representation. Thus the paternal function Lacan writes about does not refer, textual appearances to the contrary, to an actual father, parent or cultural figure but rather simply represents the localization of the mother's desire as elsewhere than the child.

Shepherdson's conception of the maternal domain as itself symbolic rather than presymbolic corresponds in important ways to Benjamin's conception of the parental other as an independent center of subjectivity. Both agree it is the infant's perception of the mother's reality beyond the mother–child relationship that acts as the guarantor of the foundation of a full-fledged subjectivity. For Benjamin, this reality is established through the mother's ability to survive the child's rage and fantasies of destruction, which in turn allows her to offer to the infant the recognition that founds subjectivity. For Shepherdson, the mother's reality beyond the parent/child dyad is represented by the symbolic localization of her desire as "elsewhere" than the child. The absence of an "elsewhere" within the maternal domain itself corresponds to the failure of recognition of the mother as cultural agent of which Benjamin writes. "Without this symbolic point of reference . . . the child will offer itself up as the object, in a sacrificial effort to fill the lack in the Other."[105] Such a sacrificial effort would place the child in the position of submission to the Other, while placing the Other in the position of the one whose need becomes determinative of the experience of the subject: the position of domination.

Although the language of primary mothers and secondary or absence-inducing paternal functions lingers on, these works point to the possibility of a psychoanalytic elucidation of subjectivity that need not remain hostage to the patriarchal and heteronormative structure of the nuclear family, since both loosen the connections between mothers as providing recognition or desire, on the one hand, and fathers as representing the absence thereof, on the other. If, as Benjamin contends, there is no undifferentiated merger out of which a separate subject emerges, and if, as Shepherdson contends, the semiotic and the symbolic are "mutually equiprimordial," then there is no site of primitive/maternal origins temporally prior to our current, lived historical time. Conceptions of the enthralled and enthralling maternal/feminine/primitive are revealed to be retrospectively constructed fantasies of archaism, arising out of the failure to recognize the primary parents as subjects of the cultural/symbolic order at the same time as they participate in the parent/child dyad. If subjectivity emerges from a state of undifferentiation through a succession of repudiating separations, eventuating in a differentiated but stable, independent and centered self, then any destabilization and decenteredness appear as *effects* of being pushed off-center somewhere later on down the line. But if differentiation and undifferentiation, the semiotic and the symbolic, are seen as equiprimordial, then stability and destabilization, centeredness and decenteredness, recognition and repudiation, all describe competing, conflicting, oscillating possibilities of a multicentered subjectivity.

Although it may be argued that any position of personal and cultural effectiveness requires the development or cultivation of some stable location of agency, psychoanalysis—even in its most positivistic readings—has always argued for the acknowledgment of, and the capacity to tolerate, those elements whose repudiation has contributed to the constitution of subjectivity. By invoking the topos of the unconscious, Freud demonstrated how potentially threatening and destabilizing elements are repressed for a particular center of subjectivity to be achieved; by developing the therapy of psychoanalysis, he pointed to the need to recuperate those very elements and to bring them back into the orbit of awareness. To envisage recognition along with repudiation as moments in the instantiation of subjectivity points to possible postcolonial conceptualizations of subjectivity where maternal/primitive differences on the psychological and social registers can exist together with, rather than having to be excluded from, a subject in relation to others.

Freud discussed the inability to recognize difference not only in terms of separation and repression but also in terms of the fetish—something whose presence masks difference while representing it in another form.[106] The fetish defends against the uncanny, which in the final instance, for Freud, was a horror of the female genitals; the sign, for the male psyche, of sexual difference. Freud believed that, under favorable conditions, the apprehension of sexual difference would eventuate in the dissolution of the oedipus complex in the male psyche. The persistence of the fetish, however, represented a pathological response to the anxiety of sexual difference, a response that denies its own cause. The fetish represents the fantasy of a phallic mother, a seemingly sexually undifferentiated mother; it comes into being at the moment that the mother's lack is noticed, yet must be denied. The fetish represents the presence of what was never there, a material embodiment to defend against recognition of the mother's sexual difference. Unable to apprehend the traumatizing reality of difference, the fetishist creates a substitution that disavows difference by displacing it onto an innocuous alternative. The fetish masks the difference it signifies, bestowing the illusion of having difference under control.

The fetish is a displacement which distorts and denies difference so the illusion of sameness can be maintained. From this perspective, we could call femininity itself a conceptual rather than a material fetish formation: a concept of women that displaces their existence as different, differentiated and symbolizing subjects, onto an innocuous "femininity," conceived of as developmentally and culturally inferior. It is interesting in this regard to revisit Joan Rivière's 1929 account of "Womanliness as a Masquerade." Expressing herself in the depressingly misogynistic terms of her time ("the exhibition in public of [her patient's] intellectual proficiency . . . signified an exhibition of herself in possession of the father's penis, having castrated him," etc.), Rivière described femininity in terms of women who are

> excellent wives and mothers, capable housewives; they maintain social life and assist culture; they have no lack of feminine interests, e.g. in their personal appearance, and when called upon they can still find time to play the part of devoted and disinterested mother-substitutes among a wide circle of relatives and friends,[107]

but she then went on to make the radical assertion that this femininity or womanliness was nothing but a masquerade. Her definition of femininity as "a mask, behind which man suspects some hidden danger"[108] echoes Freud's definition of a fetish as hiding the danger of sexual difference, and supports the suggestion of femininity itself as a conceptual fetish: a mask of subservient and appeasing behavior meant to cover over the hidden danger of difference. Femininity is a conceptual mask which itself serves to fetishize—render excessive and misplaced homage to—relations of domination and subordination that result from the denial of difference.

But sexual difference is not the only difference whose terror lies at the heart of the constitution of the subject of psychoanalysis. Psychoanalysis is overtly concerned with sexual difference but it is built on an equally foundational configuration of racial difference. Classical psychoanalysis constitutes its subject through its fantasy of women *and* of the "primitive" as "already castrated." As the stereotype of femininity functions as a fetish to substitute for the recognition of sexual difference, the stereotype of the primitive provides a substitute for the recognition of racial difference. When the unconscious is cast as prior, differences within the psyche that do not conform to the normative figuration of subjectivity are soldered together with stereotypes of racial alterity to create the fetish of the primitive as the repudiated past. The stability of the subjectivity constituted in this way depends on the disavowal, rather than the recognition, of difference. Primitivity is a conceptual fetish that functions to hide the combined fears of its overdetermined origins, a conceptual mask that fetishizes relations of domination and subordination in response to the anxiety of racial alterity.

Notes

1 Freud, *Group Psychology and the Analysis of the Ego*, SE 18:69–143.
2 Gustave LeBon, *The Crowd: A Study of the Popular Mind* (London: Unwin, 1910).
3 So-called by Edward Said, *Orientalism* (New York: Random House, 1979), 207. For more on LeBon, see Hannaford, *Race: The History of an Idea in the West*, 337–40.
4 Rieff, *Freud: The Mind of the Moralist*, 250.
5 LeBon, *The Crowd*, 16. LeBon's use of the term *communism* does not point to an economic theory of evolutionary development but to a stage in the "modification in the ideas of the peoples," 13.
6 Arendt, *Origins of Totalitarianism*, 107.
7 See Dennis Klein, *Jewish Origins of the Psychoanalytic Movement* (Chicago, IL: University of Chicago Press, 1985), for a discussion of anti-Semitism in Freud's Vienna, 55; for examples of Freud's use of the term *mob*, 83;

also Yosef Hayim Yerushalmi, *Freud's Moses: Judaism Terminable and Interminable* (New Haven, CT: Yale University Press, 1991), 54, quoting a letter of Freud's to Jacob Meitlis: "The broad masses are anti-Semitic here as everywhere." The relationship between psychoanalytic primitivity and the anti-Semitic conditions of Freud's time will be examined in greater detail in Chapter 4.

8 Arendt, *Origins of Totalitarianism*, 325.
9 Freud, *Group Psychology*, SE 18:117.
10 LeBon, paraphrased by Freud in *Group Psychology*, SE 18:74.
11 LeBon, quoted in ibid., 77.
12 Freud, *Group Psychology*, SE 18:77, 80, 79.
13 William McDougall, *The Group Mind* (Cambridge: Cambridge University Press, 1920), 45; quoted in ibid., 85.
14 Freud, *Group Psychology*, SE 18:78–80.
15 Wilfred Trotter, *The Herd Instinct in Peace and War* (London: Unwin, 1916).
16 Since the psychology of groups is, for Freud, the same as the psychology of so-called primitive communities, I will refer to the group and/or "primitive" community as "the primitive group."
17 John L. and Jean Comaroff, "On Personhood: An Anthropological Perspective from Africa," American Bar Foundation Working Paper #9903 (Chicago, IL: American Bar Foundation, 1999), 1, 17–18.
18 Albert Memmi, *The Colonizer and the Colonized* (New York: Orion, 1965 [1957]), 85.
19 For LeBon, *see The Crowd*, 30–1, 32, 36, 40; for Robertson Smith, see Beidelman, *W. Robertson Smith*, 39, 40; and for McLennan, see Stocking, *Victorian Anthropology*, 167–8, 201–2. This presumption of lack of individuality among primitive peoples was the basis of the theory of primitive promiscuity (lack of individuality leads to lack of individualized relationships), developed by McLennan and taken up by Engels in his influential history of marriage and the family. But as Stocking points out, McLennan's proposition was supported by nothing more than "a single ethnographic footnote . . . . In the absence of any ethnographic evidence for a primitive state of general promiscuity, a mélange of ethnocentrically evaluated departures from the Victorian cultural norm served as proof of its possibility" (*Victorian Anthropology*, 202). Other writers characterized the "lower" races in a more Hobbesian manner, i.e. by an excess, rather than a lack, of individualistic concern. Tylor, for instance, held that the lower cultures possessed a greater selfishness than their evolutionary betters, and Spencer held that self-preservation was replaced by sympathy toward others as one rose up the evolutionary scale. For Tylor, see Stocking, *Victorian Anthropology*, 223–4, and for Spencer, 131, 222ff.
20 Freud, *Group Psychology*, SE 18:78–9.
21 Ibid., 127.
22 Freud, *The Ego and the Id*, SE 19:29.
23 Stocking, *Victorian Anthropology*, 227. See also Chapter 1 of this book, 45–46.

24 Freud, "Thoughts for the Times on War and Death," *SE* 14:282 (my emphasis).
25 Freud, *The Ego and the Id*, *SE* 19:29, 48.
26 Diana Fuss, *Identification Papers* (New York: Routledge, 1995), 34.
27 Freud, *The Ego and the Id*, *SE* 19:31.
28 Freud, *Group Psychology*, *SE* 18:105; *The Ego and the Id*, *SE* 19:48.
29 Freud, *Introductory Lectures*, Lecture 21, *SE* 16:337.
30 Freud, *Group Psychology*, *SE* 18:114.
31 Freud, *The Ego and the Id*, *SE* 19:31.
32 Ibid., 19:314. While Arendt draws a strong distinction between "the mob" as "the residue of all classes" who criminally aspire to exercise power outside the foundations of political representation, and "the masses" as those squeezed out of civic standing and juridical protection by virtue of no longer being recognized as members of their nation's race, she sees a lack of political representation and mediation as the one quality characterizing them both. See her *Origins of Totalitarianism*, chaps. 4, 5, 9–11; quote at 107.
33 Although numerous writers on slavery have invoked Hegel's master-slave dialectic, it has generally been taken as a metaphor for a speculative history of the development of consciousness. In her recent work, however, Susan Buck-Morss contends that Hegel developed this conception out of his knowledge of the Haitian slave revolution that began in 1791 and culminated in the establishment of an independent Haiti in 1804. Susan Buck-Morss, *Hegel, Haiti, and Universal History* (Pittsburgh, PA: University of Pittsburgh Press, 2009).
34 Freud, "The Moses of Michaelangelo," *SE* 13:233.
35 Freud, *Civilization and Its Discontents*, *SE* 21:131.
36 Ibid., 21:124.
37 Freud, *Group Psychology*, *SE* 18:78–9, my emphasis.
38 Ibid., 124, 125.
39 Freud, *Phylogenetic Fantasy*, 17; *New Introductory Lectures*, *SE* 20:86–7; and *An Outline of Psychoanalysis*, *SE* 23:190, n. 1.
40 Gayle Rubin, "The Traffic in Women: Notes on the 'Political Economy' of Sex," in Rayna R. Reiter, ed., *Toward an Anthropology of Women* (New York: Monthly Review Press, 1975), 157–210. See also Luce Irigaray, "Women on the Market," in Luce Irigary, *This Sex Which Is Not One*, trans. Catherine Porter (Ithaca, NY: Cornell University Press, 1985), 170–91; and, of course, Lévi-Strauss, *The Elementary Structures of Kinship*.
41 Jean Walton, *Fair Sex, Savage Dreams: Race, Psychoanalysis, Sexual Difference* (Durham, NC: Duke University Press, 2001), 10–11; Butler, *Bodies That Matter*, 18, 181, 182.
42 Rubin, "The Traffic in Women," 192.
43 Daniel Boyarin has also arrived at this conclusion via a somewhat different route in "What Does a Jew Want," in *The Psychoanalysis of Race*, ed. Christopher Lane (New York: Columbia University Press, 1998), 211–40. The Lacanian argument concerning the phallus is said to depend on a notion of masculinity as that which, in patriarchal society, represents what

is desired although never actually attained: the male wishes, but actually fails, to have the phallus. Whether Lacanian theory consistently supports this deconstructed notion of the phallus, or actually reinforces the supremacy of masculinity through its enlistment of the male sexual organ as its master signifier, is a complex and much-debated issue. See, for instance, Judith Butler, "The Lesbian Phallus," in her *Bodies That Matter*, 57–92.

44 See, as an example, the frontispiece by Jan van der Straet of Michel de Certeau's *The Writing of History*, trans. Tom Conley (New York: Columbia University Press, 1988); and de Certeau's consideration of it (xxvff.; 232ff.). Ashis Nandy writes about "the homology between sexual and political dominance which Western colonialism invariably used," in Nandy, *The Intimate Enemy*, 4.

45 Nancy Leys Stepan, "Race and Gender: The Role of Analogy in Science," in David Theo Goldberg, ed., *Anatomy of Racism* (Minneapolis, MN: University of Minnesota Press, 1990), 38–57.

46 Freud, *The Ego and the Id*, SE 19:31.

47 Freud, *Civilization and Its Discontents*, SE 2.1:106 n. 3.

48 "On ne naît pas femme: on le devient." Simone de Beauvoir, "Enfance," from *Le Deuxième Sexe*, Tome II, *L'Expérience vécue* (Paris: Éditions Gallimard, 1976 [1949]), 15–16.

49 Freud, "Female Sexuality," SE 21:230.

50 Freud, *Three Essays on the Theory of Sexuality*, SE 7:148.

51 Freud, *New Introductory Lectures*, Lecture 33, SE 22:21; "Female Sexuality," SE 21:238.

52 Freud, "Analysis Terminable and Interminable," SE 23:250.

53 Freud, "Genital Organization of the Libido," SE 19:145.

54 Simone de Beauvoir, *The Second Sex*, trans. H.M. Parshley (New York: Vintage, 1989 [1952]), 50.

55 Judith Butler's groundbreaking formulation reconceives the nature/culture dichotomy by proposing that it is the repeated performance of sexual norms that itself produces sexual identities in culturally legible form. See her *Bodies That Matter* and *Gender Trouble*.

56 Freud, *Totem and Taboo*, SE 13:102–3, n. 1.

57 Freud, "The Unconscious," SE 14:189.

58 Adam Philips, *Terrors and Experts* (Cambridge, MA: Harvard University Press, 1995), 88.

59 Freud, "On Narcissism," SE 14:89, and "Femininity," Lecture 33, *New Introductory Lectures on Psychoanalysis*, SE 22:164.

60 For example, Freud, "The Dynamics of Transference," SE 12:106: "a high degree of [ambivalence] is certainly a special peculiarity of neurotic people."

61 Freud, "Female Sexuality," SE 21:235; *Totem and Taboo*, SE 13:66.

62 Freud, "Female Sexuality," SE 21:239.

63 Ibid., 230.

64 Freud, *Civilization and Its Discontents*, SE 21:66–7.

65 A comment of Freud's from the *Minutes of the Vienna Psychoanalytic Society*, Vol. 2: 1908–10 (1967), ed. Herman Nunberg and Ernst Federn, 432, quoted in Judith Van Herik, *Freud on Femininity and Faith*, (Berkeley, CA: University of California Press, 1982), 23.

66 Gayatri Spivak, "Can the Subaltern Speak?" in Patrick Williams and Laura Chrisman, eds., *Colonial Discourse and Post-Colonial Theory* (New York: Columbia University Press, 1994), 66–111. The term "subaltern," initially derived from the political theorist Antonio Gramsci (who in turn borrowed it from its military designation for a subordinate officer), refers to populations who subsist outside of the power structure that governs them and therefore have no voice in how they are governed. The word gained its currency as the term of art for colonized peoples largely through the group of South Asian historians called the Subaltern Studies Group, dedicated to the history of colonized peoples rather than of the elites who colonized and governed them. See Ranajit Guha and Gayatri Chakravorty Spivak, *Selected Subaltern Studies* (Oxford: Oxford University Press, 1988).

67 Freud, "Femininity," *New Introductory Lectures on Psychoanalysis*, *SE* 22:145.

68 Freud, "Some Psychological Consequences of the Anatomical Distinction Between the Sexes," *SE* 19:254; Freud, "Analysis Terminable and Interminable," *SE* 23:251–2.

69 Freud, "The Dissolution of the Oedipus Complex," *SE* 19:178 (my emphasis).

70 Freud, "Some Psychological Consequences," *SE* 19:258; "Femininity," *New Introductory Lectures on Psychoanalysis*, *SE* 22:134.

71 Freud was apparently incapable of imagining that women might have a non-pathological aversion to unsolicited and coercive sex. As he wrote about the teenager Dora, importuned for sex by her father's friend as a pawn in exchange for her father's liaison with his friend's wife: "I should without question consider a person hysterical in whom an occasion for sexual excitement elicited feelings that were preponderantly or exclusively unpleasurable." Freud, "Fragment of an Analysis of a Case of Hysteria," *SE* 7:28.

72 Quoted in Hanke, *Aristotle and the American Indians*, 47. For more context about Sepúlveda, see Chapter 1, 28–30.

73 Charles W. Mills, *The Racial Contract* (Ithaca, NY: Cornell University Press, 1997), 70–1, 94.

74 Alexander Thomas and Samuel Sillen, *Racism and Psychiatry* (New York: Brunner/Mazel, 1972), 63 and passim. This book as a whole demonstrates the role of the American psychiatric—including psychoanalytic—profession in providing scientific legitimacy for common racist attitudes.

75 Octave Mannoni, *Prospero and Caliban: The Psychology of Colonization*, trans. Pamela Powesland (Ann Arbor, MI: University of Michigan Press, 1990 [1950]). The quote is from Maurice Bloch's introduction, ix. See Frantz Fanon's famous, emphatic denunciation of Mannoni in *Black Skin, White Masks*, chap. 4, 83–108.

76 My thanks to Victoria Olwell for informing me of this law.

77 Seshadri-Crooks, "The Primitive as Analyst," 195.

78 Spivak, "Can the Subaltern Speak?"; Butler, *Bodies That Matter*, 117.

79 Butler, *Bodies That Matter*, 2.

80 Freud, *Group Psychology*, SE 18:113 (*GW* 13:125). Freud also invoked this term in his article on "The Taboo of Virginity" to describe the extreme sexual attachment that is "far more frequent and more intense in women" in a discussion of "the sexual life of primitive people" (*SE* 11:201). He also speaks of it in relation to the transference in "Dynamics of Transference" (*SE* 12:101).

81 Leela Gandhi, *Postcolonial Theory: A Critical Introduction* (New York: Columbia University Press, 1998), in a gloss on Albert Memmi, 11.

82 Nandy, *The Intimate Enemy*, 7.

83 Fanon, *Black Skin, White Masks* (New York: Grove Press, 1967; Paris: Éditions de Seuil, 1952).

84 Fanon, *Black Skin, White Masks*, 98.

85 James Baldwin, *The Fire Next Time* (New York: Vintage International, 1993 [1962]), 80.

86 Jacques Lacan, "The Mirror Stage," in *Écrits: A Selection*, trans. Alan Sheridan (New York: Norton, 1977), 1–7; Bruce Fink, *The Lacanian Subject: Between Language and Jouissance* (Princeton, NJ: Princeton University Press, 1995); Jane Gallop, *The Daughter's Seduction: Feminism and Psychoanalysis* (Ithaca, NY: Cornell University Press, 1982).

87 Lynne Layton, in her *Who's That Girl? Who's That Boy? Clinical Practice Meets Postmodern Gender Theory* (Northvale, NJ: Jason Aronson, 1998), bridges the differences between these two schools, suggesting that "'the subject' is both . . . sub-jected to the multiple and contradictory discourses of culture . . . and a multiple and contradictory being whose negotiation of early relationships will shape the meanings that these discourses take on." 26.

88 Julia Kristeva, *Powers of Horror: An Essay on Abjection*, trans. Leon S. Roudiez (New York: Columbia University Press, 1982).

89 Ibid., 94.

90 Butler, *Bodies That Matter*.

91 Judith Butler, in Gayle Rubin and Judith Butler, "Sexual Traffic" (interview), *differences: A Journal of Feminist Cultural Studies* 6, nos. 2–3 (1994): 69.

92 Nandy, *The Intimate Enemy*, 37.

93 Homi Bhabha, "The Other Question: Stereotype, Discrimination and the Discourse of Colonialism," in Bhabha, *The Location of Culture*, 66–84, quote at 81.

94 Daniel Stern, *The Interpersonal World of the Child: A View from Psychoanalysis and Developmental Psychology* (New York: Basic Books, 1985); Beatrice Beebe, Ph.D., Frank M. Lachmann, Ph.D. and Joseph Jaffe, M.D., "Mother-Infant Interaction Structures and Presymbolic Self- and Object Representations," in *Psychoanalytic Dialogues* 7, no. 2 (1997):

133–82. See Jessica Benjamin's discussion of these views in *The Bonds of Love: Psychoanalysis, Feminism, and the Problem of Domination* (New York: Pantheon, 1988), chap. 1, "The First Bond." Quote is from Benjamin, *Bonds of Love*, 49.

95 Ibid., 18.

96 D.W. Winnicott, "Playing: The Search for the Self," in his *Playing and Reality* (London: Routledge, 1989 [1971]).

97 Michael Eigen, "Dual Union or Undifferentiation?" in Michael Eigen, *The Electric Tightrope*, ed. Adam Phillips, (Northvale, NJ: Jason Aronson, 1993), 157–76; quote at 171.

98 Jessica Benjamin, "The Shadow of the Other Subject: Intersubjectivity and Feminist Theory," in Benjamin, *Shadow of the Other* (New York: Routledge, 1998), 79–108.

99 D.W. Winnicott, "The Use of an Object and Relating through Identifications," in his *Playing and Reality*, 86–94.

100 Ibid., 89.

101 Benjamin, *Bonds of Love*, 82.

102 Freud, "Female Sexuality," *SE* 21:226–7.

103 Charles Shepherdson, *Vital Signs: Nature, Culture, Psychoanalysis* (New York: Routledge, 2000).

104 Shepherdson, *Vital Signs*, 208.

105 Ibid., 127.

106 See Freud's essay on "Splitting of the Ego in the Process of Defense," *SE* 23:275–8; and "Fetishism," *SE* 21:152–8.

107 Joan Rivière, "Womanliness as a Masquerade," *International Journal of Psychoanalysis* 10 (1929); reproduced in Victor Burgin, James Donald and Cora Kaplan, eds., *Formations of Fantasy* (London: Methuen, 1986), 36–44.

108 Ibid., 43.

Chapter 4

Historicizing consciousness

Time, history and religion

The challenge of postcolonial theory to psychoanalysis

Time, timelessness and history

While Chapter 3 drew out the logic of primitivity and race internal to psycho-analysis, this chapter places these psychoanalytic issues in conversation with recent postcolonial critiques of anthropology. Postcolonial theorists have criticized the ways that anthropological writings, not only of the nineteenth but also of the twentieth century, have negotiated cultural differences by conceiving them as temporal differences: the west's cultural others, if no longer conceived of as lower on the evolutionary scale, have nonetheless continued to be cast as less advanced in their social and economic development, and as inhabiting a timeless realm altogether outside of history. Postcolonial theorists have countered this view by *historicizing* anthropology: by recognizing and recording the histories of the subjects of western anthropology who had previously been represented (by western anthropologists) as having no history at all; by recognizing that non-western peoples are not vestiges of a prehistoric past but live in our shared present and act on our shared global stage; and by questioning the universal applicability of western standards of technological development.

The placing of non-western peoples in the past through their inscription as *primitive* continues to live on in psychoanalysis not only through its perpetuation of categories imported from evolutionary anthropology but also through its conception of its relationship to the past, a relationship expressed in its aims to prevail over, by coming to terms with, the compulsions of the primitive past. This chapter begins with a discussion of the development of the anthropological and postcolonial critique and then directs this critique toward psychoanalysis. This, in turn, leads to a consideration of Freud's works on religion, together with some psychoanalytic responses to these works, since religion constitutes the crystallization of the authority of the past from which it was Freud's project to emancipate us. Finally, placing Freud's work in the religious and racial context in which he wrote allows us to see how his responses to the crises of his time and place translated into the historicizing strategies of psychoanalysis itself.

Anthropological assumptions and preoccupations have changed considerably since Freud's appropriation of the work of Tylor and Frazer. The twentieth century has seen several reorientations in the field of anthropology, from the evolutionary concerns and armchair methodologies of the first generation of anthropologists to the functionalist and structuralist paradigms that dominated the mid-twentieth century and, more recently, to the more critical and reflexive forms of anthropology whose re-examinations of the foundational assumptions not only of anthropology but of the European humanist tradition of which it is a part have opened onto the field of postcolonial studies. At the beginning of the twentieth century the pioneering anthropologist Franz Boas played an important role in discrediting the evolutionary comparative method on which early anthropology had been based. Boas, through his comparison of the cranial measurements of immigrants to the US with their offspring, demonstrated that even physical characteristics such as cranial measurements, no less than cultural phenomena, were environmentally influenced rather than evidence of a particular evolutionary stage. Bronislaw Malinowski, another leading anthropologist of the first half of the twentieth century, styled the ethnographer as a participant-observer and, along with Boas and his many students (Margaret Mead and Ruth Benedict among them), established the importance and centrality of intensive fieldwork for the development of anthropological knowledge. The ethnographer would now live "in the field" and learn the language of the people being studied, and then return to the metropolitan (European or American) university to write about them. Malinowski helped establish the influential theoretical paradigm of structural functionalism that would frame this next theoretical stage, conceptualizing the institutions and customs of so-called primitive societies in terms of how they facilitated the functioning of the community rather than in terms of where they might fit in a universal scheme of human evolution. Non-western societies were no longer to be studied as links in a grand evolutionary chain but as communities unto themselves and in their own terms.[1]

With these changes, anthropology was presumed to have shed the embarrassments of its evolutionary past, but by the 1970s the discipline began to reconsider the far-reaching implications of its colonial beginnings and to track the evolutionary assumptions still embedded in its ongoing epistemological strategies. Rather than having done away with the evolutionary conception of time, functional anthropology was recognized as having merely compressed the evolutionary scale into one timeless moment: the "ethnographic present," the present tense in which accounts of non-western peoples were commonly given. As Margaret Mead began her famous book *Coming of Age in Samoa*: "The life of the day begins at dawn . . . Babies cry, a few short wails before sleepy mothers give them the breast."[2] This use of the present tense to describe distant cultures gave the impression that such people existed in an unchanging, eternal present, untouched by the dynamics of history. This timeless, eternal present was not only outside of, but prior to, history: the ethnographic present was used to describe a *primitive* or *prehistoric* society (Mead calls the subjects of her study "primitive groups"). The pre-lapsarian past of the Noble Savage, the pre-Christian past of "the ancients" and the missing-link-between-the-animals-and-us past of evolutionary theory were now joined by the timeless, prehistoric present of functionalism. Rather than doing away with the evolutionary relationship between the west and the rest, functionalism reconfigured it: from the bottom of the evolutionary ladder, anthropology moved its subject to a position outside history altogether.[3] History was the privileged precinct of the modern west, while timelessness became a distancing framework for its racialized Other. As James Baldwin wrote, in a testament to the enduring nature of this outlook: "History is a hymn to White people, and all us others have been *discovered*—by White people, who may or may not (they suppose) permit us to enter history."[4]

A remark of Freud's in *The Interpretation of Dreams* illuminates what may be the motive underlying the use of the ethnographic present: "The present tense is the one in which wishes are represented as fulfilled."[5] The ethnographic present perpetuated the western wish to construe non-white and/or non-western peoples as continuing to live in the past, unmodified by the impact of historical reality or of internal conflict, and serving as a convenient background against which to measure the progress of modernity.

Different ways of living in time were represented as an absence of the awareness of the passage of time and thus as an absence of history and of historical consciousness. So-called primitive peoples were represented as re-enacting their timeless rituals and reproducing their social structures, but never altering or transforming them in response to internal strife or external pressures. The most intrusively historical acts—conquest and colonization, which had made the subjects of anthropological inquiry accessible to ethnographic scrutiny in the first place—were omitted from these descriptions of primitive cultures.[6]

This temporalizing of the perceived difference between colonizer and colonized—the former an agent of history, the latter a passive object out-side history—has functioned as a constitutive operation of the western concept of modernity, which has typically defined itself in terms of a past it has overcome. Timelessness became the characterization of its cardinal others: the primitive (its racial other), religion (its ideological other) and the feminine (its gendered other). For example, in his refutation of Jean-Paul Sartre's privileging of historical knowledge as the purview of the mod-ern to which primitive peoples had not yet acceded, Claude Lévi-Strauss attempted to demonstrate the parity between "modern" and "savage" thought by portraying the latter as intellectual, conceptual and scientific.[7] Lévi-Strauss's structuralism characterized the mythic thought of so-called primitive peoples as a "science of the concrete" that established codes of meaning through the paired oppositions of various totemic species of plants and animals. These paired oppositions combined to form structures of meaning to which any and all elements of life could be assimilated and by which they could be understood, and they represented the templates according to which kinship relations were arranged. Primitive societies were "synchronic" and "cold" because they assimilated the movements of history into these timeless, logical structures, whereas modern societ-ies were "diachronic" and "hot," propelled forward by the ever-changing movements of history. Although Lévi-Strauss noted that "primitive people are always at a safe distance from the Scylla and Charybdis of diachrony and synchrony,"[8] in general he identified primitive peoples with the first term in his binary oppositions: with synchrony rather than diachrony, with timelessness rather than history, and as "cold" rather than "hot." While modern peoples were seen as assimilating synchronic, repetitious elements of experience into a diachronic framework, creating history as they went along, so-called primitive peoples were seen as incorporating the diachrony of historical events into synchronous systems of meaning, continuously reproducing unchanging social and cultural systems. Not only did Lévi-Strauss's portrayal of gender relations render women as passive objects of exchange (as discussed in Chapter 3); his portrayal of non-western peoples, intended to pose a challenge to the disparagement of the primitive mind as lacking in rationality, ended up by identifying primitivity with unchanging structures of mind embedded in an eternal, timeless present. In this way he reproduced the exclusion of so-called primitive peoples from history.

The characterization of so-called primitive peoples as living in a timeless world was also given support by the work of the foremost mid-twentieth-century scholar of religions, Mircea Eliade. For Eliade, the religious consciousness participates in practices that periodically repeat the paradigmatic acts of the gods believed to have founded the world. Through this participation, the religious consciousness is re-immersed in the mythical time of beginnings which is thus made present once again. In this way, the religious consciousness "abolishes time"; that is, it "does not record time's irreversibility," does not "transfor[m] it into conscious-ness."[9] Through periodic ritual reenactments, the time of origins eternally returns: time, rather than merely passing, is regenerated, and, with it, so is the religious subject, who is born again. The ritual repetition of arche-typal events undergirds a cyclical notion of time as an eternal return of the primordial. From this perspective, time is not irreversible and diachronic, since an eternal present recurrently becomes available as "a succession of eternities."[10] Time as irreversible duration, says Eliade, time as progress, as a linear unfolding of unrepeatable events that leads inexorably toward death, is the hallmark of the secular consciousness. From this religious perspective, history is a form of suffering (or, as James Joyce had it, a nightmare) that can only be made meaningful through its assimilation to transhistorical archetypal structures of meaning.

Eliade based his convictions regarding the religious consciousness on his studies of the "archaic ontology" of "primitive" cultures and repre-sented the theological distinction between religious timelessness and secular historicity as the distinction between primitive societies and the contemporary western culture of modernity.[11] His work was intended as a challenge to the modern, secular disdain for religious experience. While revalorizing religion for an increasingly secular west, he nonetheless reproduced the binarism that aligned timelessness with primitivity, and historical consciousness with the modern, western subject.

Femininity, too, has been mapped as a modality of time(lessness): as Simone de Beauvoir was the first to point out in *The Second Sex*, women have always been identified with timeless *being* as opposed to the historical *becoming* of men in a gendered division of existential labor. In her essay on "Women's Time," Julia Kristeva provides a description of western characterizations of women that sounds remarkably like a transposition into gendered terms of Eliade's religious categories. The feminine, she tells us, has been identified with repetition, based on the biological rhythms of women's lives, and with eternity, based on "a massive presence of a monumental temporality, without cleavage or escape." The archetypal figure of the eternal feminine in western thought has identified female subjectivity, as Eliade identified primitive religiosity, with repetition and eternity; and Kristeva points to the identification of male subjectivity, as Eliade identified secular consciousness, with "linear temporality, time as project, teleology, linear and prospective unfolding."[12] The juxtaposition of Kristeva's description with Eliade's shows how the qualities that define the feminine are none other than those that define the primitive; and those qualities that define modernity are syntonic with modalities held to be masculine. This commonality between female and primitive subjectivities consists in their capacity to signify the (re)creation of life: Eliade's religious/primitive consciousness participates in rites that re-enact the creation of the universe, whereas women, in childbirth, participate in the re-creation of life itself. Life as nature—female and primitive—is contrasted to culture as history, the domain of the masculine.

As gender theory has gone on to challenge the validity of these static characterizations of gender/sexual difference, by the 1970s anthropology began to reconsider its characterizations of cultural/racial difference as timeless primitivity and to re-examine the colonialist context in which such characterizations had been forged. Anthropology's colonial origins and early theorizing came under fire in addition to its post-evolutionary epistemological strategies. Despite its mid-century rejection of cultural evolutionism, despite its participant observation and its efforts at linguistically accurate and respectful cultural translation, the primal scene of colonial conquest continued to haunt the discipline, whose practitioners sought to atone for its scandal and yet helped perpetuate its legacy by repressing it completely from their representations of so-called primitive life. As French anthropologist Georges Condimas was to write, anthropologists "could do all the research they wanted on the condition that they took no account of the global system in which the people they were studying were involved."[13] In 1950 Michel Leiris sounded the first alarm of what was to become a groundswell of anthropological concern over the relationship of anthropology to the projects of western imperialism. In 1957 Albert Memmi published his *Colonizer and the Colonized*, in which he described the timelessness of the primitive not as an ethnographic fact but as a "serious blow" imposed by the colonizers; an effect, in other words, of colonization itself.[14]

Not only the evolutionary speculations of the first generation of anthropologists but also the strategies of functionalism and structuralism of the next generation began to be recognized as having been implicated in the politics of western imperial expansion. The close connections between anthropology and the exercise of colonial power came under scrutiny, as anthropologists began to reckon with the history of their discipline's dependence on colonial regimes for access to "the field," together with the commodification of anthropological expertise to provide more effective colonial administration. Malinowski, for instance, had proposed that anthropology be "mobilized for the task of assisting colonial control."[15] Functionalist and structuralist attempts to understand so-called primitive societies and cultures in terms of how their constitutive elements facilitated the functioning of the community became increasingly suspect for being artificially represented as divorced from their larger economic and political contexts. The epistemological assumptions and strategies of anthropology were increasingly understood to be connected with its colonial and neo-colonial conditions of possibility. Anthropological discourse was criticized for having helped perpetuate, through its construction of ethnographic knowledge, the political forces against which its practitioners often imagined themselves to be ranged. The very premises of the doing of anthropology came to be questioned; as James Clifford asked, "Whose reality? Whose new world?"[16]

In 1978 Edward Said published his landmark *Orientalism*, which examined the ways in which western constructions of knowledge about "the east" served colonial and imperialist ends. This work—now a foundational text of postcolonial theory—demonstrated how representations found in oriental studies (and, by implication, in other anthropological studies of the non-west) had been generated to satisfy the west's need for a mysterious, passive other against which to delineate itself. Said marked out the underlying ideological structures of western knowledge concerning "the orient," demonstrating how these supposedly impartial forms of knowledge supported the European colonial enterprise. This work set the stage for the field of postcolonial studies which would continue to examine western epistemological assumptions undergirding the ethnographies and social histories of previously subjugated—now called subaltern[17]—populations. Said's critique reverberated across several disciplines, compelling a sharper examination of the relationship between the history of colonialism and modern western forms of power and knowledge.

An incisive critique of western anthropological representations of racial/ cultural others was leveled by Johannes Fabian in his *Time and the Other*.[18] Fabian argued that the "allachronizing" of non-western societies—that is, positioning them in "another time" (outside of history)—was the epistemological dimension of the power relations between those peoples who practice anthropology and those on whom anthropology has traditionally been practiced. Any actual intercultural communication would require both parties to recognize that they inhabit, simultaneously, the very same historical time. Yet most anthropological discourse had been predicated on the distance maintained by representing the anthropological other as in the past, through what Fabian terms "the denial of coevalness," the denial of living in and at the same time; a denial whose "key term," he points out, is "the primitive."[19] Fabian's assessment implicated British and American schools of anthropology; but his most thorough critique was of the structuralism of Lévi-Strauss, which he accused of eliding time from the picture altogether by placing the historical, diachronic west "up the temporal slope" from the totemic, synchronic non-west, thereby reproducing a continuing asymmetrical relationship between the two. Here again "primitive" populations stood outside time, neither having their own diachronous local history nor participating in the global theater of world history. Scholars of religion have pursued a similar critique of Eliade's identification of time-lessness with the primitive: Paul Ricoeur has pointed out "the multiplicity of temporal patterns opened up by comparative religion,"[20] and Jonathan Z. Smith has directly challenged Eliade's categories of the "archaic" and the "modern," cautioning that "we must be careful to . . . resist imposing even an implicit evolutionary scheme" on religious materials.[21]

Thus long after the demise of nineteenth-century evolutionary anthropology, non-western societies continued to be represented as non-contemporaries of our modern time, both in the sense of standing outside of and prior to the theater of global history and in not having their own particular, local histories. But as the anthropologists John and Jean Comaroff have pointed out, "people everywhere turn out to have had history all along":[22] rather than some societies living with a sense of time and others without, each pattern of social arrangements produces its own particular forms of temporality; and all of us exist simultaneously, at the same time and within the same world. By the end of the twentieth century it had become an anthropological commonplace to recognize that all peoples have both a local history and a role in the global history we all share. As the Comaroffs commented, "the image of 'traditional' societies, of 'cold' cultures caught up in endless cycles of social and/or semantic reproduction, is pure fiction."[23]

That the primitive seemed to stand outside time altogether turns out to have been an artifact of colonial and anthropological relationships. What appear to be differences in various cultural experiences of time actually have to do with differences in social and cultural conditions. As Dipesh Chakrabarty suggests, "different kinds of 'social'" imply "different orders of temporality as well."[24] The participation of the anthropological observer in a society under study generally remains partial (a ready exit always at hand), and the anthropologist's position remains outside the particular social arrangements under consideration. These social arrangements seem timeless because the observer is not fully subject to their connections, constraints and obligations, which are what mold a succession of events into a particular form of temporality. The purported difference between timelessness and historical temporality masks differences between various social arrangements and the subjectivities they sponsor, all of which coexist in the same coeval, contemporary time. It also masks the difference between the modern world and those who were subjugated to help create that modern world.

Postcolonial anthropology has developed various critical strategies to respond to these problems. Chief among them has been the deconstruction of the anthropological conceptualizations that placed non-western subjects in a timeless primitivity in the first place. This has resulted in dismantling the distinction between history (the story of the west) and anthropology (the stories of the west's others) by creating historicized ethnographies that represent the ethnographic subject within, rather than outside, both local and global historical forces. It has given us social histories of non-western peoples as told from their own perspectives, moving the locus of the historical gaze from Europe to those whose histories are being recorded, and revising many assumptions in the process. For example, the Subaltern Studies Group has begun to rewrite South Asian histories from the perspectives of subaltern, or previously colonized, peasant populations, rather than from the perspective of their colonizers or their elite classes. As another example, in his work on the colonization of Latin America, Walter Mignolo has challenged the widespread conception of history as composed exclusively of written narratives that are "accomplished by the agency of letters," a conception which strengthens the connection between people without letters and people without history and which provides yet another reason to portray non-alphabetic peoples as without—and thus outside of—history.[25]

Mignolo demonstrates the linkages between the conceptions of civilization, alphabetic literacy and history with which Spanish colonizers encountered and represented the indigenous inhabitants of the lands they occupied. Alphabetic writing, along with clothing, was seen by the colonizers as a sign of the civility that distinguished European, Christian civilization from these newly colonized peoples. In the sixteenth century, as now, alphabetic writing has been held to have replaced the less adequate acts and procedures through which non-alphabetic cultures constitute(d) their cultural self-understanding and communication: writing has often been understood as *the* evolutionary event that distinguished civilization from barbarity,[26] and therefore as the reason for the political triumph of European forces over the peoples of the new world.[27]

Challenging this conception of alphabetic literacy, Mignolo describes the sophisticated alternative ways in which the various peoples of Latin America recorded and transmitted the archives that constituted their self-knowledge and history. He suggests that alphabetic writing, rather than the necessary condition for the recording of history, is a "regional conceptualization" particular to the European west. He offers the conception of "cultural semiosis" as a replacement for thinking in terms of the presence or absence of alphabetic literacy as the *sine qua non* of record keeping, historical consciousness and civilization. Cultural semiosis would embrace the variety of media through which different cultures construct, keep track of and transmit their conceptions of themselves, their pasts and their interactions. Among his examples are the oral discourses of the Mexica as well as the knotted textiles by which the Inca recorded in great detail elements of their traditions and political governance (drawing the connection, evidenced to this day in much of Latin America, between "textile" and "text"). This concept of cultural semiosis implies a view of communication as performative ("cultural objects as results of activities responding to human needs") rather than representational ("artifacts by means of which the mirror of nature is extended and the nature of the world is captured in visible signs"). It negates the evolutionary schema that sees alphabetic literacy as having superseded oral and other communicative acts by understanding alphabetic representations themselves as performative communicative acts.[28]

In these and other ways, postcolonial scholars have increasingly begun to revisit the anthropological and historical archives to demonstrate how the colonizing ambitions of the west helped shape the categories of anthropological and historical knowledge concerning the colonized, to create a space in which those histories can be reimagined and rewritten, and thus to recover the voices of the colonized. They aim to disrupt the monopoly of the European gaze on the history and life-worlds of its colonized others, and to imagine postcolonial encounters that refuse the frameworks that have sustained this monopoly. The postcolonial project extends beyond the bounds of anthropology, rejecting as it does the divide between the disciplines of anthropology and history, which is itself a symptom of the very set of problems postcolonial theory seeks to address. Written from a confluence of a number of contemporary critical perspectives, particularly Marxism and poststructuralism, its applications span both the humanities and the social sciences.[29] The move from anthropology to postcolonial studies has been a move from a western anthropological discourse speaking about the non-west, to an examination of this discourse from non-western perspectives in order to excavate the distortions built into its terms; and finally, to representations of non-western histories and politics from previously excluded vantage points. Postcolonial scholars, together with critical race theorists, lay bare the construction of modernity and of modern western civilization not only as a development internal to the west but as one whose achievements have been built on materials, labor and profits wrung from Europe's various colonizing enterprises, from the Atlantic slave trade to the mines and rubber plantations of Africa and South America.[30] Gayatri Spivak and others have contended that the previously colonized peoples of the Third World (and the still colonized peoples of the fourth world, the "indigenous" nations living within modern nation states) have contributed not only to the material wealth of the west but also to its "possibility of cultural self-representation," through their crucial role as the raw material out of which universal theories of culture, society and the mind have been constructed (think of the work done by words such as *taboo, mana, fetish*).[31] Edward Said further argues that reckoning with the previously disavowed role of colonialism in the construction of modernity was the crucial, if seldom acknowledged, issue in making evident the failure of grand narratives which is said to have ushered in our era of postmodernity.[32]

But questions of representation and its authorization remain. Not only anthropology but the canons of western history and political philosophy, too, have represented non-western and non-white populations as politically immature, as pre-political, as not yet ready to assume independently the political institutions developed to safeguard liberty and equality in the west.[33] Historicization, the remedy for the othering of the non-west as timeless, turns out to reproduce a timeline similar to that of evolutionary thought, conceptualizing the non-west no longer biologically, but now historically less developed and therefore consigned to the "waiting room of history," in Dipesh Chakrabarty's felicitous phrase: still in need of "development" and the tutelage of the west.[34] "Primitive societies" have become the "third world," the un- or underdeveloped countries whose development is measured by comparison with the industrial and technological standards of the first world. It seems that the historicizing remedies of postcolonial histories and anthropologies—subaltern histories, historicized ethnographies—may still harbor some of these temporal biases. Postcolonial scholars continue to struggle with the paradox that, for subaltern histories to register on the screen of the globalized consciousness of the west, they have had to be written in the cultural codes intelligible to this consciousness; yet these codes have been founded on the exclusion of the very subjects in question.

Time and "the past" in psychoanalysis

These critiques compel us to examine the overall meaning and function of time, history and historicization in psychoanalysis, since psychoanalysis, like anthropology, placed the development of the modern subject within an evolutionary conception of the development of the human race. Freud's theory of the emergence of the modern subject from the thralldom of group psychology through the explosive impact of the primal crime was articulated within an evolutionary timeline; and his rendering of the unconscious as the timeless and primitive abode of "aboriginal populations" mirrored functional anthropology's representation of primitive peoples as outside and prior to history. Although by the end of the twentieth century the category of the primitive in anthropology has become, in James Clifford's words, "unravel[led] for good,"[35] it carries on as an assumedly unproblematic, "scientific" category, uncritiqued and unreconstructed in its psychoanalytic usage, where its ethnographic meanings have been written into the premises of psychoanalytic theory.

As one of the "grand narratives" of modernity, psychoanalysis has at the heart of its project a negotiation of the subject's relationship with the past, and thus the temporal orientation of psychoanalysis is not simply one element among many, but is its central organizing framework. The psychoanalytic gaze is fixed on the past; in a metaphor Freud was fond of evoking, the work of psychoanalysis is an archaeology of the soul: "The psychoanalyst, like the archaeologist in his excavations, must uncover layer after layer of the patient's psyche, before coming to the deepest, most valuable treasures."[36] This preoccupation with the past can be seen in the three distinct yet interdependent domains of Freud's work: the clinical, the metapsychological and the sociohistorical/cultural.

Beginning with the early assertion that his neurotic patients suffered from reminiscences, Freud sought the meaning of the anomalous present— of neurotic symptoms, slips of the tongue, dreams—in the repressed past of the subject. Dreams, neurotic symptoms, perversions and the irrational behavior of the mob were all cast as regressions to a psychological and evolutionary past that endured in the unconscious. Freud proposed a therapeutic protocol in which, through free association, the repressed memories of the past would be recovered so that the grip of prior developmental/ evolutionary stages, to which the patient had regressed through neurosis, would be loosened.

This therapeutic protocol was based on metapsychological models that also drew on evolutionary assumptions. In the unconscious was the sedimentation of the cultural legacy of humankind, understood as its evolutionary/biological inheritance, where the oedipus complex lived on as the recapitulation of the originary desire that had led to the primal crime. The oedipus complex and its eventual formation of the superego were the recapitulation of the primordial foundations of culture, so that not only the stages of development but the very agencies of the mind as Freud conceived of them were precipitates of inherited experience, legacies of a primordial (and raced) past. Repressed in the unconscious, the evolutionary past of the human race became the timeless psychological structure of the psychoanalytic subject: the unconscious, like the primitive of functionalist anthropology, lived in a present outside time, a present situated, eternally, in the prehistoric, precultural past.

Freud's metapsychological and clinical claims had their roots in the soil of the sociocultural preoccupations of psychoanalysis, where we find the basis for this foundational concern with the past. For Freud, only individuals freed from the authority of tradition, as embodied in the leader of a primitive group, could "dare to think" (in Kant's Enlightenment precept) and act autonomously, according to their own desires. Only by emerging from the group bonds of premodern, traditional communities and from the thralldom of external authority could the individual assume rational and libidinal autonomy. This emergence of the individual effected, in Freud's words, "a separation of our mental existence into a coherent ego and into an unconscious and repressed portion which is left outside it."[37] The "unconscious and repressed portion which is left outside it" became *the past*, or *the primitive*: the emergence of the subject as the individual of modernity was concurrent with the creation of its unconscious alterity as the past—what it excluded to constitute itself. The past in all its forms was the otherness against which psychoanalysis defined itself, and came to play a double role in the historicizing mission of psychoanalysis: the emergence of the psychoanalytic subject was understood to take place through the repudiation of the past ("the repressed portion" of our mental existence), while the recovery of this repudiated past (from its slumber as the eternal, timeless present of the unconscious) was central to the therapeutic project of psychoanalysis.

In its clinical, metapsychological and sociohistorical dimensions, then, psychoanalysis has been structured around a central concern with the past, often signified by the trope of primitivity whose referents were both developmental and evolutionary, both temporal and racial. Thus an understanding of the role of the primitive past, and of the temporalizing and historicizing strategies of psychoanalysis, is essential to an understanding of how psychoanalysis is positioned with regard to postcolonial critique of placing otherness in the past. Religion was the privileged example of the past within psychoanalysis: it was the topic through which Freud overtly argued for a psychoanalysis that would go beyond the religious and racial divisions that characterized the traditions of the past. Thus the postcolonial challenge to anthropology's representation of cultural difference suggests an examination of Freud's conceptualization of the past as found in his critique of religion.

Religion and the past in psychoanalysis: ideologies of enthrallment

When a group of black and white feminists convened for discussions on feminist psychoanalysis and African-American representations of female subjectivity leading to the publication of *Female Subjects in Black and White*, they discovered that the greatest of their "stubborn incompatibilities" was "the racially charged division between spiritual and psychoanalytic discourses."[38] That their attempt to deploy psychoanalysis to mediate racial and gender difference found its deepest fissures in the topic of religion was no accident: they had stumbled upon the psychoanalytic correlation between non-whiteness and religion, both of which were understood as belonging to an evolutionary past that the modern psychoanalytic subject was presumed to have overcome.

Within psychoanalysis, religions represent the ideologies of the superseded past. Freud used the term *religion* as a more or less universal category but referred mainly to the two religions among which he lived, Judaism and Christianity. His usage, however, masked the differences between these two traditions, overlooking the Christian assumptions embedded in the term *religion*, and, with the exception of *Moses and Monotheism*, ignoring the fraught historical relationship between Judaism and Christianity by subsuming them under a single category. Even within these limits, Freud seems to have concerned himself mainly with popular conceptions of religion, largely ignoring any textual, theological or rabbinic discussions of Christianity or Judaism. All this points to the polemical role the topic of religion played in his writings. For Freud, religion was "the enemy" against which the arsenal of psychoanalytic insight needed to be trained.[39]

Recent postmodern interventions have begun to elaborate significant countercurrents in Freud's thought that open up intriguing post-traditional dimensions to his writings on religion, and the growing literature on Freud's relationship to Judaism demonstrates an increased interest in the ways Freud's pronouncements on religion complicate his biographers' insistence on his identity as a "godless Jew."[40] In this examination of Freud's theories of religion, however, I am concerned with how he constructed the idea of "religion" as archaic and as characteristic of the primitivity of the mind.

As outlined in Chapter 2, in *Totem and Taboo* Freud plotted the universal development of the psyche along E.B. Tylor's evolutionary scale of the development of cultures: animism and religion were the narcissistic worldviews proper to savage and barbarian cultures. By casting animism and religion as expressions of the narcissistic stage of development, Freud psychologized them as primitive modes of perception and belief appropriate to the "darker races." More recently, ethnographies have begun to appear that reconceive so-called animistic beliefs in terms that demonstrate how they may possess a relevance for our contemporary world. Ronald Berndt revises Freud's (and Tylor's) idea of animism in his discussion of Australian aboriginals' view that "the land is a living thing, the source of all life," and Elizabeth Povinelli recasts animism as a recognition—also emergent in contemporary environmental discourse—of the sentience of the land and an empathy with this sentience derived from daily interaction with the land.[41] In psychoanalytic discourse, however, Tylor's nineteenth-century notion of animism continues to hold sway.

In Freud's later broadside written in 1927, *The Future of an Illusion* (whose conclusions are repeated in chapter 35 of the *New Introductory Lectures* [1933]), Freud supplemented his earlier phylogenetic account of religion with a corresponding ontogenetic one, dwelling on the childhood helplessness that recapitulated the earliest evolutionary outlook out of which the first religious ideologies had arisen. Here we read that even contemporary forms of religion bear "a fatal resemblance" to the "mental products of primitive peoples and times."[42] Religious symbolism expresses wishes for protection against the terrifying helplessness of childhood; it also conjures up the memory of the murdered yet longed-for primal father, whose forgiveness would provide consolation and comfort. But transcendent protection, forgiveness and consolation are merely desired illusions; by enlisting belief in them, religions restrict independent thought and perpetuate an infantile attitude toward the world. Like the child who "cannot successfully complete its development to the civilized stage without passing through a phase of neurosis," Freud believed that humanity itself had passed through a stage of religion on its (evolutionary) path to civilization. Contemporary forms of religion were "neurotic relic[s]," regressions to the mental processes of an earlier era which the human race should now outgrow.[43] As Freud put it, religion is like "a childhood neurosis, and I am optimistic enough to suppose that mankind will surmount this neurotic phase."[44]

Because both *Totem and Taboo* and *The Future of an Illusion* emphasized animism and religion as wishful illusions, more recent attempts to revise the psychoanalytic understanding of religion have often relied on an examination and re-evaluation of the concept and role of illusion.[45] But a juxtaposition of Freud's account of primitivity in *Group Psychology* with that found in *Totem and Taboo* yields a different perspective on his assessment of religion. *Totem and Taboo* mapped an ideological trajectory from animism to religion to rationality and science, while *Group Psychology* mapped a political trajectory from embeddedness within group relations in thrall to authority, toward the emergence of the modern subject free from external authority. In both trajectories, the earliest stages are understood as manifestations of an evolutionary primitivity, characterized in *Totem and Taboo* as a belief in animistic illusions, and characterized in *Group Psychology* as a submergence in relations of domination and subjugation. When we join these two trajectories, the primitive illusions of animism and religion emerge as the counterpart to primitive relationships of domination and subordination, while the postreligious scientific spirit is seen as the characteristic of the autonomous, modern individual. Thus the problem of religions for Freud does not inhere only in the limitations they place on personal intellection and experience but also in the oppressive relationships they legislate. Religions provide ideological support for the relationships of domination that define primitivity.

Since notions of the prior are inseparable from notions of domination in Freud's temporal economy of the psyche, "primitive peoples" are bound up in relations of domination, and religion is the ideology that prescribes just such a desire for domination as its desideratum. The primitive is in thrall to the illusions of religion that serve to sustain relational and political bondage. With lighter skin and the civilized ethos that is its prerogative comes the capacity to dissolve the bonds of authority and resist the comforts that religion has provided, to gain instead the ability to confront the world rationally and objectively.

The relationship of Freud's conceptions of religion to those of femininity has been explored by Judith van Herik, who has argued that Freud's notions of femininity occupy the negative pole against which the positive attainments of civilization, conceived of as masculine, can be measured.

Freud identifies instinctual renunciation with the masculine ideals of individual and civilizational progress, while fulfillment is identified with the feminine limitations of regression and dependency.[46] As can now be seen clearly, the fulfillment that van Herik places in opposition to renunciation—the fulfillment afforded by subjection to patriarchal authority—is the defining quality not only of femininity but of primitivity as well. Moreover, the pleasures of this fulfillment are always won at the price of subordination: the epistemology of illusion and the erotics of fulfillment are inescapably bound up with the politics of subordination. Religions are ideologies of enthrallment to authority that legitimate conditions of social bondage from which humankind is, or should be, struggling to free itself. The degree of enthrallment (*Hörigkeit*) with authority is the measure of the relative evolutionary positions of religions. The greater the enthrallment, the greater the primitivity.

With *Civilization and Its Discontents*, Freud introduced his mature theory of the dynamics of civilization, more complex than the straightforward evolutionary trajectories presented earlier. Opening with a discussion of Romain Rolland's plea for the validity of a religious "oceanic feeling," Freud begins *Civilization and Its Discontents* by setting up religion as the foil against which the institution of civilization will be analyzed. The oceanic feeling represents the feeling of the "infant at the breast" who "does not as yet distinguish his ego from the external world." In advocating the beneficial effects of this feeling, religious advocates seek regression, "the restoration of limitless narcissism." Freud reiterates that religion seeks to "intimidat[e] the intelligence . . . forcibly fixing [people] in a state of psychical infantilism . . . and mass delusion." The recapitulatory implications of the argument are evident once again: "We cannot fail to be struck by the similarity between the process of civilization and the libidinal development of the individual."[47]

As the essay progresses, however, the distinction between civilization and religion becomes less securely drawn, and the evolutionary optimism of Freud's earlier works gives way to the famous pessimism of his later years. As Freud anticipated in *Future of an Illusion*, where he conceded religion to be "perhaps the most important item in the inventory of a civilization,"[48] the presence of religion in a culture, however misguided, comes to indicate "a high level of civilization." The evolutionary trajectory is no longer so confidently portrayed: no longer does Freud wish to concur with "the prejudice that civilization . . . is the road to perfection pre-ordained for men." The march of evolution has now become a struggle between Eros and Thanatos waged over the course of history, whose outcome is far from certain.[49]

In *Civilization and Its Discontents* religion is no longer meant merely to console us against the helplessness of infancy and the terrors of nature; it is meant to console us for the strains of the civilizing compact that followed in the wake of the primal crime. Freud's introduction of the death instinct in this essay and his discussion of its manifestation as the aggression within each psyche add another twist to the understanding of the psychodynamics implicated in religion. More than just the internalization of the law of the father, the superego is now the mechanism that binds primary aggression: it renounces the outward expression of hatred by directing it inward to the ego in the form of guilt. Thus every renunciation of instinctual aggression becomes a new source of guilt increasing the strength and severity of the superego. Religions both prescribe these renunciations of aggression and then promise, as a compensation for their guilt-inducing effects, a return to the consolations of earlier, pre-superego (pre-oedipal) stages of development.

Religions are thus the mobilization of a pre-oedipal state in the service of the oedipal requirements of civilization. In *Civilization and Its Discontents*, as in Freud's earlier works, this regression to a pre-oedipal stage is considered neurotic: the evolutionary/developmental clock should not be turned back. To yield to religious longing is to tighten the noose of the superego, thus increasing the need for religious solace once again. As Rieff put it, religion is the symptom of that for which it claims to be the cure.[50]

Religions, then, are not only ideologies meant to keep members of primitive groups or contemporary children—who have not yet developed a superego—in thrall to an external authority. They are also the ideologies meant to keep discontented civilized subjects in thrall to the authority of society and its leaders; they are enforced not only externally but by that intrapsychic "garrison" of civilization, the superego itself. In *Civilization and Its Discontents* the emphasis has shifted from the evolutionary past of humankind to the regressive past of civilized subjectivity; but Freud's recapitulatory convictions continue to keep these two connected. Religion is the reinstatement of primitive thralldom *within* the psyche, yoking internal conscience to cultural imperative. Religion becomes not only infantile and evolutionarily inferior, or a temporary passage from which humanity will someday emerge; religion is now the possibly unavoidable neurotic regression of whole segments of contemporary civilizations, lured into the pleasures of pre-oedipal states as compensation for the burden civilization imposes on them.

Finally, Freud modifies his evaluation of religion again in *Moses and Monotheism* with his psycho-historical account of the development of Judaism and Christianity. Whereas his previous works discussed "religion" as a unitary category, *Moses and Monotheism*, Freud's self-named "histori-cal novel," attends to the comparative specifics of Judaism and Christianity. Written under the darkening shadow of the impending Holocaust, it seeks to uncover the roots of anti-Semitism in the origins of Judaism and Christianity and to explain the origins and endurance of these religious traditions in psychological, rather than theological or sociological, terms. One of the most wildly speculative of his works, it continues to be mined for the rich insights it yields into Freud's sentiments concerning Judaism, which here turn out to be not nearly as negative as those expressed con-cerning religion in general in his previous works. Religions here are seen as historically specific organizing symbolics which express a culture's par-ticular mediation of the ever-reverberating effects of the repressed primal crime. Far from being illusions, "religions are reawakened memories of very ancient, forgotten, highly emotional events of human history."[51]

As van Herik pointed out, Freud valued religious renunciation over religious fulfillment, seeing the former as masculine and characteristic of Judaism and the latter as feminine and characteristic of Christianity. And as Daniel Boyarin has perceptively observed, in this way Freud subverted the centuries-old Christian vilification of Jews and Judaism as carnal and feminine: instead of the standard Christianity view that the Christian spirit is superior to the Jewish law, Freud argues instead that it is Judaism that truly represents the greater spirituality and morality, by virtue of the greater renunciation it requires.[52]

The Mosaic renunciation of the worship of visible idols in favor of a single, invisible God—the establishment of monotheism—was, according to Freud, a triumph of this patriarchal spirituality, confirming the renun-ciatory, masculine and spiritual superiority of Judaism. This renunciation produced the inevitable increase in guilt as described in *Civilization and Its Discontents*. But whereas in *Civilization and Its Discontents* the relation-ship between renunciation and guilt was seen as the plight of civilization and of religion's role within it, here Freud accords it a more positive value: guilt may tighten the hold of the civilizing superego, but it also produces the ever greater ethical heights that contribute to moral progress. Religion as consolatory belief—Christianity—is still regressive; but religion as renunciation that leads to ethical progress—Judaism—makes a valuable progressive contribution.

By the end of Freud's work, then, religion was no longer necessarily antithetical to civilization, although there remained superior and inferior— renunciatory and progressive vs. enthralling and regressive—religions, negotiations of "reawakened memories." The standard of comparison was encoded in raced and gendered terms: masculine renunciation created spiritual and moral advances that contributed to civilization, whereas with religious fulfillment the subject regressed to a pre-oedipal, primitive and feminine compliance with external authority. Judaism was cast as the truly progressive religious force, built on renunciation and able to sustain the tension between monotheism and guilt, whereas Christianity was a return of pagan primitivity ("as though Egypt was taking vengeance once more on the heirs of Akhenaton").[53]

In his earlier works Freud presumed that civilized—and white—peoples had overcome religion and the domination it underwrote; in his middle works he no longer presumed this was the case but continued to hope it would eventually turn out to be so. In this concluding work, the possibility of overcoming the cultural formations called religion receded as religions became seen as inherited histories or transmitted memories, potentially in the service of either regression (enthrallment with domination) or ethical progress (renunciation of domination). Freud's earlier reading of the past as having been overcome by the present was modified over time to include a greater recognition of how the past lives on within us as part of the present. In the words of historian Yosef Yerushalmi, in Freud's latest works "the past not only subjugates; it also nourishes."[54]

Moses and Monotheism was written at the end of Freud's life and published posthumously, and it constitutes an exception to the rest of his work on religion. In the rest of his work, religious beliefs represent the worldview of the primitive past—in both evolutionary and developmental registers—from which psychoanalysis seeks to liberate us, whether they are ideologies that underwrite evolutionarily primitive arrangements of domination or reinstatements of such primitive ideologies within civilized societies intended to compensate for the discontents engendered by civilization. Indeed, in his 1933 summation, the *New Introductory Lectures on Psychoanalysis* (1933), Freud's claim that psychoanalysis shared the *Weltanschauung* of science was constructed in terms of its opposition religion: "religion alone is to be taken seriously as an enemy."[55]

By placing religion in the past, Freud has bequeathed us a psychoanalytic notion of religion inseparable from the many implications of racial, developmental, epistemological and political inferiority associated with its *primitivity*. No wonder, as W.W. Meissner muses, that "psychoanalysts are not comfortable with religion" and that "there is a latent persuasion, not often expressed . . . that religious ideas are inherently neurotic, self-deceptive, and illusive."[56] Such a "latent" outlook is written into the very premises of psychoanalysis.

Responses to Freud on the question of faith

Ever since Freud's time there has developed a wide-ranging literature on the topic of psychoanalysis and religion, both in agreement and disagreement with Freud. Theologians, Jewish and Christian, have made use of psychoanalysis for their religious understandings in spite of Freud's overt stance against religion. Starting with Oscar Pfister, a Protestant minister who was a good friend and staunch supporter of Freud's, several theologians and religious philosophers have managed to assimilate Freud's thought in ways that helped explain and even enlarge their theological beliefs. Using psychoanalytic concepts to enrich their theological outlooks, especially in their pastoral work with their parishioners, Protestant ministers developed the area of pastoral care and counseling, and its younger sibling, clinical pastoral education (the education of hospital chaplains). The renowned theologian Paul Tillich, a major architect of pastoral psychology, saw what Freud called neurosis—including religion as neurosis—as a way of avoiding the full, existential awareness of our radical freedom. Tillich's pastoral psychotherapy owed much to psychoanalysis in how it helped the person confront his anxieties.[57] In a different vein, the Jewish theologian Richard Rubenstein, having lost his faith after the Holocaust, used Freudian insights to deepen his understanding of Jewish aggadah and legend.[58]

Many in the first generation after Freud who wrote on psychoanalysis and religion, both in the United Kingdom and the United States, saw no difficulty in reconciling the aims of these two topics. But as time has gone on, this literature has increased and differentiated; and much of it reflects the contradictions, mentioned above, embedded in the conception of religion used by Freud. On the one hand, there are works on religion and psychoanalysis that treat Freud's arguments as a theological challenge. These writers, often clinicians, discuss Freud's writings on religion predominantly in terms of faith or the object(s) of faith, even if they attempt to bracket the ultimate truth claims of such faith.[59] Predominantly Christian, their questions are motivated by the crisis of faith in an age that has been shaped by, among other forces, the secularizing impulse of psychoanalysis: in the title of a recent book, they want to know why Freud (and psychoanalysis) "reject[ed] God,"[60] and whether and how contemporary revisions of psychoanalysis might allow for an alternative and more positive psychoanalytic understanding of religious experience. Many of these works suggest that it was Freud's scientistic framing of psychoanalysis which did not allow him to appreciate the value of religion and that the revisions of post-Freudian psychoanalysis allow a rapprochement between psychoanalysis and religion that was prevented by Freud's rationalistic and autonomous model of subjectivity.

But "religion" for Freud referred not only to matters of faith: it was also synonymous with "race" when the religion in question was Judaism in Europe in the early decades of the twentieth century. These theologically inclined writers have neglected the relationship between Judaism as religion and Jewishness as race, ethnicity or culture that allowed Freud to remain proudly Jewish while remaining staunchly antagonistic toward religion. The conjunction of meanings of religion, race, culture and nationality that came together in the concept of Judaism meant that, for Freud, religion had as much to do with the psychology of identity as it did with the psychology of faith.[61]

On the other hand, there is an ever-burgeoning literature on the Jewish dimension of Freud's identity, which analyzes Freud's relationship to Judaism in historical, sociological and even literary terms, and inquires into the influence of Judaism and Jewishness on the creation of psychoanalysis despite Freud's claims of scientific neutrality.[62] Predominantly Jewish, they are motivated by the crisis of "a (post)modern Jewish identity."[63] They do not question why Freud did not believe in God, but rather what role his Jewish identity played in the construction of psychoanalysis. Rather than accepting an ineluctable antipathy between psychoanalysis and religion, they have pursued continuities between Judaism and psychoanalysis, demonstrating the extent of Freud's involvement with

Judaism in his education and debating the role of Judaism in the formulation of his ideas. Some have demonstrated the centrality of interpretation in both rabbinic Judaism and psychoanalysis, and have shown how Jewish themes underlie central psychoanalytic concepts. Yet others do indeed analyze a spiritual or theological dimension they see already inscribed within Freud's own writings[64] or they discover resonances between recent developments in relational psychoanalysis and the more mystical dimensions of Jewish thought.[65] From these perspectives, both Freud and psychoanalysis can be seen to have been nourished by Jewish tradition.

With a few exceptions, neither group of writers seems to recognize the concerns of the other. But when each of these groups is read with and against the other, it becomes evident that Freud's concerns about faith are related to, rather than isolated from, his ongoing negotiation of the social, religious and racial context of his relationship to both Judaism and Christianity.

Among the first group who wish to reconcile the insights of psychoanalysis with a theological outlook, Paul Ricoeur's magisterial *Freud and Philosophy* stands out as one of the most eminent. Ricoeur recognized the centrality of the temporalizing impulse in Freud's work, noting that consciousness "unfolds in a direction opposite to timelessness" and that "it is obviously in the critique of religion that this archaeological character of Freudianism culminates."[66] He framed his interpretation of Freud as a debate between psychoanalysis and the phenomenology of religions, since these two represent the opposing horizons of the hermeneutical field between which he sought to mediate. On the one hand, psychoanalysis is a "hermeneutics of suspicion" that seeks to demystify religions as illusions, tracing them back to their human and infantile origins; while on the other, the phenomenology of religion seeks "the manifestation and restoration of a meaning addressed to me in the manner of a message."[67] Psychoanalysis directs the mind backward, to investigate its origins, while religion directs the mind forward, to discover its meaning in its destiny.

Ricoeur mounts a formidable challenge to an exclusively archaeological understanding of the orientation of Freud's work. Anticipating Jonathan Lear's later claim that the infantile roots of religious symbols need not invalidate the meanings that these symbols come to hold for the adult,[68] Ricoeur made the case that symbols are inherently multivalent; that is, their power and saliency arise from their ability to condense in themselves the personal, archaeological meanings out of which they have arisen together with the cultural, kerygmatic meanings toward which they gesture, with neither direction annulling the meaning of its opposite. He complements Freud's perception of religion as a regression to the infantile and the primitive with a Hegelian progressive, teleological element which, he says, resides implicitly within psychoanalysis itself (although he concedes that Freud did not and would not recognize it as such). This element would account for whatever therapeutic success psychoanalysis has as arising not only from an understanding of the past but also from a creative movement forward which emerges out of that understanding. With this progressive element in place, symbols become susceptible to a two-way interpretation, capable of revealing regressive infantile origins and prospective cultural or religious meanings at one and the same time. The fantasies of childhood become the raw material out of which are forged the figures of the spirit, "the projection of our human possibilities on to the area of imagination."[69]

For Ricoeur, the temporal orientation of psychoanalysis is a philosophical and psychological one, not a historical one: he does not address the evolutionary and social correspondences that structure Freud's understanding of the past and of religion. Questions of the subject's relation to history and domination seem to lurk in his conception of psychoanalysis as a negotiation of the relationship between the regressive pull of force (what he calls the energetics of the drives) and the prospective emergence of meaning; he also explicitly remarks that "the true problematic of the ego . . . is expressed basically in the alternative of dominating or being dominated, of being master or slave."[70] And he recognizes in the metapsychology of ego, superego and id the entrance of the forces of history and authority into the dynamics of the psyche itself, writing in sweeping terms of psychoanalysis as a history of the debate between desire and authority. This preserves the political resonances of Freud's concerns with primitivity as a state of consciousness but leaves aside the problems posed by its colonial and evolutionary correlations.

Following Ricoeur's reading of Freud in terms of a dialectic of archaeology and teleology, the anthropologist Gananath Obeyesekere has attempted to recuperate psychoanalysis not only for religious but also for cross-cultural understanding in his ethnographic work in southeast Asia. Unlike Ricoeur, Obeyesekere throws out the metapsychology wholesale, seeing it as an ethnocentric map of the modern west; but he makes significant use of Ricoeur's dialectic to discern a critical difference between (religious) symbol and (pathological) symptom.[71] His articulations of a psychoanalytic dialectic of regression and progression underlying the relationship between symptom and symbol, like Ricoeur's, productively complicate Freud's temporal framework, yet necessarily preserve it. Neither writer addresses the political and racial ramifications of the temporal poles of archê and telos that postcolonial theory has brought to our attention. So the question remains: Can we be free of the evolutionary/historicizing implications embedded within psychoanalysis if its temporal framework is maintained?

Others who have written on the topic of psychoanalysis and religion from a theological perspective have echoed Ricoeur's question: Does religion only repeat, or can it perhaps point beyond, its infantile origins? Many of them have combined clinical and theological concerns to articulate a revised, favorable psychoanalytic view of religion, stressing a framework based on Freud's developmental schema (rather than on Ricoeur's Hegelian dialectic) together with a re-evaluation of the epistemic value of illusion. Their developmental approach in general owes much to recent Anglo-American psychoanalytic perspectives—in particular, D.W. Winnicott's object relations theory and the self psychology of Heinz Kohut—which stress that dependency and object relatedness are ongoing throughout life rather than needs that must be overcome for maturity to ensue. From this perspective, the relegation of religious states to the "infantile" no longer seems so condemnatory, since needs previously seen as exclusively infantile are now understood to continue, non-pathologically, throughout the course of a lifetime.

In addition, these writers renegotiate Freud's damning epithet of religion as "illusory" through Winnicott's notion of transitional space, the relational arena between parent and child in which the first symbolic expressions are said to take place, with its paradoxical interpenetration of the real and the illusory, the given and the created. Because they are located within transitional space, religious representations are seen as neither fully internal nor fully external, but rather as an expression of the way the imagination makes sense of the world in which we find ourselves. We come to know of God through the language of our religious traditions, which have been given to us; yet each generation renews that language with its own experiences and interpretations.

These writers have shifted the focus of their attention from the origins of religion in the primal crime and infantile helplessness to its function in sustaining the stability and vitality of the self.[72] Their reliance on Anglo-American trends in contemporary psychoanalysis has allowed them to cast religious expressions hitherto characterized as regressive, infantile and primitive as integrative factors that undergo progressive reconfigurations through the developmental journey of the individual. From this perspective the capacity for religious experience is seen to develop (or not) pari passu with all the other developments of the life span.

This shift from origin to function suggests that the works of these Anglo-American writers expound what we might call a "functionalist psychoanalysis." This functionalism is closely allied to a therapeutic outlook that aspires to enable the patient to (re)gain the ability to *function* fruitfully in personal and social domains. However, in our context, this poses a critical question. For it is the same move made by the second generation of anthropologists who replaced evolutionary theories based on notions of human origins with functionalist theories concerning the social structures that facilitated the functioning of the community. Where anthropological functionalism emphasized the positive function of social and cultural forms in sustaining the cohesion of the community, psychoanalytic functionalism emphasizes the positive functions of religion in sustaining the cohesion of the self. And in the same way as anthropological functionalism considered societies in their own terms without reference to the conflictual global systems in which they were located, psychoanalytic functionalism considers subjects in their own terms—that is, in terms of their intrapsychic dynamics—without reference to the often contested social and political systems in which they are located.

As we have seen, anthropological functionalism merely reconfigured, rather than resolved, the problems inherent in the socioevolutionary perspective. We may well wonder, then, whether functionalist psychoanalysis follows suit: Does it avoid Freud's evolutionary perspective with the racial implications it entails? And, furthermore, do these approaches to the question of psychoanalysis and religion meet the challenge of Freud's critique of religion as enthrallment to relations of authority and domination?

The developmental approach of these psychoanalytic functionalists seems to avoid the temporal/evolutionary quandary simply by avoiding the question of origins. However, although psychoanalytic functionalism may not hold onto an overt evolutionary agenda, like anthropological functionalism it retains within it a temporal scale expressed in its developmental approach, which retains a primary archaic/infantile/primitive stage.

This developmentalism is understood to express the order of the unfolding of the psyche *within* the context of a contemporary western subjectivity. But can these more recent notions of development and primitivity be divested of the evolutionary and racial context out of which they arose? Does the developmental scale of functionalism order only *intra*cultural difference along the life span, or does it order *inter*cultural/racial difference as well? Does functionalist psychoanalysis, like functionalist anthropology, merely reconfigure rather than avoid the problem of primitivity?

While on the face of it there is nothing to indicate that a developmental scale necessitates a corresponding evolutionary one, the network of such colonial correspondences in Freud's thought and beyond continues to exert a strong pull. What is understood as developmentally "primitive" tends almost automatically to end up being understood as evolutionarily "primitive" as well. An argument in the mid-twentieth-century work *Psychoanalysis and Religious Experience* by W.W. Meissner, which draws largely on object relations for its theoretical framework, demonstrates how this recapitulatory correspondence continues to be reproduced in psychoanalytic thought. After explaining how each stage of the developmental life span has its own appropriate form of religious experience, Meissner suggests that each developmental stage might correspond to one or another of the world's religions. The earlier modalities of individual development would correspond to the "more primitive polytheisms," we are told, whereas the later stages would correspond to "a more advanced form of Christian theological monotheism."[73] Psychological maturity is represented here by the attainment of specifically Christian belief. Freud's antipathy toward religion has indeed been avoided but at the cost of a questionable pairing of psychoanalytic maturity with Christian supersessionism. More important for our purposes here, the evolutionary premises which underwrote Freud's perspective on religion are retained: his hoped-for postreligious scientific rationality has merely been replaced by Christian monotheism as the culmination of development and of evolution, which is here said to have begun with primitive polytheism (the author's name for the religions of the third and fourth worlds). Although most writers in this genre often refrain from making comparative statements such as this, the psychoanalytic approach demonstrating the developmental functions and value of religion, like the anthropological approach demonstrating the functional value of the practices of primitive societies, can too easily reproduce the linkage between development and evolution that Freud bequeathed to psychoanalysis.

How does the psychoanalytic functionalist approach reckon with Freud's critique of religions as ideologies of enthrallment that support relations of authority and domination? Psychoanalytic functionalism has stressed the role played by religion in helping sustain a coherent sense of self over the life span. That religions help sustain internal coherence, that they stave off the anomie that used to be treated in the name of neurosis and is now treated in the name of narcissistic disturbances of the self, is a point Freud readily conceded; but he conceded it as a point that was beside the point. In *Group Psychology and the Analysis of the Ego* he stated clearly that

> even those who do not regret the disappearance of religious illusions
> from the civilized world of today will admit that so long as they were
> in force they offered those who were bound by them the most power-
> ful protection against the danger of neurosis. Nor is it hard to discern
> that all the ties that bind people to mystico-religious or philosophico-
> religious sects and communities are expressions of crooked cures of
> all kinds of neuroses.[74]

The fact that religions perform psychological functions that stabilize the individual may be viewed as part of the problem Freud saw in them. Their very capacity to fulfill psychological needs for meaning and order makes their followers particularly vulnerable to authoritarian programs that make use of religious discourse for their own ends. Freud's concern was not merely with the epistemological folly of the illusions of religion but with the authoritarian relations underwritten by religion. This issue, like the issue of developmental/evolutionary ordering of racial/cultural/religious difference, has not been addressed by the functionalist psychoanalytic approach to religion.

These two theoretical lacunae, in turn, have to do with the neglect of the social and political contexts in which Freud lived and constructed his theories, a neglect evident in the biographical efforts of Meissner and Rizzuto, each of whom have provided a psychoanalytic explanation of the roots of Freud's (too limited) understanding of religion.[75] In these bio-graphical works the burden of Freud's views toward religion is largely seen to rest on his conflicted oedipal relationships within his extended family. The implication is that had his family configuration been less problematic, Freud would have developed a more useful God representa-tion that would have allowed him a more favorable approach to faith and to the topic of religion in general. Although they make some mention of the racist restrictions under which Freud labored, these writers accord little weight to the social and historical situation of European Jews of Freud's generation and to the anti-Semitism that was gathering force by the turn of the century. From this perspective, Freud's famous "Rome neurosis" did not involve his ambivalent ambitions to succeed in a Christian European world that excluded Jews from its institutions, and *Moses and Monotheism* did not grow out of a need to make sense of the intensification of anti-Jewish sentiment in the 1930s; rather, both are ultimately traced to childhood conflicts.

That intergenerational conflicts played a significant role in organizing Freud's affects and ideas about religion need not be in dispute, but to focus on them exclusively omits the crucial recognition that such conflicts were part of a larger struggle of the Jews of Freud's generation to negotiate their relationship to a Christian/Aryan Europe that wished to destroy them for their religious/racial status, however attenuated their relationship to Judaism may have been. Intrapsychic infantile and familial conflicts do not take place independently of social and political forces; on the contrary, they are the emotionally charged vectors through which these forces are conveyed to us as the texture of the world we are constrained to live in. Social structures condition the social and cultural environment and they are internalized through and within interpersonal object relations.[76]

The erasure of social context in these works is part and parcel of psychoanalytic functionalism. Psychoanalytic functionalism divorces its study of the subject, as anthropological functionalism divorced its study of primitive societies, from the larger and conflictual historical and political contexts in which they are formed. Intrapsychic dynamics are privileged over the social and historical contexts in and through which they are constituted.[77] Freud's emphasis on the oedipal as the moment of socialization and enculturation in the context of intergenerational conflict recedes from the horizon, and the conflict between cultural prohibition and individual desire that underpins the entire Freudian outlook fades away. Conflict, oppression, exclusion, discrimination and other forms of social influence and violence are understood as exclusively intrapsychic problems with the nuclear family as their sole sponsor. "Culture" and "religion" come to be seen as neutral or benign resources from which the self derives various sorts of sustenance that enhance its stability. If we turn, however, to the social and historical contexts of Freud's creation of psychoanalysis, the issue of

religious and racial conflict reemerges, both in the crises of his time as well
as in the ways psychoanalytic theory was constructed to meet them.

Primitivity, race and anti-Semitism

In her innovative inquiry into the applicability of psychoanalysis for an
articulation of African-American subjectivity, Hortense Spillers proposes
that "the race matrix was the fundamental interdiction within the enabling
discourse of founding psychoanalytic theory and practice itself." She suggests that this situation arose from the fact that "Freud could not 'see' his
own connection to the 'race'/culture orbit, or could not theorize it, because
the place of their elision marked the vantage point from which he spoke."[78]
But as demonstrated by the second group of writers mentioned above,
those who attend to the relationship between Freud and Judaism, Freud's
construction of psychoanalysis was itself a negotiation of his own position
vis-à-vis "the 'race'/culture orbit": as a Jew, however godless, Freud was
a member of a despised and threatened race at the most heightened period
of European anti-Semitism. Considering the social and historical context
of Freud's creation of psychoanalysis allows us to consider the broader
forces and pressures that contributed to the particular ways he configured
his theories of religion, race and gender. The mapping of the opposition
between primitive and civilized in psychoanalysis bears an intimate relationship to the mapping of Aryan and Jew of Freud's era.

The racist ideology of evolutionary theory was, by the end of the
nineteenth century, as inimical to Jews as it was to non-European others. Hannah Arendt has described European colonialism in Africa as the
"most fertile soil for the flowering of what later was to become the Nazi
elite," and Aimé Césaire and historian Victor Kiernan have characterized
Nazism as the application within Europe of practices hitherto imposed
exclusively on the non-European world.[79] The Jews had long occupied
the role of Europe's internal religious and racial other; Daniel Boyarin
suggests we understand the European Jews as having been an internally
colonized European population.[80]

By the mid-nineteenth century, as the religious distinction between Christianity and Judaism became replaced by the racial distinction between
Aryan and Jew, Jews were understood to be not only religiously but
racially inferior to white Christian Europeans. The rhetorics of colonialism
and anti-Semitism converged: in Freud's Vienna, as elsewhere in Europe,

the language of racial inferiority was used not only for dark-skinned peoples in such places as Africa, Australia and the Americas but also for the Jews of Europe, who were variously described as "Oriental," "primitive," "barbarian," "white Negroes," "mulatto" and "a mongrel race." Jews and Africans were characterized as "equivalent dangers to the 'white' races," and the Eastern European Jew, in particular, could be described "as the exemplary member of the 'dark-skinned' races."[81] There were, of course, critical differences between the racial stereotypes with which Jews and peoples of African descent were branded.[82] But by the late nineteenth and early twentieth centuries in Europe, Jews, too, were seen as evolutionarily inferior, darker-skinned and primitive; and like other colonized peoples, they, too, internalized this view of themselves to varying degrees.

The Vienna of the 1860s and 1870s of Freud's childhood had been home to an energetic liberalism that had expanded the rights of Jews to an unprecedented extent, fortifying Jewish faith in Enlightenment values and in the promise of assimilation. But this tolerant liberalism was short-lived, replaced by the virulent anti-Semitism of the 1890s championed by the municipal government of Karl Lueger, to whom Hitler later credited much of his education about the Jews. Lueger promulgated a platform demanding the exclusion of Jews from the professions and civic services.[83] As a student Freud had been faced with the anti-Semitism of his fellow students; as an academic his professorship was denied him for years on the grounds of his "denomination"; in the 1930s German universities burned his works; and, although Freud was brought to safety in England in 1938 through the intervention of his disciple, Princess Marie Bonaparte of Greece, four of his sisters were not so fortunate and met their deaths at Auschwitz and Theriesenstadt.[84]

Assimilated Jews in Germany and Austria, such as Freud, identified themselves with European civilization and Germanic culture, and internalized the Euro/Aryan language of racial inheritance with which the Jews were stigmatized. They dissociated themselves from their Eastern European counterparts, the *Östjuden*, turning their internalized self-denigration on their eastern cousins. They looked down on the *Östjuden* (not to mention the "savages" of Africa and elsewhere) in the same terms in which the dominant culture looked down on them, projecting racist terms on others as they repudiated the applicability of these terms to themselves.[85] Those Jews who had migrated westward—as had Freud's family, from Moravia to Vienna—and had replaced Yiddish with German

as their daily language came to look down on Yiddish as "the language
of the 'barbarian'" and on Yiddish speakers as primitive easterners.[86] For
German-speaking Jews, Eastern European Jews came to embody the anti-
Semitic stereotype of the Jew as primitive from which they wished to
distance themselves; the increasing anti-Semitism in Freud's Austria was
often blamed by the Jews who were already established there as due to the
continuing influx of the primitive *Östjuden*.[87] Freud, too, originally from
Eastern Europe, looked down with contempt on his culture of origin, whose
customs he found inferior, shameful and out of date.[88] Freud's son Martin,
in writing about his grandmother, wrote of "these Galician Jews [who]
had little grace and no manners" and who, "in many respects . . . would
seem to be untamed barbarians to more civilized people."[89]

As Sander Gilman and Daniel Boyarin have amply documented, the
purported inferiority of the Jews was inscribed not only in racial terms
and along an east–west orientalist axis but also in gendered terms within
the dominant popular and scientific racial discourse.[90] Male Jews were
seen as having been made feminine through circumcision; thus feminized, they were believed to be susceptible to diseases, both physical and
mental, usually associated with women. Chief among these, of course,
was hysteria, to which Eastern European Jews were said to be especially
prone.[91] Circumcision could also suggest that male Jews were neither
fully male nor female and therefore constituted a "third sex"; that is, they
were homosexual. All the elements in this chain of associations ([male]
Jews—circumcised—feminized—homosexual—hysterical) were taken
as inherited dispositions of the Jewish race. (Lamarckian theory, after all,
allowed for the inheritance of acquired characteristics: Gilman documents
extensive debates from the eighteenth to the twentieth century concerning the "congenital" circumcision of the Jews.[92]) The inferiority of the
Jews was mapped across a network of signifiers which converged in the
gendering of the Jew as female: manliness was the prerogative of the
master race of the Aryans. Boyarin suggests that the view of Jews as feminized was an internally as well as externally generated categorization: not
only an imposed racial canard, but an alternative ideal of a nonviolent
masculinity developed by the rabbinic community itself as a deliberate
resistance to norms of masculinity imposed by dominant western cultures
since Roman times.

Freud lived amid these designations, recognizing and resisting them in
himself and recasting them in his theory. By his own admission he had

hysterical tendencies (e.g., his fainting spells, his "Rome neurosis"), and his intense associations with Fliess and Jung demonstrated his susceptibility to homoerotic relationships. As a scientist he searched for ways of designating those behaviors that would release these tendencies—and himself—from their racial implications. With psychoanalysis Freud would reconfigure the psyche as universal and therefore beyond the stigmatizing racial particularities with which medical science had branded the Jew. Hysteria would no longer be seen as a disease ascribed to particular races such as the Jews through inheritance; instead it was caused by fantasies that might occur in any psyche. Freud demonstrated that men as well as women could become susceptible to hysteria: hysteria would no longer be a woman's disease and, by association, its occurrence in (Jewish) men would no longer brand them as feminine. The universal oedipal inheritance of mankind would replace the particular racial inheritances ascribed to specific races. From this perspective, Freud's Lamarckianism can be seen as a universalizing improvement over particularistic racial stigmatizing: the inheritance of oedipal memories by *all* humans took the place of the inheritance by Jews of a particular racial degeneracy; and the narrative of *Group Psychology and the Analysis of the Ego* can be seen as emplotting the emergence of the European subject from a (particular, racial, primitive) group into (universal, modern) civilization. These universalizing reconfigurations were made at considerable expense, however: the modalities of inferiority previously ascribed to the Jews did not simply disappear but were ambivalently displaced onto a series of abjected others: primitives, women and homosexuals.

For Gilman, sexual difference in psychoanalysis represents Freud's transmutation of a yet more fundamental racial trauma that haunted him: Gilman contends that underlying the oedipal fear of castration was, for Freud, the fear of circumcision. The medical discourse of Freud's day drew associations between castration and circumcision as did Freud himself, for whom circumcision was a milder form of the castration originally imposed by the primal father on his subjugated sons.[93] For Gilman, then, not sexual difference but the raced difference between circumcised and noncircumcised males aroused the fundamental horror with which the male psyche had to grapple. Circumcised males were seized by the fear that they might become and/or be seen as female; uncircumcised males were seized by the fear that they might become circumcised (Jewish and feminized). In addition, assimilated Jewish men feared that their Jewishness would be revealed by their circumcised genitalia. Gilman posits that this anxiety of circumcision—an anxiety of racial difference—was resolved by Freud and by psychoanalysis by projecting the difference *between* males onto the difference between males and females. Then the difference that could be seen to really matter was not between circumcision and noncircumcision (the racial difference between males) but between castration and noncastration (the sexual difference between men and women). Sexual difference became Freud's dissolution of his circumcision complex by becoming the cause of the castration complex, figured now in terms of the repudiation of femininity. The asymmetrical racial opposition between "Aryan" and "Jew" was transformed into the asymmetrical psychoanalytic categories of "male" and "female." The male Jew was assimilated to the universal subject, and all the limitations, incompleteness and pathologies previously associated with him were now ascribed to women (who, of course, had been the recipients of these projections all along).

Boyarin supplements this view by contending that homosexuality as well as femininity was repudiated in Freud's construction of the psychoanalytic subject. Judith Butler, too, has written at length about the refusal of homosexual desire on which the heteronormative oedipus complex is built, and has also pointed to the imbrication of its sexual prohibitions with "a complex set of racial injunctions."[94] Rather than a single, underlying exclusion from which all others follow to make possible the constitution of the psychoanalytic subject, then, we find a network of denigrated differences that both undergird, and are cast out of, Freud's construction of the subject.

The inclusion of the previously excluded Jew within the universal subject position of psychoanalysis not only depended upon a repudiated femininity and homosexuality, it included Jews in the overarching, dominant cultural/racial category—civilization—which was defined by its excluded, constitutive opposite, the racialized other as primitive. Categorized as a member of a primitive race, Freud repudiated primitivity, locating himself and his work within European civilization and replacing the opposition of Aryan/Jew with the opposition of civilized/primitive. Civilization, now including the Jews, would displace Aryanism, and the place of the excluded Jew would be taken by primitive "savages.' Boyarin tellingly juxtaposes psychoanalysis to that other political project addressed to the crisis of Judaism in modernity, Zionism, demonstrating how both aimed to remake the feminized, primitivized and queered Jew into a civilized, manly subject (in the case of Zionism, a "muscle" Jew), a member of the family of civilized and colonizing states rather than a member of a colonized population. Zionism implicitly recognized this transvaluation of categories: the Jews would "re-enter" the history they had been outside of, emerging from their primitive status by entering a "land without people" analogous to the *terrus nullius* of the Americas, Africa and Australia prior to their European settlement.[95] In psychoanalysis, the previously "colonized" Jew would now be placed in the position of the civilized subject, leaving behind a timeless, feminized, Jewish primitivity and entering the historical time of modernity. Freud would create a discourse that proclaimed itself to be both universal and universalizing: not just a "Jewish psychology" (as Jung would have had it)[96] nor simply a "Jewish national affair" (as Freud himself feared).[97]

By locating himself and his work within a hoped-for universal European civilization, Freud replaced the opposition of Aryan and Jew with the opposition of civilized and primitive, which was then mapped onto the psychic registers of conscious/unconscious. Particularities of race and religion were part of a repudiated past, repressed into the unconscious in a psychosocial process that was linked to disgust, repugnance and offensive smells. Freud, in an extended disquisition on the sense of smell in a footnote to *Civilization and Its Discontents*, speculated that civilization had been set in motion when humans first assumed an erect posture; the previously unobjectionable smells of menstruation and excreta submitted to an "organic repression"—defined as "a defence against a phase of development that has been surmounted"—which "paved the way to civilization." Once a phase of development was thus repressed, it became "worthless, disgusting, abhorrent and abominable."[98] Or as he had put it earlier in a letter to his confidant, Fliess,

> the memory stinks just as . . . the object stinks; and in the same manner as we turn away our sense organ (the head and the nose) in disgust, the preconscious and the sense of consciousness turn away from the memory. This is repression.[99]

Norbert Elias has also drawn connections between civilization, repression and repugnance, demonstrating how behaviors that came to be outside the purview of what was considered first "civil" and later "civilized" were associated with repugnance and considered shameful.[100] And as the anthropologist Mary Douglas has pointed out, what makes something repugnant is that it is anomalous to the particular structure of a specific social order.[101] "Matter out of place" arouses disgust at the same time as it helps to define the boundaries of that order. Non-European institutions and behaviors were "out of place" on the European grid and were therefore seen not as differently structured but as anomalous and repugnant. Elias reminds us that the development of behaviors that came to be known as "civil" and "civilized" were markers of social distinction within the social hierarchies of Europe, and later between Europe and its colonial others. A civilized subjectivity predicated on the repudiation of social positions considered as belonging to a superseded past had emerged out of a fear of "lapsing into" positions of social inferiority.[102] Civilized subjectivity, then, was specifically tied up with its associated repugnance toward the past to sustain positions of privilege.

As mentioned in Chapter 3, Julia Kristeva correlated repression and repugnance with the past in her consideration of how bodily wastes, newly separated from the body's interior, replicate the separation from the maternal body.[103] Following Freud, she sees the disgust aroused by bodily wastes as associated with the successive repressions required for the instantiation and maintenance of subjectivity, all of which become retrospectively looked on as disgusting, repugnant and smelly. These repudiations haunt subjectivity, threatening to undo it; as a defense, they are mapped as prior and remembered with disgust as the primitive and the maternal. What the psychoanalytic subject is not is disdained as the past from which she or he has emerged. European discourses of abjected and excluded others had long featured theories of both the "odor di femina" and the "foetor judaicus,"[104] terms expressing an offensive animalistic smell meant to distinguish its bearers from civilized man. With Freud and Kristeva, the olfactory repugnance that had been associated with Jews and women is now traced to psychic repudiations seen as universally necessary to the emergence of a modern, civilized subjectivity. These repudiations are, however, lodged as the repressed contents of the still "primitive" unconscious.

But Freud had sympathies both for and against the universalizing world of European civilization. He wanted to be a fully accepted citizen of the intellectual community of Europe, whose work would make a significant impact on the European culture he took as his own, but without abandoning his attachment to the Jewish community (the preface to the Hebrew translation of *Totem and Taboo*, where Freud claims he has "never repudiated his people" and "feels that he is in his essential nature a Jew," is often quoted in this regard).[105] He desired membership in the (ideally) racially unmarked world of European science; but he also resisted the Aryanization of that world with its castigation of the Jews in terms of primitivity, femininity and homosexuality. In Boyarin's words, he was "both the object and the subject of the racism of the civilizing mission," simultaneously a member of a colonized and a colonizing culture.[106]

As a result, his work is torn between, on the one hand, unmasking the hypocrisy of a culture that deems itself superior to subaltern populations, and on the other hand, adopting the universalized position that abjected those populations but would allow his critique to be heard and have an impact on that culture. His work reflects a struggle between acknowledging and attempting to overcome the differences between specific cultural (raced, gendered) social locations, and a universalized normative subjectivity. As a body of theory that helped to shape the modern culture of twentieth-century Europe, Freud's work became a central representative of that culture even as it expressed his abiding skepticism about it. Psychoanalysis arrived on the scene as a radical and provocative critique of European culture, but at the same time it "[built] into [its] theoretical frames aggressive Eurocentric critiques of non-western cultures" whereby "the primitive world, especially the Orient, is an anachronistic presence and represents an earlier stage of cultural order that social evolution has rendered obsolete."[107]

This bivalent perspective was augmented, as Gilman suggests, by Freud's roles as both a medical scientist and a long-term cancer patient whose diseased body was diagnosed in the anti-Semitic medical discourse of his time. Freud's double positioning as racially marked patient and racially unmarked scientist, as aspiring universalist and unrepentant particularist, became institutionalized within psychoanalysis itself through Freud's doubled position as both the first analyst and the first analysand, a position inherited by all his descendants, all of whom become analysts only by virtue of having been analyzed. The burden of this double vision is reflected in the contradictions found in all areas of psychoanalysis: Freud's ambivalences become the paradoxes of psychoanalysis. On the one hand, psychoanalysis speaks in the voice of the scientific, racially unmarked, unitary and universal subject who is the culmination of the evolutionary

and historical development of civilization. On the other hand, its revo-
lutionary innovation lies in its invocation of the paramount significance
of the heterogeneity inherent in subjectivity, whose multiple sites Freud
subsumed in the unconscious. Though it codes the multiple sites of this
heterogeneity as inferior, psychoanalysis also insists that we have to recuperate these heterogeneous elements into consciousness to free ourselves
from unwanted neurotic symptoms. Freud's situation as both outsider and
insider has yielded a unique kind of knowledge that forces us to think
together both the universal and particular and to undermine the binarism
of nature and culture.[108]

The historicizing mission of psychoanalysis

Freud negotiated the dilemma of the particular and the universal through
the psychoanalytic historicization of (un)consciousness. Historicization
in psychoanalysis is the double movement by which a repressed, unconscious, primitive timelessness would be recovered and confronted in the
present. Once rendered conscious, it would be set within a contextualiz-
ing, historical narrative, located as part of the past that was continuing to
influence the present. The neurotic psychoanalytic patient had regressed to
primitivity, where the unconscious particularities of the past dominated the
present through the compulsion to repeat. Psychoanalytic therapy would
bring about a reversal of this process of regression. By making these past
events conscious, the subject would be freed from the domination of the
past and released into a universally conceived, contemporary modernity.

As discussed in Chapter 3, subjectivity in psychoanalysis has largely
been conceptualized in terms of separation from and repudiation of a relationship of undifferentiation with mother/nature/primitivity, through the
mediation of the father/civilizing law. The abjected past from which the
psychoanalytic subject is believed to have emerged includes the maternal (infantile) past, the evolutionary (racial) past of humankind, the social
(racial/ethnic group structure) past and the cultural (religio-symbolic)
past.[109] Domination and subordination were the political relations of primitivity; enthrallment was the psychology of primitivity; religion was the
ideology of primitivity; disgust and repugnance were the emotional affects
provoked by primitivity; and non-white was the skin color of primitivity.
To regress through neurosis was to regress to a developmental primitivity that was correlated with an evolutionary primitivity. In its treatment,

psychoanalysis sought to encourage the development of an individualized subjectivity whose maturity would be measured by its release from the grip of the primitive—infantile, but also animistic, religious, racial, relationship-embedded, group-oriented—past.

For classical psychoanalysis, "the primitive" retrospectively marks a position of immersion in a past of intersubjective relationality, in the narcissistic processes that bind infants to their parents, group members to their legitimating authorities and analysands to their analysts (as will be discussed in Chapter 5). "Time" in classical psychoanalysis reveals itself as the measure of distance from the immediacy, coevalness and thralldom of intersubjective relationality. "Timelessness" becomes the temporal analog for "undifferentiation," both of which are termed *primitive* and, as such, characterize the unconscious. Religions advocate a return to this primitive "timelessness" of eternity—a return which, within a framework where subjectivity might be seen as governed by recognition as well as by repudiation, could otherwise be read as a form of connection with the sentience of the surrounding lifeworld.

When psychoanalysis conceives of pathology as a regression to the past, cure becomes synonymous with moving out of the grip of that past through the historicizing of the timelessness of the unconscious. Becoming conscious of the primitive psychic processes of the unconscious transforms and dissolves the timeless immediacy of unconscious relational bonds (object cathexes) through their temporalization or historicization. Psychoanalysis reanimates a previously abjected "primitive" immediacy in the transference neurosis and then sets it within a temporalizing narrative that historicizes it by locating it in a personal and perhaps social history. As Hans Loewald writes in a symptomatic passage:

> Through psychoanalysis man may become a truly historical being. In contrast to the ahistorical life of primitive societies and primitive man, including the primitive man in ourselves, the higher forms of memorial activity make us create a history of ourselves as a race and as individuals, as well as a history of the world in which we live.[110]

Formative, perhaps traumatic elements of a sedimented identity are relived with the full force of their immediacy and then, through interpretation, reflected on from a vantage point no longer identical to them. This reflection disrupts their immediacy by placing them in a historical narrative, creating a temporal distance between the remembering subject and the objects of remembrance, which include the relational ties—familial, social, cultural—in which these objects had been embedded. The rupture of the compelling immediacy of these relational bonds results in the traces ("precipitates of abandoned object cathexe[s]") that institute the psychological structures of a modern, civilized subjectivity. The timeless, compelling/compulsive/enthralling performances ("acting out") of unconscious desire are transformed into historicized representations of now conscious memories. Previously external objects are transformed into internalized structure, and acting out becomes replaced by verbal or textual expression, retracing the conventional view of the evolutionary history of consciousness.

A psychoanalytic coming-to-terms with emotional distress entails a reckoning with the ways in which relational configurations of the past continue on as constitutive parts of the present. But as we can see, this coming-to-terms, holding together the past and the present, may too easily collapse into a denial of the coevalness of these previously repressed relational configurations by re-fixing them in the past, re-separating contemporary subjectivity from timeless primitivity and inserting the subject into the linear, "empty, homogenous time" of historical modernity.[111] The historicizing of consciousness, then, has the potential to reinscribe the psychoanalytic subject within the same linear and temporally allachronizing framework criticized by postcolonial theory: separate from, because of having overcome, primitivity. Such a reinscription is not necessitated by psychoanalysis. However, psychoanalysis remains vulnerable to re-locating "the primitive" as a temporal and racial marker of an ever-beckoning relationality, whose recognition as coeval would compromise the dream of an autonomous subjectivity. The historicizing mission of psychoanalysis runs the risk of reinstating the same temporal distance from alterity which the postcolonial critique challenges us to annul.

Notes

1 George W. Stocking Jr., "The Critique of Racial Formalism" and "Franz Boas and the Culture Concept," in Stocking, *Race, Culture and Evolution*, chaps. 8 and 9, respectively, 161–233; Stocking, "Maclay, Kubary, Malinowski: Archetypes from the Dreamtime of Anthropology," in Stocking, ed., *Colonial Situations*, 9–74; "Radcliffe-Brown and British Social Anthropology," in Stocking, ed., *Functionalism Historicized*, 131–91.

2 Margaret Mead, *Coming of Age in Samoa: A Psychological Study of Primitive Youth for Western Civilization* (New York: William Morrow & Company, 1928), 14.

3 Johannes Fabian, *Time and the Other: How Anthropology Makes Its Object* (New York: Columbia University Press, 1983).

4 James Baldwin, *The Evidence of Things Not Seen* (New York: Henry Holt, 1985), 80.

5 Freud, *Interpretation of Dreams, SE* 5:535.

6 James Clifford, "On Ethnographic Authority," in idem, *The Predicament of Culture: Twentieth-Century Ethnography, Literature, and Art* (Cambridge, MA: Harvard University Press, 1988), 21–54; Stocking, "Maclay, Kubary, Malinowski," esp. 66; John and Jean Comaroff, *Ethnography and the Historical Imagination*, 21; Fabian, *Time and the Other*.

7 Claude Lévi-Strauss, *The Savage Mind* (Chicago, IL: University of Chicago Press, 1966 [1962]). The primary meaning of the adjective *sauvage* in French is *wild* rather than *savage*. The thesis and meaning of the title are well captured by Margaret Trawick, who writes that "Mythic thought is wild thought, and wild thought is as patterned and well-ordered as a wild plant" in Trawick, *Notes on Love in a Tamil Family* (Berkeley, CA: University of California Press, 1990), 4.

8 Lévi-Strauss, *The Savage Mind*, 73.

9 Mircea Eliade, *The Myth of the Eternal Return, or, Cosmos and History*, trans. Willard R. Trask (Princeton, NJ: Princeton University Press, 1991 [1954]), 86, 91.

10 Mircea Eliade, *The Sacred and the Profane: The Nature of Religion*, trans. Willard R. Trask (San Diego, CA: Harcourt Brace Jovanovitch, 1959 [1957]), 88.

11 Eliade, *The Myth of the Eternal Return*, 3.

12 Julia Kristeva, "Women's Time," trans. Alice Jardine and Harry Blake, in Toril Moi, ed., *The Kristeva Reader* (New York: Columbia University Press, 1986), 187–213; quotes are from 191, 192.

13 Georges Condimas, quoted in Gerrit Huizer and Bruce Mannheim, eds., *Politics of Anthropology: From Colonialism and Sexism toward a View from Below* (The Hague: Mouton, 1979), 193.

14 Michel Leiris, "L'Ethnographie devant le colonialisme," in *Les Temps Modernes* 6, no. 58 (1950): 357–74. Albert Memmi wrote, "Why must we suppose that the colonized would have remained frozen in the state in which the colonizer found him?" in *The Colonizer and the Colonized*, trans. Howard Greenfeld (New York: Orion, 1965) 91, 113. See also Talal Asad, ed., *Anthropology and the Colonial Encounter* (Atlantic Highlands, NJ: Humanities, 1973); Dell Hymes, ed., *Reinventing Anthropology* (New York: Random House, 1969); Huizer and Mannheim, *The Politics of Anthropology*;

Stocking, ed., *Observers Observed; Functionalism Historicized*; and, especially, Stocking, ed., *Colonial Situations*.

15 Bronislaw Malinowski, "The Rationalization of Anthropology and Administration," *Africa* 3, no. 4 (1930): 408.

16 Clifford, *The Predicament of Culture*, 6.

17 See Chapter 3, note 66 for an explanation of the term *subaltern*.

18 Fabian, *Time and the Other*.

19 Ibid., 82.

20 Paul Ricoeur, "The History of Religions and the Phenomenology of Time Consciousness," in Joseph Kitagawa, ed., *The History of Religions: Retrospect and Prospect* (New York: Macmillan, 1985), 16, 21.

21 Jonathan Z. Smith, "The Wobbling Pivot," in his *Map Is Not Territory*, 100, 101.

22 John and Jean Comaroff, *Ethnography and the Historical Imagination*, 5.

23 Ibid., 122.

24 Dipesh Chakrabarty, *Provincializing Europe: Postcolonial Thought and Historical Difference* (Princeton, NJ: Princeton University Press, 2000), 92.

25 Walter D. Mignolo, *The Darker Side of the Renaissance: Literacy, Territoriality and Colonization* (Ann Arbor, MI: University of Michigan Press, 1995).

26 Mignolo quotes Marshall McLuhan: "The phonetic alphabet, alone, is the technology that has been the means of creating 'civilized man'" (*The Darker Side of the Renaissance*, 323).

27 This is the thesis advanced by Tzvetan Todorov in his *Conquest of America*.

28 Mignolo, *The Darker Side of the Renaissance*, chap. 3, "Record Keeping without Letters and Writing Histories of People without History," 125–69, notes at 331–4; quotes at 334.

29 For an overview of the concerns and strategies of postcolonial studies, see Leela Gandhi, *Postcolonial Theory*.

30 See Eric Williams's *Capitalism and Slavery* (New York: Capricorn, 1966 [1944]); Charles Mills, *The Racial Contract*, 31–40; Gayatri Chakravorty Spivak, *The Post-Colonial Critic: Interviews, Strategies, Dialogues*, ed. Sarah Harasym (London: Routledge, 1990); see also Sanjay Seth, Leela Gandhi and Michael Dutton, "Postcolonial Studies: A Beginning," in *Postcolonial Studies* 1, no. 1 (1998): 7–11.

31 Spivak, *The Post-Colonial Critic*, 96; see also Seth, Gandhi and Dutton, "Postcolonial Studies: A Beginning."

32 Edward Said; "Representing the Colonized: Anthropology's Interlocutors," *Critical Inquiry* 15, no. 2 (winter 1989): 205–25. But also see Eric Santner's "Postwar/Post-Holocaust/Postmodern: Some Reflections on the Discourses of Mourning," in his *Stranded Objects* (Ithaca, NY: Cornell University Press, 1990), 1–30, for a lucid discussion of how political events internal to European history also (and perhaps more centrally) engendered the postmodern turn in western academic thought.

33 See Dipesh Chakrabarty's penetrating discussion of Marx in *Provincializing Europe*, chap. 2, "Two Histories of Capital," 47–71, as well as his remarks on John Stuart Mill, 8. See also Charles W. Mills's discussions of Hobbes, Hume, Kant and Hegel, in *The Racial Contract*, passim.

34 Chakrabarty develops this thesis in his *Provincializing Europe*; quote is at 8. See also Arturo Escobar, *Encountering Development: The Making and Unmaking of the Third World* (Princeton, NJ: Princeton University Press, 1995).

35 Clifford, *Predicament of Culture*, 212.

36 Freud, "From the History of an Infantile Neurosis," *SE* 17.

37 Freud, *Group Psychology*, *SE* 59:131.

38 Elizabeth Abel, Barbara Christian and Helene Moglen, eds., "Introduction: The Dream of a Common Language," in idem, *Female Subjects in Black and White: Race, Psychoanalysis, Feminism* (Berkeley, CA: University of California Press, 1997), 1, 7.

39 Freud, *New Introductory Lectures*, Lecture 35, *SE* 22:160.

40 See books listed in note 62, below.

41 Povinelli, *Labor's Lot*, 31; Ronald Berndt, "Traditional Concepts of Aboriginal Land," in R. Berndt, ed., *Aboriginal Sites, Rights, and Resource Development* (Perth: University of Western Australia Press, 1982), 1–12; quoted in Povinelli, *Labor's Lot*, 157.

42 Freud, *Future of an Illusion*, *SE* 21:38.

43 Ibid., 42–4, 53.

44 Ibid., 53.

45 Winnicott's work on illusion has played a pivotal if over-worked role here: see Ana Maria Rizzuto, *The Birth of the Living God: A Psychoanalytic Study* (Chicago, IL: University of Chicago Press, 1979); W.W. Meissner, *Psychoanalysis and Religious Experience* (New Haven, CT: Yale University Press, 1984).

46 Van Herik, *Freud on Femininity and Faith*.

47 Freud, *Civilization and Its Discontents*, *SE* 21:72, 84–5, 97.

48 Freud, *Future of an Illusion*, *SE* 21:14.

49 Freud, *Civilization and Its Discontents*, *SE* 21:96.

50 Rieff, *Mind of the Moralist*, 318. In *The Triumph of the Therapeutic* (Chicago, IL: University of Chicago Press, 1966; repr. 1987), Rieff describes Freud's analysis of consolation and renunciation as the constitutive dynamic of religion: "religion presents jointly and in fusion two analytically discernible alternatives: either a therapeutic control of everyday life or a therapeutic respite from that very control" (34, passim).

51 Freud, in a letter to Lou Andreas Salomé, 6 January 1935, *Briefwechsel* 224; cited in Bluma Goldstein, *Reinscribing Moses: Heine, Kafka, Freud, and Schoenberg in a European Wilderness* (Cambridge, MA: Harvard University Press, 1992), 100.

52 Daniel Boyarin, *Unheroic Conduct: The Rise of Heterosexuality and the Invention of the Jewish Man* (Berkeley, CA: University of California Press, 1995), 246ff., esp. 249.
53 Freud, *Moses and Monotheism*, *SE* 23:136.
54 Yosef Hayim Yerushalmi, *Freud's Moses: Judaism Terminable and Interminable* (New Haven, CT: Yale University Press, 1991), 78.
55 Freud, *New Introductory Lectures*, Lecture 35, *SE* 22:160.
56 Meissner, *Psychoanalysis and Religious Experience*, 5.
57 See William Parsons, "Psychology of Religion," in *The Encyclopedia of Religion*, second edition, ed. L. Jones (Detroit, MI: Macmillan Reference USA, 2005), 7477.
58 Richard Rubenstein, *The Religious Imagination: A Study in Psychoanalysis and Jewish Theology* (Lanham, MD: University Press of America, 1968).
59 This group includes, Ricoeur's philosophical study of 1970; Rizzuto, *The Birth of the Living God*; John McDargh, *Psychoanalytic Object Relations Theory and the Study of Religion* (Lanham, MD: University Press of America, 1983); Meissner, *Psychoanalysis and Religious Experience*; James W. Jones, *Contemporary Psychoanalysis and Religion: Transference and Transcendence* (New Haven, CT: Yale University Press, 1991); Jones, *Religion and Psychology in Transition: Psychoanalysis, Feminism, and Theology* (New Haven, CT: Yale University Press, 1996).
60 Ana Maria Rizzuto, *Why Did Freud Reject God? A Psychoanalytic Interpretation* (New Haven, CT: Yale University Press, 1998).
61 See Leora Batnitsky, *How Judaism Became a Religion: An Introduction to Modern Jewish Thought* (Princeton, NJ: Princeton University Press, 2013).
62 This group includes inter alia David Bakan, *Sigmund Freud and the Jewish Mystical Tradition* (Princeton, NJ: Van Nostrand, 1958); Marthe Robert, *From Oedipus to Moses: Freud's Jewish Identity*, trans. Ralph Manheim (Garden City, NY: Anchor, 1976); Dennis Klein, *Jewish Origins of the Psychoanalytic Movement*; Susan A. Handelmann, *The Slayers of Moses: The Emergence of Rabbinic Interpretation in Modern Literary Theory* (Albany, NY: State University of New York Press, 1982); Yosef Yerushalmi, *Freud's Moses*; Sander L. Gilman, *Freud, Race, and Gender* (Princeton, NJ: Princeton University Press, 1993); Boyarin, *Unheroic Conduct*; Gilman, *The Case of Sigmund Freud: Medicine and Identity at the Fin de Siècle* (Baltimore, MD: Johns Hopkins University Press, 1993); Boyarin, "*Épater l'embourgeoisement*"; Boyarin, "What Does a Jew Want?"; Jay Geller, "The Godfather of Psychoanalysis: Circumcision, Antisemitism, Homosexuality, and Freud's 'Fighting Jew'," in *Journal of the American Academy of Religion* 67, no. 2 (1999): 355–85. For a thoughtful and witty overview of works of this nature, see Jay Geller, "Identifying 'Someone Who Is Himself One of Them': Recent Studies of Freud's Jewish Identity," *Religious Studies Review* 23, no. 4 (1997): 323–31.
63 Geller, "Identifying 'Someone'," 323.
64 See Eric Santner's luminous discussion of Freud's work in the light of Jewish theologian Franz Rosenzweig, *On the Psychotheology of Everyday Life:*

Reflections on Freud and Rosenzweig (Chicago, IL: University of Chicago Press, 2001); also James DiCenso, *The Other Freud: Religion, Culture and Psychoanalysis* (London; New York: Routledge, 1999).

65 Karen Starr, *Repair of the Soul: Metaphors of Transformation in Jewish Mysticism and Psychoanalysis* (New York: Routledge, 2008).

66 Ricoeur, *Freud and Philosophy*, 452, 446.

67 Ibid., 26.

68 See Jonathan Lear, *Freud* (New York: Routledge, 2004), chapter 7.

69 Ricoeur, *Freud and Philosophy*, 496.

70 Ibid., 181.

71 Gananath Obeyesekere, *The Work of Culture: Symbolic Transformation in Psychoanalysis and Anthropology* (Chicago, IL: University of Chicago Press, 1990), esp. Lecture 1, "Representation and Symbol Formation in a Psychoanalytic Anthropology," 3–68. See also Gananath Obeyesekere, *Medusa's Hair: An Essay on Personal Symbols and Religious Experience* (Chicago, IL: University of Chicago Press, 1981).

72 See Jones, *Contemporary Psychoanalysis and Religion*, 68; Rizzuto, *Birth of the Living God*, inter alia 7, 52–3, 89, 180, 202, passim; McDargh, *Psychoanalytic Object Relations Theory and the Study of Religion*, 4; Meissner, *Psychoanalysis and Religious Experience*, 135, 132.

73 Meissner, *Psychoanalysis and Religious Experience*, 159.

74 Freud, *Group Psychology*, SE 18:142.

75 Meissner, *Psychoanalysis and Religious Experience*, 21–134; Rizzuto, *Why Did Freud Reject God?*

76 See Frantz Fanon's discussion of "sociogeny," *Black Skins, White Masks*, trans. C.L. Markham (New York: Monthly Review Press, 1967), 11 ff. Kelly Oliver argues for a "notion of the individual or psyche that is thoroughly social" in Oliver, *The Colonization of Psychic Space: A Psychoanalytic Social Theory of Oppression* (Minneapolis, MN: University of Minnesota Press, 2004), xiii, passim. See also Derek Hook's keen elucidation of the relationship between discursive structures and subjective libidinal investments in Derek Hook, *A Critical Psychology of the Postcolonial: The Mind of Apartheid* (London; New York: Routledge, 2012), ch. 2.

77 Feminist interventions from within Anglo-American psychoanalysis are the notable exceptions.

78 Spillers, "'All the Things You Could Be By Now,'" 386.

79 Hannah Arendt, *Origins of Totalitarianism*, 206; Aimé Césaire, *Discourse on Colonialism*, trans. Joan Pinkham (New York: Monthly Review Press, 1972 [1955]), 14; Victor Kiernan, *Imperialism and Its Contradictions* (London: Routledge, 1995), 101.

80 Boyarin, "*Épater l'Embourgeoisement*," 17–42.

81 Gilman, *Freud, Race and Gender*, 19; Gilman, *The Case of Sigmund Freud*, 13; Boyarin, "What Does a Jew Want?" 219, 220.

82 Frantz Fanon details the differences between the stereotypes applied to the Jew and the "Negro." See Fanon, *Black Skin, White Masks*, 162ff. See also

Elizabeth Young-Bruehl, *Anatomy of Prejudices* (Cambridge, MA: Harvard University Press, 1996) for a detailed psychoanalytic taxonomy of various forms of racial prejudice.

83 Schorske "Politics and Fratricide in Freud's *Interpretation of Dreams*," 185; Hannaford, *Race: The History of an Idea in the West*, 318, 362, 364.

84 See Peter Gay, *Freud: A Life for Our Time* (New York: Norton, 1988), 139, 447, 649; Gilman, *Freud, Race, and Gender*, 12ff.

85 See Gilman's examples in *Freud, Race, and Gender*, 12ff., and in *The Case of Sigmund Freud*, 87; see also Gay, *Freud*, 19. This internalization of anti-Semitic stereotypes by German Jews and their subsequent projection by German Jews onto Eastern European Jews is the subject of Sander Gilman's *Jewish Self-Hatred: Anti-Semitism and the Hidden Language of the Jews* (Baltimore, MD: The Johns Hopkins University Press, 1986), with particular examples on 7, 9, 10, 15, 99, 122, 138, 214. Daniel Boyarin reports that "Theodor Herzl went so far as to write explicitly that the *Östjude* was of a different 'race' from the 'evolved' German Jew" (*Unheroic Conduct*, 267).

86 Gilman, *Jewish Self-Hatred*, 99.

87 Dennis Klein, *Jewish Origins of the Psychoanalytic Movement*, chaps. 1, 2.

88 Ibid., chap. 1, 46–50.

89 Martin Freud, *Glory Reflected: Sigmund Freud, Man and Father* (London: Angus and Robertson, 1957), 10–12, quoted in Rizzuto, *Why Did Freud Reject God?*, 187.

90 The following discussion is indebted to Gilman, *Freud, Race, and Gender*, and Boyarin, *Unheroic Conduct*.

91 Gilman, *Freud, Race, and Gender*, chap. 3.

92 Ibid., 52–6.

93 See the discussion of Freud's "A Phylogenetic Fantasy" in Chapter 2, 82–83; and Chapter 3, 114.

94 Judith Butler, "Passing, Queering: Nella Larsen's Psychoanalytic Challenge," in her *Bodies That Matter*, 166. See also her "Prohibition, Psychoanalysis and the Production of the Heterosexual Matrix," in her *Gender Trouble* (New York: Routledge, 1990), 35–78.

95 The Zionist slogan was "a land without a people for a people without a land." See Boyarin, "The Colonial Drag: Zionism, Gender, and Mimicry," in his *Unheroic Conduct*, chap. 7, 271–312, for a discussion of the complex relationships between Zionism and colonialism.

96 C.G. Jung, *Two Essays on Analytical Psychology*, trans. R.F.C. Hull (Princeton, NJ: Princeton University Press, 1966 [1953]), 152, n. 8.

97 H.C. Abraham and E.L. Freud, eds., *A Psychoanalytic Dialogue: The Letters of Sigmund Freud and Karl Abraham*, trans. B. Marsh and H. Abraham (New York: Basic Books, 1965), 34.

98 Freud, *Civilization and Its Discontents*, SE 21:99–100, n. 1, 18, 68, 69.

99 Freud, *The Complete Letters of Sigmund Freud to Wilhelm Fliess, 1887–1904*, ed. and trans. Jeffrey M. Masson (Cambridge, MA: Harvard

University Press, 1985), letter of November 14, 1897, 280; quoted in Jay Geller, "(G)nos(e)ology: The Cultural Construction of the Other," in Howard Eilberg-Schwartz, ed., *People of the Body: Jews and Judaism from an Embodied Perspective* (Albany, NY: State University of New York Press, 1992), 258.

100 Elias, *The Civilizing Process*.

101 Mary Douglas, *Purity and Danger* (London: Routledge and Kegan Paul, 1966).

102 Elias, *Civilizing Process*, 415.

103 Kristeva, *Powers of Horror*, chaps. 3 and 4.

104 Gallop, *The Daughter's Seduction*, 27; Geller, "(G)nos(e)ology," 243–82; Gilman, *Freud, Race, and Gender*, 152ff.

105 Freud, *Totem and Taboo*, preface to the Hebrew translation, *SE* 13:xv.

106 Boyarin, *Unheroic Conduct*, 261.

107 Ashis Nandy, "The Savage Freud: The First Non-Western Psychoanalyst and the Politics of Secret Selves in Colonial India," in his *Savage Freud* (Princeton, NJ: Princeton University Press, 1995), 81.

108 Boyarin, *Unheroic Conduct*, 268; Shepherdson, *Vital Signs*, 87.

109 Peter Homans, in *The Ability to Mourn: Disillusionment and the Social Origins of Psychoanalysis* (Chicago, IL: University of Chicago Press, 1989), provides a detailed sociological account of the ways that psychoanalysis itself emerged out of the breakdown of traditional religious community and belief.

110 Hans Loewald, "Perspectives on Memory," in Merton M. Gill and Philip S. Holzman, eds., *Psychology versus Metapsychology: Psychoanalytic Essays in Memory of George S. Klein* (New York: International Universities Press, 1976), 298–325.

111 In the famous phrase of Walter Benjamin, "Theses on the Philosophy of History," in his *Illuminations* (New York: Schocken, 1968), 261.

Chapter 5

Race and primitivity in the clinical encounter

How does the racial subtext of psychoanalysis, constellated around its category of primitivity and embedded in its evolutionary and historicizing tendencies, effect its therapeutic practice? It seems that Freud himself was aware, however dimly, of a racial coding in psychoanalysis, as can be seen by a joke he apparently told over a period of several decades. This joke was brought to light by Claudia Tate, who discovered it (where it had been hiding in plain sight) in the third volume of Ernest Jones's biography of Freud. The joke, traced by Jones to a cartoon published in the journal *Fliegende Blätter* in 1886, featured a yawning lion muttering to himself: "Twelve o'clock and no negro." The cartoon depended for its supposed humor on the knowledge that Freud's consulting hour at that time was at noon and that among Freud and his colleagues, "for some time patients were referred to as 'negroes'."[1]

This analogy between "negroes" and psychoanalytic patients suggests that the racial subtext of psychoanalysis was not limited to its theoretical structures but filtered through to the clinical relationship as well. African Americans in particular have often suspected that psychoanalysis and its associated talk therapies were unfriendly to their interests, and their suspicions have not been without merit.[2] As we have seen in Chapter 2, the pervasive correspondence in Freud's work between human development and a racially indexed conception of human cultural evolution led to the unfortunate equivalency of pathology and non-white peoples. In addition, hidden connections in Freud's work between the psychology of primitivity and the psychology of the transference have, as we shall see in this chapter, contributed to the susceptibility of the clinical relationship to place "the doctor [in] the role of colonizer and the patients as the colonized people," as Octave Mannoni described the situation that he felt psychoanalysis was "liable to inherit."[3]

This brings us to the question of the relationship between therapeutic practices and the body of theory that guides them. Do all psychoanalytically influenced practices necessarily bring all of Freud's assumptions and conceptualizations in tow with them? The short answer to this question is that they needn't do so; but the more complex answer is that all elements of Freud's work have a porousness in relation to each other, so that while psychoanalytic clinical practice does not *necessarily* entail all of Freud's assumptions, it always remains vulnerable to those assumptions, until and unless their potential presence has been acknowledged and the usefulness of each one decided upon. (We need only think of the common psychoanalytic practice in the mid-twentieth century of diagnosing female patients with penis envy, and judging their treatment successful when the women in question were able to more happily limit themselves to their feminine roles as mothers and housewives.) We can neither dispense with the theory completely nor follow it blindly.

We cannot completely dispense with the theory behind psychoanalytic treatment, and not simply because of a commitment to Freud or to psychoanalysis. Broadly speaking, we humans are self-interpreting beings who at any time and place have a need to make sense of our experience and, especially, of our suffering. This need to make sense of our condition commonly has recourse to a codified system of interpretation—religious, psychoanalytic, medical, theoretical, scientific—which partakes of the biases and assumptions of the community that gives rise to it. Psychoanalysis and its related therapies provide us with some of our contemporary ways of doing this, distinguished from other forms of interpretation and psychological healing by their emphasis on the unconscious dimension of experience and on the transformative power of giving expression to that dimension.

There are levels of our experience and motivations that remain opaque to us under the usual conditions of everyday life, yet continue to influence our everyday feelings and actions. Psychoanalysis attempts to help us become aware of this liminal dimension of our lives and to express what we may have hitherto remained unaware of. Putting words to difficult feelings and memories that have previously remained inchoate has the effect of giving them form and endowing them with a reality—even if only the reality of a newly understood fantasy. These verbal expressions of reminiscence, fantasy, desire and fear help us better understand ourselves and in so doing, help make the intolerable become bearable.

The clinical practice of psychoanalysis is suspended between two poles: the theories on which it has been founded, on the one hand, and the open-ended and open-minded attitude it counsels for the conduct of the clinical relationship, on the other. Clinical treatment skirts a fine line between the discovery of unanticipated emotional elements and the guidance of preconceived frameworks. We need to be able to pursue the therapeutic goals of understanding the hidden dimensions of our suffering; yet we need to remain alert to the ideological propensities of our systems of interpretation.[4] Psychoanalysis and its associated psychotherapies hold the key to transformative possibilities; but they are also potentially amenable to interpretations that lean too concretely on the racial theories that underpin some of Freud's theorizing. With all of this in mind, this chapter traces the way the inescapably racial conception of primitivity can make its way into the clinical encounter.

The literature on the dynamics of racial difference within the clinical relationship has grown considerably over the last several decades. Back in 1968 Judith Schachter and Hugh Butts discussed the variety of effects that may emerge when the members of the therapeutic dyad are of different races or when both members of the therapeutic dyad are black; and in 1992 Dorothy Holmes demonstrated the range of meanings mobilized both consciously and unconsciously in the transference and countertransference around racial difference between members of the therapeutic dyad.[5] More recently Kimberlyn Leary has taken a leading role in discussing, over the course of several papers, the dynamics of race within the psychoanalytic dyad.[6] As Leary states, whiteness is the universal standard "against which a patient of color is understood to be 'different'."[7] *Psychoanalytic Dialogues* devoted an issue in 2000 to a "Symposium on Race" with articles by, among others, Muriel Dimen, Joel Kovel, David L. Eng and Ann Pellegrini; and the *Psychoanalytic Quarterly* devoted an issue in 2006 to "Race, Culture and Ethnicity in the Consulting Room," with articles by Holmes, Lynne Layton, Anne Cheng and Farhad Dalal, among others.[8] These articles begin to sketch out the hitherto unmentioned role played by racial difference in the psychoanalytic encounter. Often, they locate the problem of psychoanalytic racism in the asymmetry of the transference and in the associated ascription of all conflict experienced within that relationship to the analysand. Recognizing that questions of racial difference "are not simply the concern of those who are disadvantaged by them,"[9] these essays advocate a more mutual psychoanalytic interaction grounded in a greater awareness of the racial and social positions of both analyst and analysand.

From a different perspective, Janice O. Bennet has examined the fraught position occupied by the African-American psychoanalyst: the sense of invisibility and of finding herself "other" in the psychoanalytic community she has joined, together with a sense of otherness that has developed toward her within the African-American community from which she comes, because of its mistrust and awareness of psychoanalysis as part of a larger system of white theory and practice that is oppressive to them.[10] Following in this vein, in 2014, Basia Winograd directed the breakthrough film, *Black Psychoanalysts Speak*, which gives striking documentary evidence of the many discriminations that black patients, psychoanalytic candidates and analysts must endure on a regular basis to engage with psychoanalysis as a treatment, a training or a profession.[11]

A comprehensive treatment of the racially exclusionary dimensions of the therapeutic practice of psychoanalysis in late twentieth-century North American practice is provided by Neil Altman in his book, *The Analyst in the Inner City: Race, Class, and Culture through a Psychoanalytic Lens*.[12] Altman describes how psychoanalysis has tended to exclude racial minorities and non-middle-class subjects by viewing them as "unanalyzable." "Ego strength," through the influence of ego psychology in American psychoanalysis, became the criterion of analyzability, the requirement necessary for the patient-to-be to withstand the unsettling rigors of analysis. But ego strength, as Altman points out, presupposes "characteristics that are culture- and class-specific," and differences from the cultural/racial profiles that are correlated with "ego strength" (a disinclination to bear with the silence and neutrality of the analyst, for example) are construed as "defects" or "deficits."[13] The beliefs that ego strength, within an evolutionary framework, would have been considered rather far along the developmental/evolutionary scale, and that those considered to be racially "more primitive" would have been seen as not yet having developed a strong ego, have translated into reasons for excluding racial minorities from analytic treatment.

Altman appropriately ties this problem to the broader issues of the psychoanalytic separation of the psychological from the social register and of the hierarchical structure of the psychoanalytic relationship which itself reproduces the social hierarchies of class and race. Psychoanalysis has traditionally located the causes of psychopathology exclusively within the psyche of the patient, at the very least obscuring the crucial role of social and political factors in the psychological suffering of African Americans and other racial/cultural minorities, and at worst blaming their suffering on their own (lack of) psychological development. That the analyst, by virtue of racial, ethnic and/or socioeconomic status, often occupies a position of privilege within a social structure that is oppressive to the patient generally remains hidden and unremarked-upon in the clinical situation. Any overt manifestations of the oppressive nature of this arrangement have been cast as problems of the patient. Altman therefore advocates a psychoanalytic recognition of the social embeddedness of the self, as well as a less authoritarian and more relational form of analysis that would allow the meanings and difficulties experienced within the clinical relationship due to the racial attitudes of either of its members to be examined as such, rather than solely as projections of the patient.

While examinations of the interpersonal dynamics of the analytic/ therapeutic dyad, including their relationship to broader social and racial issues, play a crucial role in illuminating how issues of racial difference are reproduced in psychoanalytic situations, they do not reveal the full range of the systemic theoretical forces that have invisibly contributed to the potential racial bias of the analytic/therapeutic encounter. Connections between seemingly disparate theoretical elements described in previous chapters will be brought together here to show how Freud's understandings of influence, suggestion and hypnosis (with its ties to the dynamics of the primal horde) have combined with his conceptions of regression and resistance to seep into the clinical situation, rendering it vulnerable to racist enactments.

Suggestion and influence in the therapeutic relationship

Psychoanalysis can be seen as a variety of what Foucault has termed "technologies of the self": a discipline of dialogic reflection whose purpose is to transform the experience of subjectivity. Individuals engage in psychoanalysis, if not "to attain a certain state of happiness, purity, wisdom, perfection or immortality,"[14] then at least to attain the "common unhappiness" of everyday life.[15] In psychoanalysis, the clinical relationship provides the relational framework that regulates the contours of the subjectivity it aims to cultivate. In turn, the clinical relationship is molded by the theoretical understandings that guide the comportment of the analyst and the production of his or her interpretations. These underlying theoretical understandings point to norms of psychological well-being which treatment aspires to approximate.

This might seem to imply that psychoanalysis is a technique of persuasion or suggestion, but such a notion was forcefully rejected by Freud himself.[16] Psychoanalysis was to be a treatment that replaced suggestion (which, at the time, was associated with hypnosis) with a therapy based on self-discovery through the emergence of free associations. The idea that psychoanalysis has a set of norms (e.g. oedipal resolution; the depressive position; a cohesive sense of self) toward which its therapy is meant to lead could seem to imply that it is the analyst's covert suggestions concerning these norms, rather than an emergent self-understanding of the patient, that bring about change in the patient's subjectivity. Moreover, if the norms toward which psychoanalytic therapy leads are represented by what lies at the apex of its developmental models, and if developmental models are, as suggested earlier, temporal arrangements of normative social behaviors and practices, then the use of suggestion and influence in psychoanalysis would be deeply allied with a tendency to encourage the patient to adapt to reigning social conditions. Critics from varying perspectives—from Erich Fromm to Herbert Marcuse to Jacques Lacan—have warned against the adaptationalist potential of such uses of psychoanalysis.

The history of psychoanalysis has many cautionary tales of the use of suggestion in the service of adapting patients to the theories of their analysts as well as to the larger social conventions of the time. An early example was the alarming and almost fatal nasal surgery prescribed by Freud himself, and performed on his patient Emma Eckstein in the 1890s. At the time, Freud adhered to a theory propounded by his friend, Wilhelm Fliess, which attributed the etiology of neurosis to the pharyngeal passages (a theory Freud was subsequently to reject, but not in time for Emma).[17] We might also consider Freud's attempts to encourage his patient Dora to adapt to and play a part in her father's complex sexual intrigues.[18] The recent proliferation of feminist psychoanalytic writings should not allow us to forget earlier feminist charges brought against psychoanalysis for its role in diagnosing female desire and agency as pathology, and for using its diagnostic and interpretive powers to further bind its women patients to the conventional social structures that enforced their subordination.

But Freud also cautioned against the use of psychoanalysis to help patients adapt to social norms. In *Civilization and Its Discontents* (1930) he depicted the requirements of civilized life as hostile to the libidinal desires of its members, and indicated that the role of the analyst was often to side with the patient *against* the demands of conventional social mores. Here, psychoanalytic self-knowledge was to provide a bulwark against the burdensome pressures of the norms of civilized life, rather than an adaptation to them. Psychoanalysis was to deconstruct internalized social prohibitions, helping to free the patient from their grip. This line of thought gave rise to various utopian attempts to see psychoanalysis as a practice that would undo the repressions of civilization to uncover an underlying, uncorrupted libidinal nature, freeing up the fullness of the potential to love (as in the work of Wilhelm Reich, Marcuse and Norman O. Brown). Clinical psychoanalysis has steered a course between the extremes of both adaptationalism and utopianism, trends toward both of which can be found in Freud's thought.

Charges of adaptation to social norms and related questions of influence and suggestion have occurred again and again: What is, and what should be, the role of suggestion, influence and authority in psychoanalysis? Is its therapy meant to help people find relief from suffering by helping them to comply with social norms or by helping them to free themselves from social dictates? Is psychoanalysis prescriptive or descriptive, normative or analytic, suggestive or deconstructive?

Two significant recent sites for debates about these questions have been the feminist engagement with psychoanalytic theory, and late twentieth-century developments in Anglo-American psychoanalysis. American feminists of the 1960s and 1970s lambasted Freud and his American followers for their perceived role in enforcing female subordination through a prescriptive use of psychoanalytic theory and practice.[19] They brought out the ways in which, as often as not, the role of the analyst was to reconcile women to their conventional subordinate position.[20] After all, Freud had written that femininity was identified with passivity and with the position of object rather than that of subject,[21] and that the female oedipal complex led to a defective superego lacking "the strength and independence which give it its cultural significance."[22] Freud had agreed with Ferenczi who wrote that, in a successful analysis, a woman "must emotionally accept without a trace of resentment the [maternal] implications of her female role," although Freud added that he doubted that this could frequently be achieved.[23]

However, recent feminist interventions have recuperated psychoanalysis for its value in contributing to a critical understanding of the construction of sexuality and gender, pointing toward the possibility that psychoanalysis could aid in emancipation from gender-based oppression. Forging the transition, in 1974 Juliet Mitchell advocated a Lacanian psychoanalysis for a feminist agenda on the grounds that psychoanalysis describes (the effects of patriarchy on female psyches) but does not prescribe (the reproduction of these effects).[24] The following year Gayle Rubin also mined the radical insights psychoanalysis had to offer for a theory of female oppression, as described in Chapter 3, but still admitted that psychoanalysis had been as much part of the problem as part of the solution; "one of the most sophisticated ideologies of sexism around."[25] There has been an explosion of further feminist engagements with psychoanalysis ever since, which have influenced further changes in the theoretical conception of the therapeutic relationship. Finding on balance that the usefulness of psychoanalysis lies with its use as description and analysis of gender and sexuality rather than as prescription for the role of women, the focus of feminist attention has moved away from issues of influence in clinical psychoanalysis.

Recent developments in Anglo-American psychoanalysis have taken up the issues of suggestion, of whether and how psychoanalytic theory influences the experience of its patients by the way it regulates the conduct of the therapeutic relationship, and related debates concerning what authority the analyst does and should or should not wield.[26] Although the generation of psychoanalysts who succeeded Freud customarily insisted on the absence of any prescriptive influence on the part of the analyst even more strongly than did Freud himself, there has been a broad shift toward an acknowledgment of the inevitability of the analyst's influence on the patient's experience of subjectivity. Rather than seeing this as a fatal flaw, advocates of this shift see it as in keeping with recent epistemological trends throughout the human sciences and even in the physical sciences, which recognize the inevitable impact of the outlook of the observer on the observed as part of any encounter—scientific, psychoanalytic or otherwise.

Prior to this shift, mainstream forms of American psychoanalysis had analogized the role of the analyst to that of the medical doctor and scientist. As Freud himself had written,

I cannot advise my colleagues too urgently to model themselves during psycho-analytic treatment on the surgeon, who puts aside all his feelings, even his human sympathy, and concentrates his mental forces on the single aim of performing the operation as skillfully as possible.[27]

The model of the analyst as surgeon was melded with the model of the analyst as research scientist, leading to the conception of psychoanalysis as an operation or a scientific experiment in which the body on which the operation was to be performed or the data that was to be analyzed—the free associations of the patient—were to remain antiseptic and uncontaminated by "personal bits from the analyst's life."[28] Psychoanalytic data were believed to reside exclusively within the patient's mind, from which they would emerge via free association to be interpreted by the analyst. Analytic treatment was to facilitate the emergence of this personal interiority, the coming into consciousness of hitherto unconscious contents. In specific contradistinction to both hypnosis and religion, the subject of analysis was not to be influenced, persuaded or manipulated to a particular, authoritative and/or conventional point of view.

To reach an uncontaminated, objective understanding of the unconscious data emerging in treatment, qualities of abstinence, detachment, anonymity and neutrality on the part of the analyst were cultivated throughout the mid-century North American practice of psychoanalysis. Emboldened by these tools, the analyst could claim "a singular scientific knowledge and authority vis-à-vis the patient's mind."[29] According to this view, any difficulties that arose in treatment could have nothing to do with the analyst, who was only a neutral, anonymous blank screen on which the patient's conflicts were projected. Difficulties were solely the result of intrapsychic conflicts within the patient that caused him or her to distort reality, and these distortions would be resolved through the understanding gained from the analyst's interpretations.

Recent currents in Anglo-American psychoanalysis have challenged this view of analytic authority; and the inevitability of influence and even the possibility of domination in the psychoanalytic relationship has begun to be more broadly recognized. Merton Gill, a proponent of mainstream American ego psychology, wrote a treatise in 1982 on the transference in which he insisted that, however restrained the analyst's behavior might be, it could not help but contribute to the experience of the patient in the transference which was, therefore, "an interpersonal experience."[30]

Contemporary analysts are challenging the philosophies of mind that supported a scientistic construal of the psyche, of the clinical relationship and of the analyst as a detached observer. They have begun to reintegrate a previously disavowed history going back to Ferenczi's heretical experiments with "mutual analysis," a history which includes the work of the interpersonal psychiatrist Harry Stack Sullivan, who, in the 1950s, introduced the Malinowskian term *participant observation* to characterize the analytic relationship.[31] The British school of object relations has developed models pointing to the possibility of mutual influence in the analytic relationship. Melanie Klein's concept of projective identification, for example, suggested that disavowed parts of the unconscious lives of patient and analyst found their way into the psyches of each other, and Winnicott's description of the transference as a "holding environment" suggested the impact of the analyst's comportment itself in providing the atmosphere which would allow the patient to risk revealing unknown parts of him- or herself.

The schools of psychoanalysis referred to as relational and intersubjective have gone the furthest in considering the construction of psychoanalytic knowledge as an intersubjective and mutual process that privileges neither analyst nor patient. Instead, they see the analytic experience of each partner as constituted through their relationship to the other, each "contributing to shaping the relationship in a particular way among many ways that are possible . . . entail[ing] the creation of meaning, not merely its discovery."[32] As Stephen Mitchell has written of contemporary Anglo-American psychoanalysis:

> There has been a striking convergence over the past decade in all the major schools of analytic thought in the broad-scale, dramatic shift from a view of mind as monadic, a separable, individual entity, to a view of mind as dyadic, emerging from and inevitably embedded within a relational field.[33]

Feminist critiques of normative models of subjectivity and their proposals for alternate, more relational models have also played an important role in the development of this shift in focus.[34]

These developments have approached the question of influence and authority in psychoanalysis from an epistemological perspective, challenging the view that the patient's mind alone is the source of whatever goes on in the analytic relationship. They have come a great distance in conceiving the clinical encounter as a mutual one whose understanding is contributed to in equal measure by both partners. But only a few have linked these changes to issues of race, in spite of the fact that the connections of the clinical relationship with the racial discourse of primitivity are embedded in the foundational structures of psychoanalysis. Therefore, let us now investigate these connections by returning to Freud's formulations of the topics of suggestion, hypnosis, regression and resistance, relating his technical considerations concerning these topics as found largely in his *Papers on Technique*,[35] to his discussions of the same topics in *Group Psychology and the Analysis of the Ego* and elsewhere.

Freud's use of suggestion

Although psychoanalysis was not conceived as a form of suggestion in the service of social norms, there was, historically, a close and highly ambiguous connection between psychoanalysis and the techniques of influence and suggestion.[36] Suggestion was the mode of intervention proper to hypnosis, and the clinical technique of psychoanalysis had its roots in hypnosis. Early on in his career Freud went to France to study with the famed French hypnotists, Jean Martin Charcot and Hippolyte Bernheim. In his early *Studies on Hysteria* (1895) we see Freud making his first forays into the clinical treatment of hysteria—as a hypnotist. And, as a hypnotist, Freud was frank about his use of suggestion: "As is the usual practice in hypnotic psychotherapy, I fought against the patient's pathological ideas by means of assurances and prohibitions."[37] As he moved away from the practice of hypnosis, Freud took his cue from Bernheim's work with *non*-hypnotized patients: through insistence alone, Bernheim had been able to elicit from them memories that had previously appeared only with patients placed under hypnosis. Freud began to replace hypnosis with "insistence" and "concentration." He would have patients lie down and close their eyes, whereupon he would place his hands on their foreheads and apply a slight pressure. Faced with recalcitrance on the part of a patient, Freud "became insistent" and then "became still more insistent: . . . I then found that . . . it would in fact be possible for the pathogenic groups of ideas . . . to be brought to light by mere insistence."[38] In his first post-hypnotism ventures into what was to become psychoanalysis, Freud's original tool was suggestion in the form of insistence.

In *Group Psychology and the Analysis of the Ego* Freud had written that insistence and suggestion, as found in groups and in hypnosis, depended on "a conviction which is not based upon perception and reasoning but upon an erotic tie."[39] There he had linked the practice of hypnosis to the relationship between the group member and the patriarchal leader: both the hypnotic relationship and the group relationship were formed by an erotic tie that excluded sexual consummation. In fact, the suggestibility of hypnosis was, according to Freud, the same as the erotically based contagion that formed the bond within group relationships. Thus what Freud ascribed in *Group Psychology* to members of primitive communities vis-à-vis their leaders applied to the hypnotic relationship as well. The subject of hypnosis, like the primitive group member, was in thrall to the hypnotist who, in turn, occupied a role analogous to the patriarchal group leader. The hypnotist, like the group leader, usurped the psychic space of the hypnotized subject's superego, as described in Chapter 3. Both the hypnotic relationship and the group relationship were "primitive" relationships, awakening patterns of submissive devotion on the part of the group member and of domination on the part of the leader. Subjects under hypnosis regressed to the narcissistic levels of psychosexual development characteristic of the primitive group members of *Group Psychology* and *Totem and Taboo*. Suggestion, the technique of hypnosis, was also the technique of primitivity.

The mature psychoanalytic technique that Freud developed by the time he wrote his *Papers on Technique* (1911–15) seemed to move decisively away from suggestion and insistence as central therapeutic devices. In their place was the "fundamental rule" of the psychoanalytic patient who was enjoined to say everything that came to mind, and the analyst's corresponding "evenly suspended attention," which was not to focus exclusively on any particular element of the patient's associations. Neurosis was an acting out of unconscious wishes and prohibitions impelled by the compulsion to repeat. Through free association and the fundamental rule, and without the benefit of suggestion and insistence, these unconscious motivations would be revealed; through the analyst's interpretations they would be transformed into memories. Rather than repeating and acting out unconscious desires, the patient was to recognize and remember them: memory was to replace repetition.

Although the "primitive" technique of suggestion was replaced by these advances in psychoanalysis, the emergence of the central role of the transference threw the distinction between the two into question once more. Freud discovered that during the course of treatment, the patient's unconscious infantile patterns of desire were "transferred" to the analyst, forming the transference, an erotic feeling on the part of the patient for the analyst. Through free association, the patient was understood to regress to the earliest levels of desire which, once reawakened, became focused on the analyst. And since infantile sexuality was the substratum of these earliest levels of desire, it became, as Freud wrote, the "inescapable fate"[40] of many psychoanalytic (female) patients to fall in love with their (male) doctor. (The vexed contradiction of a largely female clientele forming the empirical basis of the psychoanalytic theory of the male psyche is nowhere more acutely in evidence than in the *Papers on Technique*.)

Although he took pains to distinguish the transference from forms of love that take place outside the consulting room, Freud was forced to recognize the genuineness of love in the transference. "It is true that the [transference] love consists of new editions of old traits and that it repeats infantile reactions. But this is the essential character of every state of being in love." Nevertheless, for the analyst to give in to transference love would be a diversion from the therapeutic aims of psychoanalysis: it would be a repeating and an acting out of what was meant to be transformed into memory. Because the desired gratification would be "a complete defeat for the treatment," Freud saw the transference as a form of resistance, a ploy of the patient to avoid the labor of insight and working through. (In the transference the female patient exhibited a far-too-active—one might say, a masculine—desire: in contradistinction, "genuine love," Freud wrote, "would make her docile.") The transference would be distinguished from other forms of love not by its form or content but by the manner in which it was to be understood and responded to: "not to be attributed to the charms of [the analyst's] own person" but evoked, impersonally, by the clinical situation itself and purposely frustrated to transform the desire to act—the compulsion to repeat—into memory.[41]

Transference love was not only a resistance to analysis, however; it was also the path toward cure: it provided the raw material on which the analysis worked, painstakingly making conscious and turning into memories the previously repressed wishes of which the transference itself was constituted. The transference was an "intermediate region between illness and real life through which the transition from the one to the other is made."[42] The working through of the transference was the transformative labor of psychoanalysis itself; psychoanalysis took advantage of a relationship of awakened desire to perform its curative work.

This relationship of unsatisfied desire on which the work of psycho-analysis rested shared the same psychological structure as the hypnotic relationship: the transference and the hypnotic relationship were both "based upon . . . an [unsatisfied] erotic tie." And in spite of the self-defini-tion of psychoanalysis in contradistinction to hypnosis, traces of influence and suggestion showed up yet again in the transference. Indeed, as Freud admitted, "this transference . . . [is] the same dynamic factor which the hypnotists have named suggestibility."[43] Thus the transference relationship characterized *both* hypnosis and psychoanalysis. Transference was a form of love, and in *Group Psychology* Freud had linked not only group rela-tions, but also love, to hypnosis. Both hypnosis and being in love exhibited "the same humble subjection, the same compliance, the same absence of criticism . . . the same sapping of the subject's own initiative" and the same "unlimited devotion."[44] Both hypnosis and love made people susceptible to forms of influence based on eros rather than on reason. Psychoanalysis, too, relied on a relationship of love, and through transference love patients became susceptible to influence and suggestion.

Banished from the official lexicon of psychoanalysis, suggestion entered through the back door of transference love. Although Freud dis-dained therapies of suggestion, claiming they were "not a psycho-analysis at all,"[45] he nevertheless conceded that psychoanalysis, like hypnosis, relied on suggestion to some extent. He wrote that "in our technique we have abandoned hypnosis only to rediscover suggestion in the shape of transference"[46] and that "analytic treatment . . . uses suggestion in order to alter the outcome of those conflicts."[47] He distinguished erotic and hostile transferences from positive but non-erotic ones, and observed that once the first two are "removed" by becoming conscious the positive transfer-ence remains and

> is the vehicle of success in psychoanalysis exactly as it is in other methods of treatment. To this extent we readily admit that the results of psychoanalysis rest upon suggestion; by suggestion, however, we must understand, as Ferenczi (1909) does, the influencing of a person by means of the transference phenomena which are possible in his case. We take care of the patient's final independence by employing suggestion in order to get him to accomplish a piece of psychical work which has as its necessary result a permanent improvement in his psy-chical situation.[48]

Thus psychoanalysis shared with hypnosis the phenomenon of transference and its associated techniques of suggestion and influence, a fact that has been recognized over the years by some analysts, who, far from objecting, have seen in these traces the reasons for the effectiveness of analytic treatment.[49]

Still, a cardinal difference remained between hypnosis and psychoanalysis. Freud was well aware of the charge that psychoanalysis was simply a sophisticated form of suggestive therapy, and he spelled out the differences between the two in a number of instances.[50] Although the transference bond of analysis is the same as the bond linking hypnotic subject to hypnotist, the crucial difference between the two lies in the attitude taken by each toward the transference. Both hypnosis and psychoanalysis take advantage of the transference to bring about their cures, but hypnosis allows the transference to remain unconscious, not recognizing that it is an incarnation of the original causes of the problem for which the patient is being treated. Psychoanalysis, on the other hand, *analyzes* the transference, making it conscious and thereby gaining access to the causative elements of the neurosis. Only after unconscious conflict has been analyzed should suggestion be used to help mobilize the patient's capacities to move in a different manner than the one he or she has hitherto been accustomed to. The transference relationship bond is deconstructed, rather than exploited, in the main part of analytic treatment. The relational glue that constitutes the hypnotic transference bond is to be dissolved through the work of analysis.

But even with *this* cardinal distinction between hypnosis and psychoanalysis, similarities remained. It seems that Freud himself did not demur from the use of suggestion at any stage during analytic treatment. He gave his patients "the appropriate anticipatory ideas"[51] and reflected that "the communication of repressed material to the patient's consciousness . . . sets up a process of thought in the course of which the expected influencing of the unconscious recollection eventually takes place."[52] Although Freud replaced hypnosis with psychoanalysis, pressure to the forehead with free association, suggestion with freely hovering attention and insistence with working through, the mature form of psychoanalytic treatment continued to bear the vestiges of the suggestion associated with hypnosis.

As we have seen in Chapter 3, the bond of suggestion created in hypnosis is the same as the erotic bond that links the primitive group members to their leader. Thus the bond that characterizes the relationship of patient to analyst is the same as the bond that links hypnotized subject to hypnotist, as well as primitive horde member to patriarchal group leader. The "numerous points of agreement" between primitivity and neurosis of which Freud spoke in *Totem and Taboo* thus emerge in the clinical relationship: in the transference the patient is in a position analogous to that of the primitive group member. The patient is in the position of primitivity, a position indexed to race and characterized by both regression and resistance.

Regression and resistance

By conceiving of the unconscious in terms of primitivity, Freud placed the unconscious within a temporal framework where it could be seen as developmentally prior to the secondary processes of consciousness, and within a dynamic framework understood as structured by relations of domination and subjugation. In the clinical relationship, the temporal relationship between the unconscious and consciousness was mediated by regression, whereas the dynamic relations of domination and subjugation were mediated by resistance.

Through the concept of regression Freud explained the mechanism by which the patient reached the position of primitivity. The neurosis that the patient brought to the analytic situation had resulted from an intrapsychic impasse along the route of psychosexual development: symptoms were the neurotic compromises to this repressed conflict. The free associations of analytic treatment would eventually lead the patient back to the repressed, unconscious, infantile—primitive—events that had originally prompted the impasse. As noted in Chapter 2, regression was understood as a movement from the rational thought of consciousness to the sensory and imaginal modes associated with the unconscious; from more recent to earlier infantile psychic structures; from "the psychical sphere . . . into the motor sphere,"[53] which is to say, from mentation to acting out; and, finally, from ontogenetic, contemporary life to the phylogenetic childhood of the human race. Inducing regression through free association, the psychoanalytic relationship regressed the patient to an infantile primitivity, enlisting him in a relationship analogous to the primitive group bond. In the same way as primitive, narcissistic processes were elicited by the horde/group leader who "awakens in the subject a portion of his archaic heritage,"[54] so were they elicited by the analyst in the transference relationship.

Like the subject of hypnosis and the primitive group member, then, the analysand in the throes of the transference becomes enthralled with an external object (the analyst), setting in motion the psychic structures of primitivity as Freud defined them. Governed by these structures, the repertoire of primitivity emerges: narcissistic processes of subjectivity and animistic modes of belief in which wish fulfillment predominates. The primitive group member, the subject of hypnosis, and the subject of the transference were all understood as constituted by these same relational dynamics and therefore as exhibiting the same psychic processes of a developmental/evolutionary primitivity, expressed through enthrallment with and submission to a dominant male figure.

The position of the analyst can also be seen to be linked to the structures of primitivity set in motion by the transference. While the patient was placed in the position of the hypnotized subject and, by extension, in the position of a member of the primitive horde, the analyst was placed in the position of hypnotic leader and of the primitive patriarch. The analyst was in the position of influence, of domination, of authority; through him, the authority of psychoanalysis was now to replace the authority of the past. As an *analyzed* patriarch, however, the analyst was to renounce his patriarchal prerogatives, as Moses had, using his authority not to maintain the patient in primitivity but to lead him out of it; to develop in the patient the capacity for an autonomous individuality. The analyst was to occupy the position of authority but to use that authority to deconstruct the relationship that supported it. This was the wager of the transference: a faith that a reintroduction of a homeopathic tincture of the original pathology would engender its cure rather than merely reproducing its effects. But this wager brings into play the possibility that each analytic relationship may be an instance *either* of the dissolution *or* of the reproduction of the domination characteristic of the regression to primitivity.

Freud's language concerning the transference, as well as the mainstream twentieth-century psychoanalytic literature that grew out of it, reflected the possibility, if not the likelihood, that the analytic relationship would reproduce domination on the part of the analyst and submission on the part of the patient. The "scientific" qualities of neutrality, abstinence and frustration, which were, through the mid-twentieth century, the mainstay of psychoanalytic technique, had long been believed to be in the service of protecting the autonomy of the patient from the danger of contamination or domination by the analyst's influence. More recently, however, these qualities themselves have been recognized as ways in which analysts have actually insured their authority over their patients. As Foucault has written concerning the ritual of confession, which he sees as reconfigured in the psychoanalytic encounter, "the agency of domination does not reside in the one who speaks . . . but in the one who listens and says nothing."[55] And as the eminent psychoanalyst Otto Kernberg has written, the traditional analytic attitude "contributed to . . . a nonanalyzed submission of the patient to the idealized analyst."[56]

In many of Freud's writings, the transference is described in metaphors of combat and legal authority. "Every conflict has to be fought out in the sphere of the transference."[57] Treatment is a "struggle,"[58] a "battlefield"[59] in which the analyst must "subdue portions of [the] id"[60] in the hopes that "victory . . . be won";[61] the core neurotic conflict is likened to "the enemy's key fortresses" and to "a hostile capital."[62] In such a combat, "victory is . . . on the side of the big battalions."[63] The transference is "the strongest weapon of the resistance";[64] the analyst's task is "that of the examining magistrate."[65] Interventions and admissions of error are to be made "without sacrificing any of our authority."[66] Freud reports that he learned "to stand obstinately by my suspicions til I had overcome the patients' disingenuousness and compelled them to confirm my views"[67] and observed that "where there is a dispute with the patient . . . the doctor is usually in the right."[68]

Although the transference was to be analyzed rather than exploited, a closer examination reveals a less detached role prescribed for the analyst. At first, in Freud's work, the transference appears as an unexpected and unwelcome intrusion. As its instrumentality for analytic work is recognized, it moves into focus as the central feature of psychoanalytic treatment, with the analyst aiding in its emergence. Soon Freud is writing that "[a]ll the libido, as well as everything opposing it, is made to converge solely on the relation with the doctor"; libido is "forced from the symptoms into the transference"; "we get hold of the whole of the libido . . . by attracting a portion of it to ourselves by means of the transference"; the analyst has to "gain control" of the libido. We read of the necessity of "*creating* in the patient's relation to the doctor—in the 'transference'—new editions of old conflicts," and we are informed that repeating is "*induced* in analytic treatment" through the transference.[69] The analyst not only influences; he seems to be an active creator and manipulator of the transference. Here is no neutrality, no detachment, no blank screen onto which unconscious contents are transferred: here is someone who induces the transference and forces libido onto it—that is, encourages the patient's love—and creates "new editions" of conflict within the relationship. "Contamination" is everywhere.

This adversarial configuration of the analytic relationship arises out of Freud's understanding of the transference as resistance. Resistance is the psychic force that seeks to maintain the repression which created the contents of the unconscious in the first place. It is the defense mechanism that opposes the coming-to-consciousness of unconscious contents, preferring that the subject act out rather than reflect on his desires. If the analyst is considered to be an impartial and uninvolved observer and interpreter, any opposition to the analyst is understood to be resistance to making the unconscious conscious. And since an analysis of the patient's resistance will reveal the fears and hostility of his or her earliest relationships, any response on the part of the patient that objects to the analyst's behavior or interpretations is understood to be a projection of infantile emotions.

But how did the concept of resistance arise in Freud's work? We recall that Freud first arrived at his understanding of resistance in his early work as he was making the transition from hypnotism to psychoanalysis. As mentioned earlier, when mere questioning proved to be of no avail in these early attempts to elicit memories of the causes of a patient's symptoms, Freud tried "insisting":

> This insistence involved effort on my part and so suggested the idea that I had to overcome a resistance . . . by means of my psychical work I had to overcome a psychical force in the patients which was opposed to the pathogenic ideas becoming conscious (being remembered).[70]

Reluctance on the part of the patient to reveal whatever came to mind was "resistance," and on this basis, clinical work was construed as a struggle in which the analyst had to overcome this resistance. Insistence on the part of the analyst was initiated to overcome resistance on the part of the patient. Therapeutic change came about through overcoming resistances, which was "the essential function of analytic treatment";[71] the clinical task became easier once the patient's "resistance [was] for the most part broken."[72] Significantly, the concepts of resistance and insistence describe relations of force and, as such, are intimately tied to Freud's characterization of primitivity. The primitivity of the unconscious suggests that it is inaccessible to rational appeal and that, like members of the primitive groups described in *Group Psychology*, the only kind of relationship in which it can be engaged is one of domination and subjugation. The concept of resistance legitimated the analyst's coercive authority within the transference.

The emergence of the concept of resistance from Freud's therapeutic use of insistence points to a possibility that has been increasingly acknowledged by contemporary developments in psychoanalysis: resistance may, in part, be an effect of the technique of insistence, rather than that which necessitates it.[73] Without denying our deep-seated reluctance to face painful fears, memories or desires, we may still recognize in the therapeutic concept of resistance a form of defense caused by the imposition of relations of psychological force and power within the analytic situation itself. Indeed, resistance may arise as a response to the unwelcome constitution of oneself as *primitive*—i.e. in a position of subordination.

As mentioned in Chapter 3, the psychological processes described as primitivity can be seen as having been created by domination, whether in "primitive" groups or in the therapeutic relationship. Freud defines his famous "bedrock of the psyche" as the rejection by male and female patients alike of "passivity towards a male,"[74] precisely his definition of both femininity and primitivity, which are his categories of subordination. Although projections of infantile defiance toward parental figures may very well manifest themselves in the transference, we may also see in Freud's "bedrock of the psyche" a fundamental resistance to the position of subordination per se and, in particular, a resistance to the analyst's imposed authority or domination. The patient whose resistance is "for the most part broken"[75] is the one who complies with the submission required by the transferential situation; and the resolution of the transference becomes the patient's subordination to the analyst's system of meaning.

The temporalization of the understanding of the transference—conceiving it exclusively in terms of familial relationships from "the past"—can itself contribute to the imposition of a "primitive" position of submission, as was demonstrated in psychoanalyst Abram Kardiner's memoirs of his analysis with Freud. Wrote Kardiner,

> Yes, I was afraid of my father in childhood, but the one whom I feared now was Freud himself. He could make me or break me, which my father no longer could. By his statement, [Freud] pushed the entire reaction [of Kardiner's fear of Freud] into the past, thereby making the

analysis a historical reconstruction . . . I made a silent pact with Freud. "I will continue to be compliant provided that you will let me enjoy your protection."[76]

Compliance in return for protection: an apt description of the psychology of the primitive group member.

The return of *Totem and Taboo*

When Freud wrote of "the necessity of creating in the patient's relation to the doctor—in the 'transference'—new editions of the old conflicts,"[77] it was the analyst's prior understanding, based on his theoretical commitments, of what those old conflicts must have been that allowed him to create, rather than simply to discover, their new editions. Freud's later writings point even further in this direction. In "Constructions in Analysis" (1937), Freud openly acknowledged the ambiguity inherent in the analyst's attempt to represent the patient's unconscious through the interpretation of free associations. Interpretations had generally been understood as faithful translations into psychoanalytic concepts of the patient's recollections from the unconscious. In this essay, however, Freud wrote that interpretations were actually the analyst's "constructions," explaining that the task of the analyst was "to make out what has been forgotten from the traces which it has left behind, or, more correctly, to *construct* it."[78] This paper can be read as signaling a shift away from a positivist conception of the unconscious as an already formed, knowable and retrievable entity awaiting scientific discovery, and toward a more sophisticated conception of the unstable and retrospectively constructed character of memory. However, if the unconscious is understood as a text whose basic contours are already known by the analyst *avant la lettre*, this designation of interpretations as constructions strengthens, rather than moderates, the analyst's authoritarian role: it extends the analyst's interpretative authority by licensing him to fill in the blanks created by the absence of actual recollections:

> Quite often we do not succeed in bringing the patient to recollect what has been repressed. Instead of that, if the analysis is carried out correctly, we produce in him an assured conviction of the truth of the construction which achieves the same therapeutic result as a recaptured memory.[79]

How does the analyst "produce an assured conviction of the truth of the construction"? The "assured conviction" may well arise out of the fact that the construction meshes seamlessly with other unconscious elements of the patient's experience that become revealed during the course of the analysis; as Freud puts it, "indirect confirmation from associations that fit in with the content of a construction . . . provide a valuable basis for judging whether the construction is likely to be confirmed."[80] But such conviction may equally well arise from the analyst's efforts to convince the patient of memories that he or she otherwise might not recollect. Interpretations themselves may be independently constructed by the analyst, who also "produces" the "assured conviction" that confirms them. Again we see that suggestion is not simply adjunct to the work of analysis; it is part of the very fabric of the analytic work itself. The analyst can use his authority to direct the shape of the analysand's associations, producing constructions that conform to his theoretical template. As we have seen, this theoretical template—a theory of psychopathology and of therapeutic technique imbricated with psychoanalytic models of libidinal development—has been indexed to evolutionary coordinates. Now we can see more fully the clinical implications of the evolutionary comparative method and its associated recapitulatory assumptions that Freud had borrowed from the evolutionary anthropologists. For "what has been forgotten" on the ontogenetic level was, as Freud had stated so many times, a recapitulation of our phylogenetic inheritance. Thus gaps in memory of ontogenetic development could be filled in by the predetermined record, elaborated in detail by Freud, of our shared phylogenetic past.

A particular case in point can be found in the case of the Wolf Man (1918), where the evolutionary premises of psychoanalysis, as laid out in *Totem and Taboo*, are pressed into service as interpretations/constructions within the therapeutic relationship. Three-quarters of the way through his discussion of this famous case, we find Freud attempting to consolidate the Wolf Man's childhood experiences into a picture of a typical oedipal complex. His difficulties, and his solution to them, are evident in the following passage:

> At this point the boy had to fit into a phylogenetic pattern, and he did so, *although his personal experiences may not have agreed with it*. Although the threats of hints of castration which had come his way had emanated from women, this could not hold up the final result for long.

In spite of everything it was his father from whom in the end he came to fear castration. In this respect *heredity triumphed over accidental experience*; in man's prehistory it was unquestionably the father who practiced castration as a punishment and who later softened it down into circumcision.[81]

Later, in the same case, Freud justifies the chain of reasoning by which the boy's memory of urination in the presence of his maid "would be evidence of the influence of an earlier impression, which might equally have been the actual occurrence of the primal scene" by remarking that

scenes of observing parental intercourse, of being seduced in child-hood, and of being threatened with castration are unquestionably an inherited endowment, a phylogenetic heritage, but they may just as easily be acquired by personal experience. With my patient, his seduc-tion by his elder sister was an indisputable reality; why should not the same have been true of his observation of his parents' intercourse? All that we find in the prehistory of neuroses is that a child catches hold of this phylogenetic experience where his own experience fails him. He fills in the gaps in individual truth with prehistoric truth; he replaces occurrences in his own life by occurrences in the life of his ancestors.[82]

A string of hypotheses—the memory of urination *might* have been evidence of an earlier impression which itself *might* have been the primal scene—is confirmed by knowledge of "phylogenetic experience," so that the Wolf Man's memories may be, however laboriously, made to conform to the theory. We may suspect that it was the analyst, rather than the boy, who had to "fill in the gaps with prehistoric truth." If the experiences and memories of a patient do not fit into the theory, the theory provides them by fiat, invok-ing them as phylogenetic inheritances. Freud goes on in this passage to caution that phylogenetic explanation be used only secondarily, once "onto-genetic possibilities have been exhausted."[83] Nonetheless, these passages make clear the resources that can provide material for the constructions the analyst resorts to when faced with a difficulty "in bringing the patient to recollect what has been repressed."[84] The analyst's interpretive inventory is poised to supplement fantasies and memories with elements of our "phy-logenetic inheritance" as established by psychoanalysis' origin myth of the inauguration of the modern social and psychic order, *Totem and Taboo*.

Freud conceived of his therapy as unbinding the knots tied by trauma and fantasy through an elucidation of their history, within the trusted intimacy of the psychoanalytic dyad. Nevertheless, he also conceived of the analytic patient as having regressed to primitivity and therefore as having traced backward the psychosexual scale of individual development that he had correlated with the racially coded scale of cultural evolution: in this latter sense, the analysand was indeed "a negro." If the patient was seen as having regressed down the psychocultural scale, treatment was to lead him out of the timeless thralldom of primitivity through its own recapitulation of (Freud's view of) the evolutionary development of individual subjectivity. Present urgencies would be understood as recapitulations or repetitions of past desires, educating the subject as to the history of his or her suffering and thereby helping free him or her from domination by the past. The replacement of repeating (acting out) by remembering (mentation) would parallel the shift from external cathexis to internalized structure that, for Freud, marked the transition of the primitive group member to civilized individuality. The bond with the analyst—the transference—would be progressively dissolved, leaving in its wake the internalized traces out of which new internal psychic structures would be created. The subjectivity of the patient would be restructured along the lines of an unimpeded developmental scale, covertly indexed to a racial evolutionary scale. Gaps in this restructuring could be filled in by references to this reconstructed phylogenetic, racial, evolutionary scale. Thus the transference of classical psychoanalysis spanned the transition not only "between illness and real life"[85] but also between primitivity and an evolutionarily conceived modernity. The relationship of colonizer to colonized encoded in the raced figure of the primitive, having filtered through the theoretical edifice of psychoanalysis, is able to be reborn in the consulting room. It is up to us to recognize this undesirable potential, woven into the hidden connections within psychoanalytic theory, rather than unwittingly reproducing it.

Notes

1 Ernest Jones, *The Life and Work of Sigmund Freud*, vol. 3 (New York: Basic Books, 1957), 105. Claudia Tate, "Freud and His 'Negro': Psychoanalysis as Ally and Enemy of African Americans," *Journal for the Psychoanalysis of Culture and Society* 1, no. 1 (1996): 53–62, provides an insightful analysis of the implications of this joke within Freud's context as well as for the alliance of the first generation of émigré psychoanalysts in the US with white privilege.

2 Phillis Isabella Sheppard, *Self, Culture and Others in Womanist Practical Theology* (New York: Palgrave Macmillan, 2011), 82–4.

3 Octave Mannoni, "Psychoanalysis and the Decolonization of Mankind," in Jonathan Miller, ed., *Freud: The Man, His World, His Influence* (London: Weidenfeld and Nicolson, 1972), 85–96, quote at 93.

4 For arguments concerning the human sciences as based on interpretation and critique, see Charles Taylor, *Philosophy and the Human Sciences* (Cambridge: Cambridge University Press, 1985), esp. chap. 1, "Interpretation and the Sciences of Man," 15–57; and Paul Ricoeur, *Hermeneutics and the Social Sciences*, ed. and trans. John B. Thompson (Cambridge: Cambridge University Press, 1981), esp. chap. 2, "Hermeneutics and the Critique of Ideology," 63–100.

5 Judith S. Schachter and Hugh F. Butts, "Transference and Countertransference in Interracial Analyses," *Journal of the American Psychoanalytic Association* 16, no. 4 (1968): 792–808; Dorothy Evans Holmes, "Race and Transference in Psychoanalysis and Psychotherapy," *International Journal of Psychoanalysis* 73, pt. 1 (1992): 1–11.

6 Kimberlyn Leary, "Race in Psychoanalytic Space," *Gender and Psychoanalysis* 2, no. 2 (1997): 157–72; "Racial Enactments in Dynamic Treatment," *Psychoanalytic Dialogues* 10, no. 4 (2000): 639–53; "Racial Insult and Repair," *Psychoanalytic Dialogues* 17, no. 4 (2007): 539–49; "Race as an Adaptive Challenge: Working with Diversity in the Clinical Consulting Room," *Psychoanalytic Psychology* 29, no. 3 (2012): 279–91.

7 Kimberlyn Leary, "Race in Psychoanalytic Space," 159. See also Rafael Art Javier and William G. Herron, "Psychoanalysis and the Disenfranchised: Countertransference Issues," *Psychoanalytic Psychology* 19, no. 1 (2002): 149–66; Rafael Art Javier and Michael Moskowitz, "Notes from the Trenches," *Psychoanalytic Psychology* 19, no. 1 (2002): 144–8.

8 *Psychoanalytic Dialogues* 10, no. 4 (2000); *Psychoanalytic Quarterly*, 75, no. 1 (2006).

9 Ann Pellegrini, "Normalizing Citizenship, Forgetting Difference," in *Psychoanalytic Dialogues* 10, no. 4 (2000), 704.

10 Janice O. Bennett, "The Analyst at the Intersection of Multiple Cultures," *Psychoanalytic Perspectives* 3, no. 2 (2006): 55–63.

11 Basia Winograd, director and producer, *Black Psychoanalysts Speak* (PEP Video Grants, 2014).

12 Neil Altman, *The Analyst in the Inner City: Race, Class, and Culture through a Psychoanalytic Lens* (New York: Routledge, 1995, 2010).

13 Altman, *Analyst in the Inner City*, xvi, 43, 45. See also Javier and Moskowitz, "Notes from the Trenches," 145.

14 Michel Foucault, *Technologies of the Self: A Seminar with Michel Foucault*, ed. Luther H. Martin, Huck Gutman and Patrick H. Hutton (Amherst, MA: University of Massachusetts Press, 1988), 17–18.

15 Josef Breuer and Sigmund Freud, *Studies on Hysteria*, SE 2:305.

16 Rebuttals of this notion can be found throughout Freud's *Papers on Technique*, SE 12:89–203; see also the end of Lecture 27, "Transference,"

and the first half of Lecture 28, "Analytic Therapy," in *Introductory Lectures*, *SE* 16:431–47, 448–63, for a fuller discussion of the differences between psychoanalysis and suggestion.

17 The gory story is recounted in Janet Malcolm's *In the Freud Archives* (New York: Knopf, 1984), 44–50; and in Jeffrey Moussaieff Masson's contentious *Assault on Truth* (New York: Farrar, Straus and Giroux, 1984), 55–106. For details in Freud's own words, see *The Complete Letters of Sigmund Freud to Wilhelm Fliess*, ed. and trans. Jeffrey Masson, 113–31.
18 Freud, "Fragment of an Analysis of a Case of Hysteria," *SE* 7: 1–122.
19 Classic American instances of these charges are to be found, among others, in Betty Friedan, *The Feminine Mystique* (New York: Dell, 1974 [1963]); Kate Millett, *Sexual Politics* (Garden City, NY: Doubleday, 1970); Germaine Greer, *The Female Eunuch* (London: MacGibbon and Kee, 1970); Phillis Chesler, *Women and Madness* (New York: Avon, 1973); and Mary Daly, *Gyn/Ecology* (Boston, MA: Beacon, 1978). Gloria Steinem repeated these charges as recently as 1995 in *Ms.* magazine. Nor is the use of psychoanalytic perspectives to control the social position of women limited to the beginnings of psychoanalysis or to the mid-century United States: David Macey cites the example of the French women's group of the 1970s, *psych et po*, which advocated that women not vote in the 1979 elections because "we are not representable." This claim derived from a Lacanian-derived view according to which women lack the means to represent themselves within the system of signification that constitutes patriarchal society. For this and other woeful tales of Lacanian misogyny, see David Macey, *Lacan in Contexts* (London: Verso, 1988), chap. 6.
20 For a history of the interconnections and struggles between feminism and psychoanalysis, see Mary Jo Buhle, *Feminism and Its Discontents: A Century of Struggle with Psychoanalysis* (Cambridge, MA: Harvard University Press, 1998).
21 Freud, "The Infantile Genital Organization," *SE* 19:145.
22 Freud, "Femininity," *New Introductory Lectures on Psychoanalysis*, *SE* 22:129.
23 Ferenczi, quoted in Freud, "Analysis Terminable and Interminable," *SE* 23:251, n. 3.
24 Juliet Mitchell, *Psychoanalysis and Feminism: Freud, Reich, Laing, and Women* (New York: Random House, Pantheon, 1974), 338–9, 362, passim.
25 Rubin, "The Traffic in Women," 200.
26 For overviews of these developments, see Lewis Aron, *A Meeting of Minds: Mutuality in Psychoanalysis* (Hillsdale, NJ: Analytic Press, 1996); and Stephen A. Mitchell, *Influence and Autonomy in Psychoanalysis* (Hillsdale, NJ: Analytic Press, 1997).
27 Freud, "Recommendations to Physicians Practicing Psycho-Analysis," *SE* 12:115.
28 Phillis Greenacre, "The Role of Transference: Practical Considerations in Relation to Psychoanalytic Therapy," in Aaron H. Esman, ed., *Essential Papers on the Transference*, (New York: New York University Press, 1990) 127.

29 As described and critiqued by Stephen A. Mitchell, "The Analyst's Knowledge and Authority," *Psychoanalytic Quarterly* 67 no. 1 (1998): 6.

30 Merton M. Gill, *Analysis of Transference*, vol. 1: *Theory and Technique* (New York: International Universities Press, 1982), 178.

31 Harry Stack Sullivan, *The Interpersonal Theory of Psychiatry* (New York: Norton, 1953), 13–14, 175–6.

32 Irwin Z. Hoffman, "Discussion: Toward a Social-Constructivist View of the Psychoanalytic Situation," in *Psychoanalytic Dialogues* 1, no. 1 (1991): 91. See Aron, *Meeting of Minds*; and Mitchell, *Influence and Autonomy*, passim.

33 Mitchell, *Influence and Autonomy*, 28.

34 Aron, *Meeting of Minds*, 20–3; Ilene Philipson, *On the Shoulders of Women* (New York: Guilford, 1993).

35 The *Papers on Technique* (*SE* 12:89–173), written between 1911 and 1914, are "The Handling of Dream-Interpretation in Psycho-Analysis," *SE* 12:89–96; "The Dynamics of Transference," *SE* 12:97–108; "Recommendations to Physicians Practising Psychoanalysis," *SE* 12:109–20; "On Beginning the Treatment," *SE* 12:121–44; "Remembering, Repeating, and Working Through," *SE* 12:145–56; and "Observations on Transference Love," *SE* 12:157–71. Freud's chapters, "Transference" and "Analytic Therapy," in the *Introductory Lectures on Psychoanalysis*, *SE* 16:431–47, 448–63, respectively, cover similar areas.

36 Henri Ellenberger places Freud within a long tradition of therapies of suggestion in his classic *Discovery of the Unconscious: The History and Evolution of Dynamic Psychiatry* (New York: Basic Books, 1970). On the other hand, psychoanalysts have, with certain exceptions, tended to see their discipline as having emerged in contradistinction to hypnosis; as Stephen Mitchell argues, "the use of hypnotism as a counteridentification . . . has allowed analysts to feel that their very methodology, unlike hypnotism, protects their patients from the problems of influence." Mitchell, *Influence and Autonomy*, 9.

37 Freud, *Studies on Hysteria*, *SE* 2:101.

38 Ibid., 256, 268.

39 Freud, *Group Psychology*, *SE* 18:128.

40 Freud, "Observations on Transference Love," *SE* 12:161.

41 Ibid., 168, 166, 167, 161.

42 Freud, "Remembering, Repeating and Working Through," *SE* 12:154.

43 Freud, "An Autobiographical Study," *SE* 20:42.

44 Freud, *Group Psychology*, *SE* 18:114–15.

45 Freud, "On Beginning the Treatment," *SE* 12:143.

46 Freud, "Transference," *Introductory Lectures, SE* 16:446.

47 Freud, "Analytic Therapy," *Introductory Lectures, SE* 16:451.

48 Freud, "Dynamics of the Transference," *SE* 12:105–6.

49 For example, Ida Macalpine, "The Development of the Transference" (1950), and Herman Nunberg, "Transference and Reality" (1951), in Esman, ed., *Essential Papers on Transference*, 188–220, 221–35, respectively.

50 See the last four paragraphs of Lecture 27, "Transference," in *Introductory Lectures*, *SE* 16, where Freud anticipates the critique of psychoanalysis as a form of hypnosis owing to its use of suggestion; and his rebuttal in Lecture 28, "Analytic Therapy"; see also "On Beginning the Treatment," *SE* 12:143.

51 Freud, "Transference," *Introductory Lectures*, *SE* 16:437.

52 Freud, "On Beginning the Treatment," *SE* 12:142 (my emphasis).

53 Freud, "Remembering, Repeating and Working Through," *SE* 12:153.

54 Freud, *Group Psychology*, *SE* 18:127.

55 Michel Foucault, *History of Sexuality*, trans. Robert Hurley (New York: Vintage, 1980), 1:62.

56 Otto Kernberg, "The Analyst's Authority in the Psychoanalytic Situation," *Psychoanalytic Quarterly* 65 (1996): 137–57.

57 Freud, "Dynamics of the Transference," *SE* 12:104.

58 Ibid., 108.

59 Freud, "Analytic Therapy," *Introductory Lectures*, *SE* 16:454.

60 Freud, "Analysis Terminable and Interminable," *SE* 23:235.

61 Freud, "Dynamics of the Transference," *SE* 12:108.

62 Freud, "Analytic Therapy," *Introductory Lectures*, *SE* 16:456.

63 Freud, "Analysis Terminable and Interminable," *SE* 23:240.

64 Freud, "Dynamics of Transference," *SE* 12:104.

65 Freud, "Psychoanalysis and the Establishment of the Facts in Legal Proceedings," quoted in Adam Phillips, *Terrors and Experts* (Cambridge, MA: Harvard University Press, 1995), 66.

66 Freud, "Constructions in Analysis," *SE* 23:261–2.

67 Freud, "The Common Neurotic State," *SE* 16:386.

68 Freud, "Recommendations to Physicians Practising Psycho-analysis," *SE* 12:113.

69 Freud, "Analytic Therapy," *Introductory Lectures*, *SE* 16:454–6; "Dynamics of the Transference," *SE* 12:108; "Repeating, Remembering and Working Through," *SE* 12:152 (my emphasis).

70 Freud, *Studies on Hysteria*, *SE* 2:268.

71 Freud, "Analytic Therapy," *Introductory Lectures*, *SE* 16:451.

72 Freud, *Studies on Hysteria*, *SE* 2:294, 295.

73 The reformulation of resistance as an effect of analytic technique has been part of a broad shift in Anglo-American psychoanalytic thinking, to which many contributions have been and continue to be made. Some of the signal contributions to this shift stem from D.W. Winnicott's recognition that resistance can be a response to a mistake made by the analyst and Heinz Kohut's understanding of the use of resistance as a defense against the analyst's failure to empathize. See Winnicott, "On Transference," in Esman, ed., *Essential Papers on Transference*, 246–51, quote at 250; and Heinz Kohut, "The Two Analyses of Mr. Z," *International Journal of Psychoanalysis* 60 (1979):3–28. For an overview, see Mitchell, *Influence and Autonomy*; and Aron, *Meeting of Minds*, esp. 184–7.

74 Freud, "Analysis Terminable and Interminable," *SE* 23:252.

75 Freud, *Studies on Hysteria*, *SE* 2:294, 295.
76 Abram Kardiner, *My Analysis with Freud* (New York: Norton, 1977), 58–9. Similarly, in his classic work on the transference, Heinrich Racker warned that the failure to recognize the contemporaneity and equality between analyst and analysand would run the risk that "certain remnants of the 'patriarchal order' will contaminate the analytic situation." Heinrich Racker, *Transference and Countertransference* (New York: International Universities Press, 1968), 132, quoted in Aron, *Meeting of Minds*, 255.
77 Freud, "Analytic Therapy," *Introductory Lectures*, *SE* 16:454.
78 Freud, "Constructions in Analysis," *SE* 23:258–9.
79 Freud, "Constructions in Analysis," *SE* 23:265–6.
80 Ibid., 264.
81 Freud, "From the History of an Infantile Neurosis," *SE* 17:86–7 (my emphasis).
82 Ibid., 96, 97.
83 Ibid., 97.
84 Freud, "Constructions in Analysis," *SE* 23:265.
85 Freud, "Remembering, Repeating, and Working Through," *SE* 12:154.

Epilogue

Over the last decades of the twentieth century and the first decades of the twenty-first, the authoritarian tendencies of the traditional structures of psychoanalysis, like the colonial influences of early anthropology with which they are linked, have increasingly come under question, and alternative forms of conceiving both the analytic encounter and the knowledge it generates have been taking shape. Although American psychoanalysis has not been subject to a postcolonial critique from within its ranks as has anthropology, epistemological questions similar to those that have been raised in the anthropological field are being raised among certain schools of psychoanalysis, challenging the traditionally unchallengeable authority of the analyst and paving the way for a revision of the associated evolutionary and racial tendencies discussed in this book. The image of the analyst as the neutral, observing scientist producing authoritative interpretations of the patient's unconscious is being replaced by a recognition of the analytic relationship as one that is unavoidably intersubjective, and whose knowledge is "co-created and negotiated" by both of its members.[1]

These critical movements in both disciplines have taken place against a background of an increased globalization which has seen the intensified transnational dispersion, forced and voluntary, of peoples, goods and cultural practices. The traditional opposition between "us" and "them" that gave rise to the discipline of anthropology in the first place has in many places broken down, along with the associated binarisms of modern and primitive, global and local, central and peripheral. In the US, differences between black and white persist, but have increasingly been challenged as grounds for discriminatory behavior, violent and otherwise. In anthropological circles there is now an increasing recognition of multiple, alternative modernities or postmodernities governed by differing but mutually implicating regimes of knowledge, and occupying differing positions of power and wealth within a common global historical framework. The "local" is a site where globally disseminated signs and goods appear, and peoples historically identified with particular geographic locations are now to be found in diasporic communities around the globe. Indigenous peoples and cultures previously "reserved" as remnants of the past are making their contemporary cultural and legal presence known (as an example, as of this rewriting in 2016–17, demonstrations by the Standing Rock Sioux Tribe against the Dakota Access Pipeline have gained national, and in some cases international, attention).[2]

Anthropology is no longer the study of humanity's past but of our common and globally interpenetrating present as well. The contemporary anthropologist is no longer considered an unimplicated authority but a socially positioned interlocutor, a co-constructor of anthropological knowledge, increasingly called on to bring an awareness of his or her own culture's historical as well as present, political role in the production of the anthropological situation under consideration.

The authority of early anthropologists and psychoanalysts alike had been bolstered by the attempts of their respective disciplines to model themselves along scientific lines as a way of placing their new forms of knowledge within a recognizable framework of legitimacy. Contemporary anthropology now distances itself not only from its colonial ancestry but from the positivism of earlier social science approaches—attempts to ground knowledge of social worlds in the observation, measurement and quantification of elements of human behavior. Similarly, certain trends in contemporary psychoanalysis have begun to distance themselves from the model of the natural sciences, which attempts to ground knowledge of the natural world by studying phenomena in laboratory conditions that ensure an uncontaminated source of data.[3] In the same way as anthropologists have come to recognize that in the human sciences both the subject and object of investigation contribute to the meanings that emerge from their interaction, some contemporary schools of psychoanalysis have begun to grapple with the ways in which psychoanalytic knowledge is produced by and through the dynamics of the psychoanalytic encounter.[4] Interactions within analytic and therapeutic relationships modify their members and, in so doing, contribute to the constitution of their members' understanding of each other and of themselves. Psychoanalytic representations, like anthropological ones, are no longer seen as scientific facts dependably deduced from raw human data but as interpretations given form and substance by both subjects in the relationship.

The contamination from which Freud aimed to preserve his patients thus turns out to be merely a pejorative name for the fact that both participants in the psychoanalytic encounter (as in any human encounter) necessarily have an effect on each other, each modifying the other and contributing to the understanding generated by their encounter. The influence of interpretation cannot be avoided, nor can the structures of power in which it is enfolded. There is no knowledge that can be had of the subject, of identity or of the unconscious that is immune to the impact of any interaction it undergoes. Contamination and influence are the concomitants of connection to others.

These schools of contemporary psychoanalysis—largely the relational and intersubjective schools—no longer deny that the analyst finds him- or herself in a position of authority, nor do they disavow the analyst's influence. Instead, they continue to search for ways to live out the recognition that psychoanalytic knowledge, like anthropological knowledge, is constructed, "contested, temporal, and emergent,"[5] the result of ongoing, multileveled exchanges between politically asymmetrical interlocutors, exchanges in which understanding is negotiated rather than imposed. This, in turn, has resulted in interpretations that are tentative rather than authoritative, and that are available for criticism, revision and even retraction in the face of the responses they elicit. This does not mean, as Janet Malcolm has derisively suggested, that "the patient is always right,"[6] but that, more to the point, the patient is not always wrong, as Freud often seemed to suggest. Indeed, it is this rendering of psychoanalytic (or anthropological) authority vulnerable to the interpretations of the object of investigation that is the hallmark of these postmodern encounters. However, the analytic relationship remains an asymmetrical one, and, like most (perhaps all) relationships, is charged with inequities of power. How, then, can we differentiate the "co-construction of meaning" from domination and the imposition of meaning?

As the philosopher Charles Taylor has pointed out, an interpretive discipline needs to steer a path between two dangers: on the one hand, the misapprehension that the scientist or authority can "have the last word" and, on the other, the misapprehension "that understanding the agent involves adopting his point of view." Similarly, the analyst needs neither to negate nor submit to the patient. Taylor suggests that what is required are interactions in which the emergent knowledge takes the form of "a new mutual understanding [that] involves a new self-understanding" on the part of the human scientist, a challenge to his or her self-definitions.[7] And this is the refrain we find both in current postcolonial and interpretive anthropology as well as in certain trends in psychoanalysis. Current anthropology requires that its practitioners "plac[e] their own reality in jeopardy" in their intercultural encounters;[8] psychoanalysis now looks for "a willingness on the part of the analyst continually to question his or her own participation, an openness to criticism and self-reflection."[9] Both see the knowledge concerning all participants that emerges from their respective engagements as contested and continuously negotiated.

As suggested in Chapter 4, the distinctive form of understanding of psychoanalysis requires a doubled vision, as was inaugurated by Freud's simultaneous positioning as both patient and scientist, analyst and analysand, social/racial outsider and insider, authoritative and abjected subject all in one. "The involvement of the analyst in the analysis is different from that of scholar, engineer or judge . . . because the analyst's knowledge . . . is applicable . . . to himself."[10] Freud not only saw himself as a combatant with big battalions struggling to compel the analysand to accept his vision of the psyche; he also understood that the unreasonable hysteria of his patients had reasons of its own of which reason itself was not aware. Instead of "placing all the reason on the side of the doctor and all the unreason on the side of the patient,"[11] he understood both patient and doctor to be rational and irrational, sick and healthy, both having their "dependencies, anxieties, and pathological defenses."[12]

And, as suggested by the discussion of enthrallment and domination in Chapter 3, the impulse to dominate that runs through Freud's writings on the transference, rather than the full potential of the analytic encounter, represents the *breakdown* of the possible recognition of the other, caused, in turn, by the breakdown of this doubled vision. If the analyst disavows this doubled vision and takes just one side of what Ann Pellegrini has called "the constitutive ambivalence" of psychoanalysis,[13] he or she can, unfortunately, feel supported by those elements of Freud's writings outlined in Chapter 5. But the analyst needs to engage the encounter from both sides of this double position, as both insider and outsider, purveyor of psychoanalytic insight as well as subject of investigation and critique. It is the task of psychoanalysis to work with the actualities that emerge when these oppositions are held together in tension.

A fuller acknowledgment of the colonial and racial contexts of these constitutive oppositions calls us to negate the idea of the primitive, with its inescapably racial connotations, as the precultural past on which its subject has been founded, through its successive separations from this primitive past. When we imagine recognition as a psychic operation that is equiprimordial with separation, we can begin to conceptualize subjectivity as *in relation with*, rather than separated from, the so-called maternal/primitive registers: we can imagine a subject in relation with its others.

"The unconscious" is a way of talking about what is unknown, unacknowledged, disavowed, indeterminate, unformulated and potential—what lies beyond the horizon of consciousness yet abides at the heart of subjective experience. The intrusion of elements of the unconscious into awareness via symptoms or dreams unsettles the certainties of consciousness, revealing it to be partial and limited. Freud correlated the unconscious with the primary process because of its "chronological priority"—it had been there from the beginning, whereas the secondary process, identified with consciousness, appeared only "belated[ly]."[14] But from a clinical perspective, the psychoanalytic narrative actually begins with consciousness, which is compelled, by the intrusion of symptomatic acts (the persistence of suffering), to recognize its partial nature, and therefore to posit, to acknowledge and to reckon with the forces of the unconscious. The psychoanalytic trajectory begins with this challenge to the sovereign self-confidence of consciousness. Consciousness without awareness of the unconscious is in a positivistic thralldom, for which psychoanalysis presents itself as cure: psychoanalysis is meant to decenter and dethrone "His Majesty the Ego." As Freud wrote in "The Unconscious," we have to "emancipate ourselves from the importance of the symptom of 'being conscious'."[15]

In his discussion of the unconscious, Freud remarked that "repression . . . cannot arise until a sharp cleavage has occurred between conscious and unconscious mental activity."[16] It is this cleavage that produces, simultaneously, both consciousness and the unconscious. Thus the unconscious as prior and primitive came to be apprehended as such, by Freud's own admission, only through the retrospectively temporalizing operations of consciousness that had arisen along with it. Rather than the state of the earliest beginnings of subjectivity or society, primitivity is constituted simultaneously with the subject (or society) as that which is then repudiated in the service of independence or autonomy. The primitive is the temporalized expression of what has been repudiated; a subject or a society produces, as Judith Butler has written, "as an *effect* of its own procedure" that which it "claims to discover as that which *precedes* its own action";[17] in this case, the figure of the primitive.

By casting the unconscious as primitive and prior, a concrete, prehistoric meaning with racist associations is ascribed to what might be better thought of as an ongoing, contemporary signified and signifying *otherwise*. In the guise of the primitive, the unconscious is shorn of this dynamic *otherwise* that can cure consciousness of its illusions of self-sufficiency. Rather than that which always uncannily disrupts whatever ways we may posit ourselves in the world, when conceived as "the primitive," the unconscious becomes merely *another thing*, developmentally prior and therefore safely inferior to the agency confronting it. Through Freud's evolutionary and historicizing frameworks this now reified other of consciousness was conjoined with the history of western colonialist representations of the racial/cultural other, incorporating this allachronizing misrepresentation into psychoanalysis and forming the doubled fetish of the *primitive* that would protect against the anxiety of both inner and outer, psychological and racial, alterity.

When psychoanalysis supplies a phylogenetic content to the unconscious, it dictates a universal, ahistorical and precultural stratum of the human mind, repressed or repudiated since infantile or "primitive" times, as the cost for the inauguration of an enculturated subjectivity. Although there may always be some exclusions brought into being through the inauguration of subjectivity, these exclusions would vary with culture and history, and therefore be open to some degree of alteration. To assert that we already know the contents (phylogenetic or otherwise) of the unconscious in all cases and in all cultures denies the risk of the unknown that a true encounter with alterity always poses to our own certainties of knowledge. In addition, the formulation of subjectivity as predicated on a repudiation of a universal, precultural primitivity reinforces the binarism of nature and culture, since it understands our entry into culture as condemning us to be forever and inescapably alienated from the "natural"—primitive—part of ourselves (and thus from those peoples identified as part of nature), setting the scene for the analyst as the authority who can inform us about the contents of this inaccessible part of ourselves.

But if the unconscious can be released from a developmental framework in which subjectivity is premised exclusively on repudiation or separation, then it need not be imagined as an abjected, inaccessible primitivity. Then the emergence of unconscious contents in the analytic encounter need not be inscribed as a regression back down the developmental and evolutionary scale but can be seen as the emergence of dimensions of experience whose existence has been obscured by, but is nonetheless coeval with, the preoccupations of consciousness. The encounter with the unconscious is a return to moments of the past simply insofar as it allows us to de-sediment the identifications that have contributed to subjectivity; insofar as it allows us to consider subjectivity from the vantage point of its contingency, from the vantage point of how it became fixed as that which it now is; insofar as it allows us to recognize, as James Baldwin has said, that "History is not the past. It is the present."[18] The analytic relationship need not be about the imposition of authoritative knowledge nor about disabusing the analysand of the fantasy of the analyst's authority. It can be a way of coming to know oneself, of becoming capable of feeling more fully alive and of engaging more fully with the world through *being with* rather than being separated from, and rather than being dominated or fearing domination by another. The interminability of analysis, rather than due to a bedrock of resistance to a primitivity that can never be overcome, would then have to do with the fact that the unconscious always exceeds our capacity to understand it: no analysis can ever exhaust it and thus truly come to an end.

Disengaging the unconscious from an evolutionary/developmental discourse would disarticulate representations of subjectivity from the racially indexed map to which it has been correlated. Some forms of such disengagement can be seen in the contemporary schools within psychoanalysis to which I have referred, where the long-held evolutionary distinction between external act and internal mentation is beginning to come undone. According to this distinction, which began with Spencer and was held by Freud along with so many others, the degree to which external compulsion was internalized placed peoples higher on the evolutionary scale; and the degree to which "acting out" or "enactments" could be replaced by "remembering" placed the psychoanalytic subject further along the way to psychoanalytic cure. But interpretations are now no longer regarded as superior to "enactments," as has been long taken for granted.

Interpretations impact and influence the patient: they are now coming to be seen as acts in their own right, as "forms of enactments themselves."[19] As Lewis Aron has written:

> We began by describing enactment as a fairly infrequent event that occurs only with very disturbed patients who need to use primitive [*sic*] forms of communication. Before long we realized that healthier patients too use this mechanism, and later we realized that analysts do too. And now we may begin to wonder whether speech is ever used only to communicate and not also as a form of action.[20]

Speech itself—interpretation—is a form of action, having its effects on both members of the relationship; therefore "the patient and the analyst are always enacting."[21] In place of the distinction between the neurotic "enactments" that are to be replaced by mentation, we find increasing reference to the performative nature of the interpretations and interactions—or enactments—of analysis, or to "relationship-transforming 'performatives'."[22] Psychoanalytic communication is becoming recognized as performative rather than merely representational as the evolutionary dichotomy between enactment and mentation has become unbound.[23]

Performativity refers to the "iterative power" of discourse—the power of a discourse to constitute its subjects through compelling their repeated performance, verbal and nonverbal, of its norms. Psychoanalytic therapeutics provide a theater in which the iteration of particular forms of relational events contributes to the reconstitution of the psychoanalytic subject's sense of self.

What then of "primitivity" as a term of art in psychoanalysis? Because it is so embedded in the foundational texts of psychoanalysis and because it is so widely considered to be a neutral, scientific term within the orbit of psychoanalytic practice, the work of confronting its colonial and racial encoding must always be ongoing. And let us not be fooled that a change in vocabulary alone can change the racist implications embedded within our theoretical frameworks. But if we are able to discard the idea of the primitive as the precultural past on which the modern subject has been founded, a past that has been indexed to a racially conceived evolutionary scale, then what has hitherto been called "primitive" can come to be seen as our inherent, contemporaneous, ongoing vulnerability and precarity. Clinically, "primitivity" has been used to represent a radical vulnerability characterizing the earliest stages of our psychic life. But this "primitivity" is merely vulnerability seen from a position in which we presume that we have superseded it. Vulnerability or precarity refer to the same condition as "primitivity" referred to, but now seen from within its own vantage point rather than from a fantasized place beyond it. Like "primitivity," vulnerability and precarity are brought to the fore by trauma and suffering. But unlike "primitivity," vulnerability and precarity cannot be limited to specific stages of development or evolution any more than they can designate specific groups of people based on skin color or cultural difference.

If we think something is primitive, we think we have overcome it. Once we recognize that vulnerability cannot be overcome once and for all (which would be a fantasy of omnipotence), then we can recognize that what we used to call primitive is never fully past. This recognition can go some way in helping us to eschew the inescapably raced concept of primitivity. By doing so, and by disengaging the unconscious from an evolutionary/developmental framework, psychoanalysis can begin to shed its racist baggage and use its performative abilities in the service of its ever powerful potential for the alleviation of mental suffering.

Notes

1 Mitchell, *Influence and Autonomy*, 139.
2 See, for example, Arjun Appadurai, *Modernity at Large: Cultural Dimensions of Globalization* (Minneapolis, MN: University of Minnesota Press, 1996); John Comaroff, "Politics of Difference in an Age of Revolution," in Edwin N. Wilmsen and Patrick McAllister, eds., *The Politics of Difference: Ethnic Premises in a World of Power* (Chicago, IL: University of Chicago Press, 1996), 162–83; and Burrows, "Indian Agency." For a fascinating and incisive analysis of the contemporary, modern situation of Canadian First Nations, see Glen Sean Couthard, *Read Skin White Masks: Rejecting the Colonial Politics of Recognition* (Minneapolis, MN: University of Minnesota Press, 2014).
3 Charles Taylor has written extensively about the unsuitability of the natural science model for the human sciences. See his *Philosophy and the Human Sciences*, esp. the introduction, 1–12, and chap. 1, "Interpretation and the Sciences of Man," 15–57.
4 I refer largely to the Anglo-American schools of relational and intersubjective psychoanalysis, represented in the essays collected in Stephen A. Mitchell and Lewis Aron, eds., *Relational Psychoanalysis: The Emergence of a Tradition* (Hillsdale, NJ: Analytic Press, 1999); and in the separate works of, among many others, Jessica Benjamin, *The Bonds of Love* and *Shadow of the Other*; Aron, *A Meeting of Minds*; and Stephen Mitchell, *Influence and Autonomy*.

This view of the human sciences as constructed through the interaction of its participants is spreading to the physical sciences as well: see Bruno Latour, *We Have Never Been Modern*, trans. Catherine Porter (Cambridge, MA: Harvard University Press, 1993 [1991]).

5 James Clifford, "Introduction," in Clifford and Marcus, *Writing Culture*, 19.
6 Malcolm elegantly but mercilessly skewers Merton Gill in her essay of this name in the collection of her essays entitled *The Purloined Clinic* (New York: Vintage, 1993), 48–62.
7 Taylor, *Philosophy and the Human Sciences*, chap. 4, "Understanding and Ethnocentricity," 116–33, quotes at 130; see also Jessica Benjamin, "Recognition and Destruction," in Mitchell and Aron, *Relational Psychoanalysis*, 181–210.
8 Clifford, *The Predicament of Culture*, 41.
9 Mitchell, *Influence and Authority*, 53.
10 Cornelius Castoriadis, "Epilegomena to a Theory of the Soul Which Has Been Presented as a Science," in *Crossroads in the Labyrinth*, (Cambridge, MA: MIT Press, 1984), 7.
11 Ibid., 6.
12 Racker, *Transference and Countertransference*, 132, quoted in Aron, *Meeting of Minds*, 255.
13 Ann Pellegrini, *Performance Anxieties: Staging Psychoanalysis, Staging Race* (New York: Routledge, 1997), 1.
14 Freud, *Interpretation of Dreams*, SE 5:603.
15 Freud, "The Unconscious," *SE* 14:172.
16 Freud, "Repression," 1915, *SE* 14:147.
17 Butler, *Bodies That Matter*, 30.
18 Castoriadis, "Epilegomena to a Theory of the Soul," 11. James Baldwin, in the movie *I Am Not Your Negro*.
19 Mitchell, *Influence and Autonomy*, 182.
20 Aron, *Meeting of Minds*, 212.
21 Ibid.
22 Mitchell, *Influence and Autonomy*, 182.
23 Judith Butler is the premiere theoretician of performativity; see her influential *Gender Trouble* and *Bodies That Matter*. Lynne Layton has provided a closely argued bridge between Butler's poststructuralist accounts of performativity and contemporary Anglo-American accounts of subjectivity in her *Who's That Girl?*

Bibliography

Abel, Elizabeth, Barbara Christian, and Helene Moglen, eds. *Female Subjects in Black and White: Race, Psychoanalysis, Feminism*. Berkeley, CA: University of California Press, 1997.

Ackerman, Robert. *J. G. Frazer: His Life and Work*. Cambridge: Cambridge University Press, 1987.

Adams, Michael Vannoy. *The Multicultural Imagination: "Race," Color, and the Unconscious*. London: Routledge, 1996.

Alexander, Michelle. *The New Jim Crow: Mass Incarceration in the Age of Colorblindness*. New York: The New Press, 2010.

Altman, Neil. *The Analyst in the Inner City: Race, Class, and Culture through a Psychoanalytic Lens*. Hillsdale, NJ: Analytic Press, 1995, 2010.

Appadurai, Arjun. *Modernity at Large: Cultural Dimensions of Globalization*. Minneapolis, MN: University of Minnesota Press, 1996.

Arendt, Hannah. *The Origins of Totalitarianism*. San Diego, CA: Harcourt Brace, 1979 [1948].

Aron, Lewis. *A Meeting of Minds: Mutuality in Psychoanalysis*. Hillsdale, NJ: Analytic Press, 1996.

—— and Karen Starr. *A Psychotherapy for the People*. London and New York: Routledge, 2013.

Asad, Talal, ed. *Anthropology and the Colonial Encounter*. Atlantic Highlands, NJ: Humanities Press, 1973.

——. *Genealogies of Religion: Discipline and Reasons of Power in Christianity and Islam*. Baltimore, MD: The Johns Hopkins University Press, 1993.

Baldwin, James. *The Evidence of Things Not Seen*. New York: Henry Holt, 1985.

——. *The Fire Next Time*. New York: Vintage International, 1993 [1962].

Batnitsky, Leora. *How Judaism Became a Religion: An Introduction to Modern Jewish Thought*. Princeton, NJ: Princeton University Press, 2013.

Baudet, Henri. *Paradise on Earth: Some Thoughts on European Images of Non-European Man*. Translated by Elizabeth Wentholt. New Haven, CT: Yale University Press, 1965.

de Beauvoir, Simone. "Enfance," in *Le Deuxième Sexe*, Tome II, *L'Expérience vécue*. Paris: Éditions Gallimard, 1976 [1949]).

——. *The Second Sex*. Translated by H.M. Parshley. New York: Vintage, 1989 [1949].

Beebe Beatrice, Frank M. Lachmann, and Joseph Jaffe, "Mother-Infant Interaction Structures and Presymbolic Self- and Object Representations," in *Psychoanalytic Dialogues*, 7(2): 133–82, 1997.

Beidelman, T.O. *W. Robertson Smith and the Sociological Study of Religion*. Chicago, IL: University of Chicago Press, 1974.

Benjamin, Jessica. *The Bonds of Love: Psychoanalysis, Feminism, and the Problem of Domination*. New York: Pantheon, 1988.

——. "The Shadow of the Other Subject: Intersubjectivity and Feminist Theory." In Jessica Benjamin, *Shadow of the Other*, 79–108. New York: Routledge, 1998.

Benjamin, Walter. "Theses on the Philosophy of History." In *Illuminations*, 253–64. New York: Schocken, 1968.

Bennett, Janice O. "The Analyst at the Intersection of Multiple Cultures," *Psychoanalytic Perspectives*, 3(2) (2006): 55–63.

Benveniste, Emile. "Civilization: A Contribution to the History of the Word." In *Problems in General Linguistics*, trans. Mary Elizabeth Meek, 289–96. Coral Gables, FL: University of Miami Press, 1971.

Berkhofer, Robert F., Jr. *The White Man's Indian: Images of the American Indian from Columbus to the Present*. New York: Vintage, 1979.

Bernheimer, Richard. *Wild Men in the Middle Ages: A Study in Art, Sentiment, and Demonology*. New York: Octagon, 1970.

Bhabha, Homi. *The Location of Culture*. London: Routledge, 1994.

Boas, Franz. *Race, Language, and Culture*. New York: Free Press, 1966 [1940].

Bolt, Christine. *Victorian Attitudes toward Race*. London: Routledge and Kegan Paul. Toronto: University of Toronto Press, 1971.

Bowler, Peter J. *Evolution: The History of an Idea*. Berkeley, CA: University of California Press, 1984.

——. *Biology and Social Thought: 1850–1914*. Berkeley, CA: Office for History of Science and Technology, University of California at Berkeley, 1993.

Boyarin, Daniel. "*Épater l'Embourgeoisement*: Freud, Gender, and the (De) Colonized Psyche." *Diacritics*, 24(1) (spring 1994): 17–42.

——. *Unheroic Conduct: The Rise of Heterosexuality and the Invention of the Jewish Man*. Berkeley, CA: University of California Press, 1995.

——. "What Does a Jew Want?; or, The Political Meaning of the Phallus." In Christopher Lane, ed., *The Psychoanalysis of Race*, 211–40. New York: Columbia University Press, 1998.

Brandon, William. *New Worlds for Old: Reports from the New World and Their Effects on the Development of Social Thought in Europe, 1500–1800.* Athens, OH: Ohio University Press, 1985.

Brantlinger, Patrick. "Victorians and Africans: The Genealogy of the Myth of the Dark Continent." *Critical Inquiry*, 12(1) (autumn 1985): 166–203.

Breman, Jan, ed. *Imperial Monkey Business: Racial Supremacy in Social Darwinist Theory and Colonial Practice.* Amsterdam: Vrije University Press, 1990.

Brodkin, Karen. *How Jews Became White Folks and What That Says about Race in America.* New Brunswick, NJ: Rutgers University Press, 1998.

Buck-Morss, Susan. *Hegel, Haiti, and Universal History.* Pittsburgh, PA: University of Pittsburgh Press, 2009.

Buhle, Mari Jo. *Feminism and Its Discontents: A Century of Struggle with Psychoanalysis.* Cambridge, MA: Harvard University Press, 1998.

Burrow, J.W. *Evolution and Society: A Study in Victorian Social Theory.* Cambridge: Cambridge University Press, 1966.

Burrows, John. "Indian Agency: Forming First Nations Law in Canada." *Political and Legal Anthropology Review*, 24(2) (2001): 9–24.

Butler, Judith. *Gender Trouble: Feminism and the Subversion of Identity.* New York: Routledge, 1990.

——. *Bodies That Matter: On the Discursive Limits of "Sex."* New York: Routledge, 1993.

de las Casas, Bartolomé. *The Devastation of the Indies: A Brief Account.* Translated by Herma Briffault. Baltimore, MD: The Johns Hopkins University Press, 1992 [1552].

Castoriadis, Cornelius. *Crossroads in the Labyrinth.* Translated by Kate Soper and Martin H. Ryle. Cambridge, MA: MIT Press, 1984 [1978].

——. *The Imaginary Institution of Society.* Translated by Kathleen Blamey. Cambridge, MA: MIT Press, 1998 [1975].

Cavalli-Sforza, Luigi Luca. *Genes, Peoples, and Languages.* Translated by Mark Seielstad. New York: North Point Press/Farrar, Straus and Giroux, 2000.

Césaire, Aimé. *Discourse on Colonialism.* Translated by Joan Pinkham. New York: Monthly Review Press, 1972 [1955].

Chakrabarty, Dipesh. *Provincializing Europe: Postcolonial Thought and Historical Difference.* Princeton, NJ: Princeton University Press, 2000.

Chodorow, Nancy. *The Reproduction of Mothering: Psychoanalysis and the Sociology of Gender.* Berkeley, CA: University of California Press, 1978.

Clifford, James. "On Ethnographic Authority." *Representations*, 1(2) (1983): 118–46.

——. *The Predicament of Culture: Twentieth-Century Ethnography, Literature, and Art*. Cambridge, MA: Harvard University Press, 1988.

—— and George Marcus, eds. *Writing Culture: The Poetics and Politics of Ethnography*. Berkeley, CA: University of California Press, 1986.

Coates, Ta-Nehisi. *Between the World and Me*. New York: Spiegel and Grau, Random House, 2015.

Comaroff, John. "Politics of Difference in an Age of Revolution." In Edwin N. Wilmsen and Patrick McAllister, eds. *The Politics of Difference: Ethnic Premises in a World of Power*, 162–183. Chicago, IL: University of Chicago Press, 1996.

Comaroff, John, and Jean Comaroff. *Ethnography and the Historical Imagination*. Boulder, CO: Westview, 1992.

——. "On Personhood: An Anthropological Perspective from Africa." American Bar Foundation Working Paper #9903. Chicago, IL: American Bar Foundation, 1999.

Darwin, Charles. *The Origin of Species*. New York: Gramercy, 1979 [1859].

——. *The Descent of Man, and Selection in Relation to Sex*. New York: New York University Press, 1989 [1871].

Davis, David Brion. *The Problem of Slavery in Western Culture*. Ithaca, NY: Cornell University Press, 1966.

——. *In the Image of God: Religions, Moral Values, and Our Heritage of Slavery*. New Haven, CT: Yale University Press, 2001.

Devereux, G. "Normal and Abnormal: The Key Problem of Psychiatric Anthropology." In G. Devereux, *Basic Problems of Ethnopsychiatry*. Translated by Bassia M. Gulati and Georges Devereux. Chicago, IL: University of Chicago Press, 1980.

DiCenso, James. *The Other Freud: Religion, Culture and Psychoanalysis*. London, New York: Routledge, 1999.

Dimen, Muriel, and Neil Altman, eds. *Symposium on Race. Psychoanalytic Dialogues: A Journal of Relational Perspectives* (Special Issue), 10(4) (2000).

Doane, Janice, and Devon Hodges. *From Klein to Kristeva: Psychoanalytic Feminism and the Search for the "Good Enough" Mother*. Ann Arbor, MI: University of Michigan Press, 1992.

Doane, Mary Ann. "Dark Continents: Epistemologies of Racial and Sexual Difference in Psychoanalysis and Cinema." In Mary Ann Doane, *Femmes Fatales: Feminism, Film Theory, Psychoanalysis*, 209–48. New York: Routledge, 1991.

Donovan, Bill M. "Introduction." In Bartolomé de las Casas, *The Devastation of the Indies: A Brief Account*, trans. Herma Briffault. Baltimore, MD: Johns Hopkins University Press, 1992.

Dudley, Edward, and M.E. Novak, eds. *The Wild Man Within: An Image in Western Thought from the Renaissance to Romanticism*. Pittsburgh, PA: University of Pittsburgh Press, 1972.

Durkheim, Emile. *The Elementary Forms of the Religious Life*. Translated by Joseph Ward Stain. New York: Free Press, 1965 [1915].

Eliade, Mircea. *The Sacred and the Profane*. Translated by Willard R. Trask. New York: Harcourt Brace Jovanovich, 1959.

——. *Myth and Reality*. Translated by Willard R. Trask. New York: Harper Torchbooks, 1963.

——. *The Myth of the Eternal Return; or, Cosmos and History*. Translated by Willard R. Trask. Princeton, NJ: Princeton University Press, 1991 [1954].

Elias, Norbert. *The Civilizing Process: Sociogenetic and Psychogenetic Investigations*. Edited by Eric Dunning, Johan Goudsblom, and Stephan Mennell. Translated by Edmund Jephcott. Oxford: Blackwell, 2000 [1939].

Ellenberger, Henri F. *The Discovery of the Unconscious: The History and Evolution of Dynamic Psychiatry*. New York: Basic Books, 1970.

Elliot, Patricia. *From Mastery to Analysis: Theories of Gender in Psychoanalytic Feminism*. Ithaca, NY: Cornell University Press, 1991.

Escobar, Arturo. *Encountering Development: The Making and Unmaking of the Third World*. Princeton, NJ: Princeton University Press, 1995.

Esman, Aaron H., ed. *Essential Papers on Transference*. New York: New York University Press, 1990.

Esprey, Yvette M. "Penetrating Subjectivity: Response to Commentaries." *Psychoanalytic Dialogues, 27* (2017): 52–60.

Evans-Pritchard, E.E. *Theories of Primitive Religion*. Oxford: Clarendon, 1965.

Fabian, Johannes. *Time and the Other: How Anthropology Makes Its Object*. New York: Columbia University Press, 1983.

Fairchild, Hoxie Neale. *The Noble Savage*. New York: Columbia University Press, 1928.

Fanon, Frantz. *The Wretched of the Earth*. Translated by Constance Farrington. New York: Grove, 1963.

——. *Black Skin, White Masks*. Translated by Charles Lam Markmann. New York: Grove Weidenfeld, 1967 [1952].

Feit, Harvey A. "The Construction of Algonquian Hunting Territories: Private Property as Moral Lesson, Policy Advocacy, and Ethnographic Error." In George W. Stocking Jr., ed., *Colonial Situations: Essays on the Contextualization of Ethnographic Knowledge*. Volume 7, *History of Anthropology*, 109–34. Madison, WI: University of Wisconsin Press, 1991.

Ferenczi, Sandor. *Thalassa: A Theory of Genitality*. Translated by Henry Alden Bunker. Albany, NY: *Psychoanalytic Quarterly*, 1938.

Fink, Bruce. *The Lacanian Subject: Between Language and Jouissance*. Princeton, NJ: Princeton University Press, 1995.

Foucault, Michel. *The History of Sexuality*. Volume 1. Translated by Robert Hurley. New York: Vintage, 1980.

——. "Nietzsche, Genealogy, History." In Paul Rabinow, ed., *The Foucault Reader*, 76–100. Trans. Donald F. Bouchard and Sherry Simon. New York: Pantheon, 1984.

——. *Technologies of the Self: A Seminar with Michel Foucault*. Edited by Luther H. Martin, Huck Gutman, and Patrick H. Hutton. Amherst, MA: University of Massachusetts Press, 1988.

Frazer, Sir James George. *Totemism and Exogamy: A Treatise on Certain Early Forms of Superstition and Society*. London: Macmillan, 1910.

——. *The Golden Bough: A Study in Magic and Religion*. 12 vols. London: Macmillan, 1911–15.

Freud, Sigmund. *Gesammelte Werke* (*GW*). Ed. Anna Freud et al. Vols. 1–18. Frankfurt am Main: S. Fischer, 1961–86.

——. "Psychoanalystiche Bemerkungen uber einen autobiographisch beschriebenen Fall von Paranoia (Dementia paranoides)." *GW* 8:239–316, 1911.

——. *Totem und Tabu*. *GW* 9, 1913.

——. *Das Unbewusste*. *GW* 10:264–303, 1915.

——. *Massenpsychologie und ich-analyse*. *GW* 13:71–161, 1921.

——. *The Standard Edition* [*SE*] *of the Complete Psychological Works of Sigmund Freud*. Edited and translated by James Strachey. Volumes 1–24. London: Hogarth Press, 1953–74. Works are listed according to their original date of publication.

—— with Joseph Breuer. *Studies on Hysteria*. *SE* 2:1–305, 1893–5.

——. *The Interpretation of Dreams*. *SE* 4:1–338; 5:339–625, 1900.

——. "Fragment of an Analysis of a Case of Hysteria." *SE* 7:7–122, 1905.

——. *Three Essays on the Theory of Sexuality*. *SE* 7:25–245, 1905.

——. "Analysis of a Phobia in a Five-year-old Boy." *SE* 10:3–149, 1909.

——. "Psycho-analytic Notes on an Autobiographical Account of Case of Paranoia (Dementia paranoides)." *SE* 12:12–82, 1911.

——. *Papers on Technique*. *SE* 12:89–203, 1911–15.

——. "The Handling of Dream-Interpretation in Psycho-Analysis." In *Papers on Technique, SE* 12:89–96, 1911.

——. "The Dynamics of Transference." In *Papers on Technique, SE* 12:97–108, 1912.

——. "Recommendations to Physicians Practising Psychoanalysis." In *Papers on Technique, SE* 12:109–20, 1912.

——. "On Beginning the Treatment." In *Papers on Technique, SE* 12:121–44, 1913.

——. *Totem and Taboo*. *SE* 13:1–164, 192–13.

——. "Remembering, Repeating and Working Through." In *Papers on Technique, SE* 12:145–56, 1914.

——. "Observations on Transference-Love." In *Papers on Technique*, SE 2:157–71, 1914.

——. "The Moses of Michaelangelo." *SE* 13:211–38, 1914.

——. "On Narcissism: An Introduction." *SE* 14:73–102, 1914.

——. "The Unconscious." *SE* 14:159–215, 1915.

——. "Thoughts for the Times on War and Death." *SE* 14:273–300, 1915.

——. *Introductory Lectures on Psychoanalysis. SE* 15:15–239; 16:243–463, 1916–17.

——. "The Taboo of Virginity." *SE* 11:193–207, 1918.

——. "From the History of an Infantile Neurosis." *SE* 17:7–122, 1918.

——. "A Child Is Being Beaten." *SE* 17:179–204, 1919.

——. *Group Psychology and the Analysis of the Ego. SE* 18:69–143, 1921.

——. *The Ego and the Id. SE* 19:3–66, 1923.

——. "The Dissolution of the Oedipus Complex." *SE* 19:173–9, 1924.

——. "Some Psychological Consequences of the Anatomical Distinction Between the Sexes." *SE* 19:248–58, 1925.

——. "An Autobiographical Study," SE 20:1–74, 1925.

——. "Fetishism." *SE* 21:152–7, 1927.

——. *Future of an Illusion. SE* 21:5–56, 1927.

——. *Civilization and Its Discontents. SE* 21:64–145, 1930.

——. "Female Sexuality." *SE* 21:225–43, 1931.

——. *New Introductory Lectures on Psychoanalysis. SE* 22:5–182, 1933.

——. "Analysis Terminable and Interminable." *SE* 23:216–53, 1937.

——. "Constructions in Analysis." *SE* 23:255–69, 1937.

——. *Moses and Monotheism. SE* 23:7–137, 1939.

——. *An Outline of Psycho-Analysis. SE* 23:144–207, 1940.

——. *A Phylogenetic Phantasy: An Overview of the Transference Neuroses.* Edited by Ilse Grubrich-Simitis. Translated by Axel Hoffer and Peter T. Hoffer. Cambridge, MA: Harvard University Press, 1987 [1915].

Freud, Sigmund, and Karl Abraham. *A Psycho-Analytic Dialogue: The Letters of Sigmund Freud and Karl Abraham, 1907–26.* Edited by Hilda C. Abraham and Ernst L. Freud. Translated by Bernard Marsh and Hilda C. Abraham. New York: Basic Books, 1965.

Freud, Sigmund, and Wilhelm Fliess. *The Complete Letters of Sigmund Freud to Wilhelm Fliess, 1887–1904.* Edited and translated by Jeffrey M. Masson. Cambridge, MA: Harvard University Press, 1985.

Freud, Sigmund and C. G. Jung. *The Freud/Jung Letters: The Correspondence between Sigmund Freud and C. G. Jung.* Edited by William McGuire, translated by R.F.C. Hull and Ralph Mannheim. Princeton, NJ: Princeton University Press, 1974/94.

Fuss, Diana. *Identification Papers.* New York: Routledge, 1995.

Gallop, Jane. *The Daughter's Seduction: Feminism and Psychoanalysis*. Ithaca, NY: Cornell University Press, 1982.

Gandhi, Leela. *Postcolonial Theory: A Critical Introduction*. New York: Columbia University Press, 1998.

Gay, Peter. *Freud: A Life for Our Time*. New York: Norton, 1988.

Geller, Jay. "(G)nos(e)ology: The Cultural Construction of the Other." In Howard Eilberg-Schwartz, ed., *People of the Body: Jews and Judaism from an Embodied Perspective*, 243–82. Albany, NY: State University of New York Press, 1992.

——. "Identifying 'Someone Who Is Himself One of Them': Recent Studies of Freud's Jewish Identity." *Religious Studies Review*, 23(4) (October 1997): 323–31.

——. "The Godfather of Psychoanalysis: Circumcision, Antisemitism, Homosexuality, and Freud's "Fighting Jew." *Journal of the American Academy of Religion*, 67(2) (1999): 355–85.

George, Katherine. "The Civilized West Looks at Primitive Africa: 1400–1800: A Study in Ethnocentrism." *Isis*, 49 (1958): 62–72.

Gill, Merton M. *Analysis of the Transference*. Volume 1, *Theory and Technique*. New York: International Universities Press, 1982.

Gilman, Sander L. *Jewish Self-Hatred: Anti-Semitism and the Hidden Language of the Jews*. Baltimore, MD: The Johns Hopkins University Press, 1986.

——. *Freud, Race, and Gender*. Princeton, NJ: Princeton University Press, 1993.

——. *The Case of Sigmund Freud: Medicine and Identity at the Fin de Siècle*. Baltimore, MD: The Johns Hopkins University Press, 1993.

Glick, Thomas, ed., *The Comparative Reception of Darwinism*. Austin, TX: University of Texas Press, 1972.

—— , ed. *Anatomy of Racism*. Minneapolis, MN: University of Minnesota Press, 1990.

Goldstein, Bluma. *Reinscribing Moses: Heine, Kafka, Freud, and Schoenberg in a European Wilderness*. Cambridge, MA: Harvard University Press, 1992.

Gould, Stephen Jay. *Ontogeny and Phylogeny*. Cambridge, MA: Harvard University Press, 1977.

——. "Spin-Doctoring Darwin." *Natural History*, 104(7) (1995): 6–9, 70–1.

——. *The Mismeasure of Man*. New York: Norton, 1996 [1981].

Greenacre, Phyllis. "The Role of Transference: Practical Considerations in Relation to Psychoanlytic Therapy." In Aaron H. Esman, ed., *Essential Papers on Transference*, 124–35. New York: New York University Press, 1990.

Greenblatt, Stephen. *Marvelous Possessions: The Wonder of the New World*. Chicago, IL: University of Chicago Press, 1991.

Grubrich-Simitis, Ilsa. "Metapsychology and Metabiology." In Sigmund Freud, *A Phylogenetic Fantasy: An Overview of the Transference Neuroses*. Edited by

Ilse Grubrich-Simitis. Translated by Axel Hoffer and Peter T. Hoffer, 73–113. Cambridge, MA: Harvard University Press, 1987.

Guha, Ranajit. "The Prose of Counter-Insurgency." In Ranajit Guha and Gayatri Chakravorty Spivak, eds., *Selected Subaltern Studies*, 45–86. Oxford: Oxford University Press, 1988.

—— and Gayatri Chakravorty Spivak, eds. *Selected Subaltern Studies*. Oxford: Oxford University Press, 1988.

Hall, Stuart. "When Was 'the Post-Colonial'? Thinking at the Limit." In Iain Chambers and Lidia Curti, eds., *The Postcolonial Question: Common Skies, Divided Horizons*, 242–60. New York: Routledge, 1996.

Haller, John S., Jr. *Outcasts from Evolution: Scientific Attitudes of Racial Inferiority, 1859–1900*. Carbondale, IL: Southern Illinois University Press, 1971.

Hanke, Lewis. *Aristotle and the American Indians: A Study in Race Prejudice in the Modern World*. Bloomington, IN: Indiana University Press, 1975 [1959].

Hannaford, Ivan. *Race: The History of an Idea in the West*. Baltimore, MD: The Johns Hopkins University Press, 1996.

Haraway, Donna. *Primate Visions: Gender, Race, and Nature in the World of Modern Science*. New York: Routledge, 1989.

Harris, Marvin. *The Rise of Anthropological Theory: A History of Theories of Culture*. New York: Columbia University Press, 1968.

Herdt, Gilbert, Lucia Villela, and Waude Kracke. Introduction to *Cultural Imagination and Individual Creativity: New Directions in Psychoanalytic Anthropology*. *The Psychoanalytic Review* (Special Issue), 84(2) (April 1997): 165–8.

Herzog, Dagmar. *Cold War Freud*. Cambridge: Cambridge University Press, 2017.

Hoffman, Irwin Z. "Discussion: Toward a Social-Constructivist View of the Psychoanalytic Situation." *Psychoanalytic Dialogues*, 1(1) (1991): 74–105.

Holmes, Dorothy Evans. "Race and Transference in Psychoanalysis and Psychotherapy." *International Journal of Psychoanalysis*, 73(1) (spring 1992): 1–11.

Homans, Peter. *The Ability to Mourn: Disillusionment and the Social Origins of Psychoanalysis*. Chicago, IL: University of Chicago Press, 1989.

Hook, Derek. *A Critical Psychology of the Postcolonial: The Mind of Apartheid*. London and New York: Routledge, 2012.

Hoxie, Frederick E. *A Final Promise: The Campaign to Assimilate the Indians, 1880–1920*. Lincoln, NE: University of Nebraska Press, 1984.

Huizer, Gerrit, and Bruce Mannheim, eds. *The Politics of Anthropology: From Colonialism and Sexism toward a View from Below*. The Hague: Mouton, 1979.

Hymes, Dell, ed. *Reinventing Anthropology*. New York: Random House, 1969.

Irigaray, Luce. *This Sex Which Is Not One*. Translated by Catherine Porter, with Carolyn Burke. Ithaca, NY: Cornell University Press, 1985 [1977].

——. *Speculum of the Other Woman*. Translated by Gillian C. Gill. Ithaca, NY: Cornell University Press, 1985 [1974]).

Jaimes, M. Annette. *The State of Native America: Genocide, Colonization, and Resistance*. Boston, MA: South End, 1992.

Javier, Rafael Art, and Michael Moskowitz. "Notes from the Trenches." *Psychoanalytic Psychology*, 19(1) (2002): 144–8.

Javier, Rafael Art, and William G. Herron, "Psychoanalysis and the Disenfranchised: Countertransference Issues." *Psychoanalytic Psychology*, 19(1) (2002): 149–66.

Jones, Ernest. "Review of *Sex and Repression in Savage Society*, by Bronislaw Malinowski." *International Journal of Psycho-Analysis*, 9 (1928): 365–9.

——. *The Life and Work of Sigmund Freud*. Volume 2, *Years of Maturity, 1901–1919*. New York: Basic Books, 1955; Volume 3, *The Last Phase, 1919–1939*. New York: Basic Books, 1957.

Jones, Greta. *Social Darwinism and English Thought: The Interaction between Biological and Social Theory*. Brighton, UK: Harvester, 1980.

Jones, James W. *Contemporary Psychoanalysis and Religion: Transference and Transcendence*. New Haven, CT: Yale University Press, 1991.

——. *Religion and Psychology in Transition: Psychoanalysis, Feminism, and Theology*. New Haven, CT: Yale University Press, 1996.

Jordan, Winthrop D. *White over Black: American Attitudes toward the Negro, 1550–1812*. Chapel Hill, NC: University of North Carolina Press, 1968.

Kardiner, A. *My Analysis with Freud: Reminiscences*. New York: Norton, 1977.

Kelly, Alfred. *The Descent of Darwin: The Popularization of Darwinism in Germany, 1860–1914*. Chapel Hill, NC: University of North Carolina Press, 1981.

Kiernan, V.S. *The Lords of Human Kind: European Attitudes to Other Cultures in the Imperial Age*. London: Serif, 1995 [1969].

——. *Imperialism and Its Contradictions*. London: Routledge, 1995.

Kernberg, Otto. "The Analyst's Authority in the Psychoanalytic Situation," *Psychoanalytic Quarterly*, 65 (1996): 137–57.

Khanna, Ranjana. *Dark Continents: Psychoanalysis and Colonialism*. Durham, NC: Duke University Press, 2003, 2004.

Klein, Dennis B. *Jewish Origins of the Psychoanalytic Movement*. Chicago, IL: University of Chicago Press, 1985.

Kohn, David, ed. *The Darwinian Heritage*. Princeton, NJ: Princeton University Press, 1985.

Kohut, Heinz. *The Restoration of the Self*. Madison, CT: International Universities Press, 1977.

——. "The Two Analyses of Mr. Z." *International Journal of Psychoanalysis*, 60 (1979): 3–28.

Kovel, Joel. *White Racism: A Psychohistory*. London: Free Association Books, 1988 [1970].

Kristeva, Julia. *Powers of Horror: An Essay on Abjection*. Translated by Leon S. Rondiez. New York: Columbia University Press, 1982.

——. "Women's Time." Translated by Alice Jardine and Harry Blake. In Toril Moi, ed., *The Kristeva Reader*, 187–213. New York: Columbia University Press, 1986.

Kuklick, Henrika. "Contested Monuments: The Politics of Archaeology in Southern Africa." In George W. Stocking, Jr., *Colonial Situations: Essays on the Contextualization of Ethnographic Knowledge*. Volume 3, *History of Anthropology*, 135–69. Madison, WI: University of Wisconsin Press, 1991.

Lacan, Jacques. *Écrits: A Selection*. Translated by Alan Sheridan. New York: Norton, 1977.

Lane, Christopher, ed. *The Psychoanalysis of Race*. New York: Columbia University Press, 1998.

Latour, Bruno. *We Have Never Been Modern*. Translated by Catherine Porter. Cambridge, MA: Harvard University Press, 1993.

Latour, B., and S.C. Strum. "Human Social Origins: Oh Please, Tell Us Another Story." *Journal of Social and Biological Structures*, 9 (1986): 169–87.

Lawrence-Lightfoot, Sara. *Balm in Gilead: Journey of a Healer*. New York: Penguin, 1988.

Layton, Lynne. *Who's That Girl? Who's That Boy? Clinical Practice Meets Postmodern Gender Theory*. Northvale, NJ: Jason Aronson, 1998.

Leary, Kimberlyn. "Race in Psychoanalytic Space." *Gender and Psychoanalysis*, 2(2) (1997): 157–72.

——. "Racial Enactments in Dynamic Treatment," *Psychoanalytic Dialogues*, 10(4) (2000): 639–53.

——. "Racial Insult and Repair," *Psychoanalytic Dialogues*, 17(4) (2007): 539–49.

——. "Race as an Adaptive Challenge: Working with Diversity in the Clinical Consulting Room," *Psychoanalytic Psychology* 29(3) (2012): 279–91.

LeBon, Gustave. *The Crowd*. London: T. Fischer Unwin, 1910 [1896].

Leeds, Anthony. "Darwin and 'Darwinian' Evolutionism in the Study of Society and Culture." In Thomas Glick, ed., *The Comparative Reception of Darwinism*, 437–85. Austin, TX: University of Texas Press, 1972.

Leiris, Michel. "L'Ethnographie devant le colonialisme." *Les Temps Modernes*, 6(58) (August 1950): 357–74.

Lévi-Strauss, Claude. *Totemism*. Translated by Rodney Needham. Boston, MA: Beacon, 1963.

——. *The Savage Mind*. Chicago, IL: University of Chicago Press, 1966.

———. *The Elementary Structures of Kinship*. Edited by Rodney Needham. Translated by James Harle Bell and John Richard von Sturmer. Boston, MA: Beacon, 1969 [1949].

Lincoln, Bruce. *Theorizing Myth: Narrative, Ideology, and Scholarship*. Chicago, IL: University of Chicago Press, 1999.

Lloyd, Genevieve. *The Man of Reason: "Male" and "Female" in Western Philosophy*. Minneapolis, MN: University of Minnesota Press, 1993 [1984].

Long, Charles H. "Primitive/Civilized: The Locus of a Problem." In Charles H. Long, *Significations: Signs, Symbols, and Images in the Interpretation of Religion*, 79–96. Philadelphia, PA: Fortress, 1986.

Lovejoy, Arthur O. *The Great Chain of Being: A Study of the History of an Idea*. Cambridge, MA: Harvard University Press, 1961 [1936].

—— and George Boas. *Primitivism and Related Ideas in Antiquity*. Baltimore, MD: The Johns Hopkins University Press, 1935.

Macalpine, Ida. "The Development of the Transference." In Aaron H. Esman, ed., *Essential Papers on Transference*, 188–220. New York: New York University Press, 1990 [1950].

Macey, David. *Lacan in Contexts*. London: Verso, 1988.

Malcolm, Janet. *In the Freud Archives*. New York: Knopf, 1983.

———. *The Purloined Clinic*. New York: Vintage, 1993.

Malinowski, Bronislaw. "Rationalization of Anthropology and Administration." *Africa*, 3(4) (1930): 405–29.

———. *Sex and Repression in Savage Society*. Chicago, IL: University of Chicago Press, 1985 [1927].

Mannoni, Octave. "Psychoanalysis and the Decolonization of Mankind." In Jonathan Miller, ed., *Freud: The Man, His World, His Influence*, 85–96. London: Wiedenfeld and Nicolson, 1972.

———. *Prospero and Caliban: The Psychology of Colonization*. Translated by Pamela Powesland. Foreward by Maurice Bloch. Ann Arbor, MI: University of Michigan Press, 1990 [1950].

Manuel, Frank E. *The Eighteenth Century Confronts the Gods*. New York: Atheneum, 1967.

Masson, Jeffrey Moussaieff. *Assault on Truth*. New York: Farrar, Straus and Giroux, 1984.

Mayr, Ernst. *The Growth of Biological Thought: Diversity, Evolution, and Inheritance*. Cambridge, MA: Harvard University Press, 1982.

Mead, Margaret, *Coming of Age in Samoa: A Psychological Study of Primitive Youth for Western Civilization*. New York: William Morrow & Company, 1928.

Meek, Ronald L. *Social Science and the Ignoble Savage*. Cambridge: Cambridge University Press, 1976.

Meissner, W.W. *Psychoanalysis and Religious Experience.* New Haven, CT: Yale University Press, 1984.

Memmi, Albert. *The Colonizer and the Colonized.* Translated by Howard Greenfeld. New York: Orion, 1965.

Mignolo, Walter D. *The Darker Side of the Renaissance: Literacy, Territoriality, and Colonization.* Ann Arbor, MI: University of Michigan Press, 1995.

Mills, Charles W. *The Racial Contract.* Ithaca, NY: Cornell University Press, 1997.

Mitchell, Juliet. *Psychoanalysis and Feminism: Freud, Reich, Laing, and Women.* New York: Random House, 1974.

Mitchell, Stephen A. *Influence and Autonomy in Psychoanalysis.* Hillsdale, NJ: Analytic Press, 1997.

——. "The Analyst's Knowledge and Authority." *Psychoanalytic Quarterly,* 67 (1998): 1–31.

Morrison, Toni. *Playing in the Dark: Whiteness and the Literary Imagination.* New York: Vintage, 1990.

Morss, John R. *Growing Critical: Alternatives to Developmental Psychology.* London: Routledge, 1996.

Muensterberger, W., ed. *Man and His Culture: Psychoanalytic Anthropology after "Totem and Taboo."* New York: Taplinger, 1970.

Nandy, Ashis. *The Intimate Enemy: Loss and Recovery of Self under Colonialism.* Oxford: Oxford University Press, 1983.

——. "The Savage Freud: The First Non-Western Psychoanalyst and the Politics of Secret Selves in Colonial India." In Ashis Nandy, *The Savage Freud and Other Essays on Possible and Retrievable Selves,* 81–144. Princeton, NJ: Princeton University Press, 1995.

Nash, Gary B. "Red, White, and Black: The Origins of Racism in Colonial America." In Donald Noel, ed., *The Origins of American Slavery and Racism,* 131–52. Columbus, OH: Merrill, 1972.

——. "The Image of the Indian in the Southern Colonial Mind." In Edward Dudley and M.E. Novak, eds., *The Wild Man Within: An Image in Western Thought from the Renaissance to Romanticism,* 55–86. Pittsburgh, PA: University of Pittsburgh Press, 1972.

Noriega, Jorge. "American Indian Education in the United States: Indoctrination for Subordination to Colonialism." In M. Annette Jaimes, *State of Native America: Genocide, Colonization, and Resistance,* 371–402. Boston, MA: South End, 1992.

Nunberg, Herman. "Transference and Reality." In Aaron H. Esman, ed., *Essential Papers on Transference,* 221–35. New York: New York University Press, 1990 [1951].

Obeyesekere, Gananath. *Medusa's Hair: An Essay on Personal Symbols and Religious Experience.* Chicago, IL: University of Chicago Press, 1981.

——. *The Work of Culture: Symbolic Transformation in Psychoanalysis and Anthropology*. Chicago, IL: University of Chicago Press, 1990.

Ogden, Thomas H. *The Primitive Edge of Experience*. Northvale, NJ: Jason Aronson, 1989.

Olender, Maurice. *The Languages of Paradise: Race, Religion, and Philology in the Nineteenth Century*. Translated by Arthur Goldhammer. Cambridge, MA: Harvard University Press, 1992.

Oliver, Kelly. *The Colonization of Psychic Space: A Psychoanalytic Social Theory of Oppression*. Minneapolis, MN: University of Minnesota Press, 2004.

Pagden, Anthony. *The Fall of Natural Man: The American Indian and the Origins of Comparative Ethnology*. Cambridge: Cambridge University Press, 1986.

Paul, Robert A. "Psychoanalytic Anthropology." *Annual Review of Anthropology*, 18 (1989): 177–202.

Pellegrini, Ann. *Performance Anxieties: Staging Psychoanalysis, Staging Race*. New York: Routledge, 1997.

Phillips, Adam. *Terrors and Experts*. Cambridge, MA: Harvard University Press, 1995.

Poliakov, Léon. *The Aryan Myth: A History of Racist and Nationalist Ideas in Europe*. Translated by Edmund Howard. New York: Barnes and Noble, 1971.

Povinelli, Elizabeth A. *Labor's Lot: The Power, History, and Culture of Aboriginal Action*. Chicago, IL: University of Chicago Press, 1993.

Prucha, Francis Paul. *Documents of United States Indian Policy*. Lincoln, NE: University of Nebraska Press, 1990 [1975].

Purchas, Samuel. *Purchas His Pilgrimes*. Glasgow: J. MacLehose, 1905–7 [1625].

Racker, Heinrich. *Transference and Countertransference*. New York: International Universities Press, 1968.

Ricoeur, Paul. *Freud and Philosophy: An Essay on Interpretation*. Trans. Dennis Savage. New Haven, CT: Yale University Press, 1970.

——. "The History of Religions and the Phenomenology of Time Consciousness." In Joseph Kitagawa, ed., *The History of Religions: Retrospect and Prospect*, 13–30. New York: Macmillan, 1985.

——. *Hermeneutics and the Human Sciences*. Edited and translated by John B. Thompson. Cambridge: Cambridge University Press, 1989.

Rieff, Philip. *Freud: The Mind of the Moralist*. Garden City, NY: Anchor Books, 1961.

——. *The Triumph of the Therapeutic: Uses of Faith after Freud*. Chicago, IL: University of Chicago Press, 1966.

Ritvo, Lucille. *Darwin's Influence on Freud: A Tale of Two Sciences*. New Haven, CT: Yale University Press, 1990.

Rivière, Joan. "Womanliness as a Masquerade." *International Journal of Psychoanalysis*, 10 (1929). Repr. in Victor Burgin, James Donald, and Cora Kaplan, eds., *Formations of Fantasy*, 36–44. London: Methuen, 1986.

Rizzuto, Ana Maria. *The Birth of the Living God: A Psychoanalytic Study.* Chicago, IL: University of Chicago Press. 1979.

——. *Why Did Freud Reject God? A Psychoanalytic Interpretation.* New Haven, CT: Yale University Press, 1998.

Robert, Marthe. *From Oedipus to Moses: Freud's Jewish Identity.* Translated by Ralph Manheim. Garden City, NY: Anchor, 1976.

Robinson, Paul A. *The Freudian Left: Wilhelm Reich, Geza Roheim, Herbert Marcuse.* New York: Harper and Row, 1969.

Robertson Smith, William. *Lectures on the Religion of the Semites.* Edited and with an introduction by T.O. Beidelman. Foreword by E.E. Evans-Pritchard. Chicago, IL: University of Chicago Press, 1974 [1894].

Rosaldo, M.Z. "The Use and Abuse of Anthropology: Reflections on Feminism and Cross-Cultural Understanding." *Signs: Journal of Women in Culture and Society*, 5(3) (1980): 389–417.

Rosaldo, Michelle Zimbalist, and Louise Lamphere, eds. *Woman, Culture and Society.* Stanford, CA: Stanford University Press, 1974.

Rubin, Gayle. "The Traffic in Women: Notes on the 'Political Economy' of Sex." In Rayna R. Reites, ed., *Toward an Anthropology of Women*, 157–210. New York: Monthly Review Press, 1975.

Rubin, Gayle, and Judith Butler. "Sexual Traffic" (interview). *differences: A Journal of Feminist Cultural Studies*, 6(2–3) (summer/fall 1994): 62–99.

Sachs, Wulf. *Black Hamlet.* Introductions by Saul Dubow and Jacqueline Rose. Baltimore, MD: The Johns Hopkins University Press, 1996 [1938].

Said, Edward. *Orientalism.* New York: Vintage, 1979.

——. "Representing the Colonized: Anthropology's Interlocutors." *Critical Inquiry*, 15(2) (winter 1989): 205–25.

——. *Culture and Imperialism.* New York: Vintage, 1993.

Santner, Eric L. "Postwar/Post-Holocaust/Postmodern: Some Reflections on the Discourses of Mourning," *Stranded Objects*, 1–30. Ithaca, NY: Cornell University Press, 1990.

——. *On the Psychotheology of Everyday Life: Reflections on Freud and Rosenzweig.* Chicago, IL: University of Chicago Press, 2001.

Scarry, Elaine. *The Body in Pain: The Making and Unmaking of the World.* New York, Oxford: Oxford University Press, 1985.

Schachter, Judith S., and Hugh F. Butts. "Transference and Countertransference in Interracial Analyses." *Journal of the American Psychoanalytic Association*, 16(4) (October 1968): 792–808.

Schorske, Carl E. *Fin-de-Siècle Vienna: Politics and Culture.* New York: Vintage, 1981 [1961].

Scott, David. "The Re-Enchantment of Humanism: An Interview with Sylvia Wynter," *Small Axe*, 8 (September 2000): 119–207.

Seshadri-Crooks, Kalpana. "The Primitive as Analyst: Postcolonial Feminism's Access to Psychoanalysis." *Cultural Critique*, 28 (fall 1994): 175–218.

——. "The Comedy of Domination: Psychoanalysis and the Conceit of Whiteness." In Christopher Lane, ed., *The Psychoanalysis of Race*, 353–79. New York: Columbia University Press, 1998.

——. *Desiring Whiteness: A Lacanian Analysis of Race*. London: Routledge, 2000.

Seth, Sanjay, Leela Gandhi, and Michael Dutton. "Postcolonial Studies: A Beginning." *Postcolonial Studies*, 1(1) (1998): 7–11.

Shepherdson, Charles. *Vital Signs: Nature, Culture, Psychoanalysis*. New York: Routledge, 2000.

Sheppard, Phillis Isabella. *Self, Culture and Others in Womanist Practical Theology*. New York: Palgrave Macmillan, 2011.

Smith, Jonathan Z. "The Wobbling Pivot." In Jonathan Z. Smith, *Map Is Not Territory*, 88–103. Chicago, IL: University of Chicago Press, 1978.

Spillers, Hortense J. "'All The Things You Could Be By Now, If Sigmund Freud's Wife Was Your Mother': Psychoanalysis and Race." In Spillers, *Black, White and in Color: Essays on American Literature and Culture*, 376–427. Chicago IL: University of Chicago Press, 2003.

Spiro, Melford. *Oedipus in the Trobriands*. Chicago, IL: University of Chicago Press, 1982.

Spivak, Gayatri Chakravorty. "Can the Subaltern Speak?" In Patrick Williams and Laura Chrisman, eds., *Colonial Discourse and Post-Colonial Theory*, 66–111. New York: Columbia University Press, 1984.

——. *The Post-Colonial Critic: Interviews, Strategies, Dialogues*. Edited by Sarah Harasym. London: Routledge, 1990.

Sprengnether, Madelon. *The Spectral Mother: Freud, Feminism, and Psychoanalysis*. Ithaca, NY: Cornell University Press, 1990.

Stannard, David E. *American Holocaust: Columbus and the Conquest of the New World*. New York: Oxford University Press, 1992.

Starr, Karen. *Repair of the Soul: Metaphors of Transformation in Jewish Mysticism and Psychoanalysis*. New York: Routledge, 2008.

Stepan, Nancy. *The Idea of Race in Science: Great Britain, 1800–1960*. Hamden, CT: Archon, 1982.

——. "Race and Gender: The Role of Analogy in Science." In David Theo Goldberg, ed., *Anatomy of Racism*, 38–57. Minneapolis, MN: University of Minnesota Press, 1990.

Stern, Daniel N. *The Interpersonal World of the Infant: A View from Psychoanalysis and Developmental Psychology*. New York: Basic Books, 1985.

Stocking, George W., Jr. *Race, Culture, and Evolution: Essays in the History of Anthropology*. Chicago, IL: University of Chicago Press, 1982 [1968].

——. *Victorian Anthropology*. New York: Free Press, 1987.

——, ed. *The Shaping of American Anthropology, 1883–1911: A Franz Boas Reader*. New York: Basic Books, 1974.

——, ed. *Observers Observed: Essays on Ethnographic Fieldwork*. Volume 1, *History of Anthropology*. Madison, WI: University of Wisconsin Press, 1983.

——, ed. *Functionalism Historicized: Essays on British Social Anthropology*. Volume 2, *History of Anthropology*. Madison, WI: University of Wisconsin Press, 1984.

——, ed. *Romantic Motives: Essays of Anthropological Sensibility*. Volume 6, *History of Anthropology*. Madison, WI: University of Wisconsin Press, 1989.

——, ed. *Colonial Situations: Essays on the Contextualization of Ethnographic Knowledge*. Volume 7, *History of Anthropology*. Madison, WI: University of Wisconsin Press, 1991.

Suchet, Melanie. "Unraveling Whiteness." *Psychoanalytic Dialogues, 17* (2007): 867–86.

Sullivan, Harry Stack. *The Interpersonal Theory of Psychiatry*. New York: Norton, 1953.

Sulloway, Frank. *Freud: Biologist of the Mind*. New York: Basic Books, 1979.

Tate, Claudia. "Freud and His 'Negro': Psychoanalysis as Ally and Enemy of African Americans." *Journal for the Psychoanalysis of Culture and Society*, 1(1) (spring 1996): 53–62.

Taylor, Charles. *Philosophy and the Human Sciences: Philosophical Papers 2*. Cambridge: Cambridge University Press, 1985.

Thomas, Alexander, and Samuel Sillen. *Racism and Psychiatry*. New York: Brunner/Mazel, 1982.

Todorov, Tzvetan. *The Conquest of America*. New York: Harper and Row, 1992.

Trautmann, Thomas R. *Lewis Henry Morgan and the Invention of Kinship*. Berkeley, CA: University of California Press, 1987.

Tylor, Edward B. *Primitive Culture: Researches into the Development of Mythology, Philosophy, Religion, Language, Art, and Custom*. New York: Brentano's, 1924 [1871].

Van Herik, Judith. *Freud on Femininity and Faith*. Berkeley, CA: University of California Press, 1982.

Wallace, Edwin, IV. *Freud and Anthropology: A History and Reappraisal*. New York: International Universities Press, 1983.

Walton, Jean. *Fair Sex, Savage Dreams: Race, Psychoanalysis, Sexual Difference*. Durham, NC: Duke University Press, 2001.

White, Hayden. "Forms of Wildness: Archeology of an Idea." In Hayden White, *Tropics of Discourse: Essays in Cultural Criticism*, 150–82. Baltimore, MD: The Johns Hopkins University Press, 1978.

——. "The Noble Savage as Fetish." In Hayden White, *Tropics of Discourse: Essays in Cultural Criticism*, 183–96. Baltimore, MD: The Johns Hopkins University Press, 1978.

Williams, Patrick, and Laura Chrisman, eds. *Colonial Discourse and Post-Colonial Theory: A Reader*. New York: Columbia University Press, 1994.

Williams, Raymond. *Keywords: A Vocabulary of Culture and Society*. New York: Oxford University Press, 1976.

Williams, Robert A., Jr. *The American Indian in Western Legal Thought: The Discourse of Conquest*. New York: Oxford University Press, 1990.

Winnicott, D.W. *Playing and Reality*. London: Routledge, 1989 [1971].

———. "On Transference." In Aaron H. Esman, ed., *Essential Papers on Transference*, 246–51. New York: New York University Press, 1990.

Winograd, Basia, director and producer. *Black Psychoanalysts Speak*. PEP Video Grants, 2014.

Wolf, Eric R. *Europe and the People without History*. Berkeley, CA: University of California Press, 1982.

Yerushalmi, Yosef Hayim. *Freud's Moses: Judaism Terminable and Interminable*. New Haven, CT: Yale University Press, 1991.

Young, Robert M. *Darwin's Metaphor: Nature's Place in Victorian Culture*. Cambridge: Cambridge University Press, 1985.

Young-Bruehl, Elisabeth. *Anatomy of Prejudices*. Cambridge, MA: Harvard University Press, 1996.

Zamora, Margarita. *Reading Columbus*. Berkeley, CA: University of California Press, 1993.

de Zengotita, Thomas. "The Functional Reduction of Kinship in the Social Thought of John Locke." In George W. Stocking Jr., ed., *Functionalism Historicized: Essays on British Social Anthropology*. Volume 2, *History of Anthropology*, 10–30. Madison, WI: University of Wisconsin Press, 1984.

Index

colonial context of European
representations of, 22–49; as
conceptual fetish, 141; in
contemporary western institutions,
105, 114; correlated with
femininity, 115–26, 153; correlated
with neurosis, 73–5, 77, 79, 80–1,
85, 89–92, 160, 186, 211;
development of the concept in
European thought, 15–57; as effect
of power, 100–1, 113–14, 154, 156,
230; as a key term of colonial
discourse, 78, 156; as a racial
concept, 40–9; in religion, 152,
163, 164–6, 175
progress, idea of, 38–9, 43, 45–6, 47,
49, 64, 108, 111, 150, 168
property, *see* land use
psychoanalyst: as blank screen, 204;
medical and scientific models for,
203–4; mutuality with, 205–6, 228;
neutrality of, 196, 204, 212;
opposition to, viewed as resistance,
214; in a position of primitivity,
212; suspended attention of, 207;
use of suggestion and influence,
200–11; *see also* transference
psychoanalytic patients (analysands):
analogy between "Negroes" and,
196, 219; in a position of
primitivity, 187, 196–224 (passim),
211–12, 219; *see also* transference
psychoanalytic treatment, *see*
transference
psychopathology, 2, 5, 11; as
characterization of primitive
peoples, 36; and race, 59, 92, 94,
196; as regression to the past, 90–2,
187; *see also* neurosis

race: anti-Semitism and, 178–83;
biological theories of, 40–9; in
early anthropological thought,
59–68; evolutionary theories of,

43–9; in Freud's construction of
psychoanalysis, 76–7, 115, 116–17,
125; and gender in psychoanalytic
theory, 115–32; and racism in
psychoanalytic treatment, 196,
198–200, 211, 219; as scientific
category, 12n1; and slavery, 26–30;
see also color, skin; phylogenetic
inheritance; "primitive peoples";
primitivity
rationality, 42, 63, 65, 164;
civilization associated with, 38;
lack of, in unconscious, 86–7; the
primitive as restricted in, 31, 35,
121, 152
recapitulation hypothesis, 13n6, 44–5,
63–4, 69; in Freud's work, 72–6,
78, 80–4, 88–9, 92–4, 98n43, 103,
109, 120, 123, 160, 163, 165–6,
175, 217, 219; *see also* biogenetic
theory; Haeckel, Ernst
recognition, as constitutive of
subjectivity, 133–8; *see also*
Benjamin, Jessica
regression, 12, 59, 73, 88–94,
102n106, 103, 105, 113, 120–1,
130–1, 160, 186; to earlier stages of
evolution, 92–3; as a feature of
religion, 163–9, 172–4, 176; in
hypnosis, 207; neurosis as, 89, 91,
92, 187; racial difference as, 92–3;
in the therapeutic relationship, 208,
211–16, 219, 231; *see also*
neurosis; psychopathology
relational psychoanalysis, 171, 200,
205, 227, 233n4
*Religion of the Semites, Lectures on
the* (Robertson Smith), 61, 67
religion(s): as the authority/ideology
of the repudiated past, 149, 151,
161, 162, 183; early anthropological
study of, 61, 65–8; as the
"enemy" of psychoanalysis, 162;
evolutionary stages of correlated